T0373159

THE NEW COLLEGE CLASSROOM

The New College Classroom

Cathy N. Davidson

and

Christina Katopodis

Harvard University Press

Cambridge, Massachusetts & London, England 2022

Printed in the United States of America
First printing
Publication of this book has been supported through the generous provisions
of the Maurice and Lula Bradley Smith Memorial Fund.

Library of Congress Cataloging-in-Publication Data
Names: Davidson, Cathy N., author. | Katopodis, Christina, author.
Title: The new college classroom / Cathy N. Davidson and Christina Katopodis.
Description: Cambridge, Massachusetts: Harvard University Press, 2022. |
Includes bibliographical references and index. |
Identifiers: LCCN 2022002816 | ISBN 9780674248854 (cloth)
Subjects: LCSH: Active learning—Handbooks, manuals, etc. | College teaching—
Handbooks, manuals, etc. | Effective teaching—Handbooks, manuals, etc. |
Classroom management—Handbooks, manuals, etc.
Classification: LCC LB1027.23 .D386 2022 | DDC 371.3—dc23 / eng / 20220217
LC record available at https://lccn.loc.gov/2022002816

To all students and teachers who fight for more

Contents

Preface

This book is an invitation to change—ourselves, our classrooms, our society. It's a practical book dedicated to a lofty mission, a step-by-step "how to" for transformation.

We've spent the last few years reading, observing, talking to, and interacting with literally thousands of dedicated researchers and inspiring instructors who have made changes large and small to their classrooms in order to teach *every* student. We have distilled what we have discovered into easy and efficient ideas that really work, both for instructors and for students, and that you will be able to choose from and put into practice tomorrow. We start from the assumption that every instructor spends a lot of time in office hours and the classroom—sometimes too much. It's easy to feel jaded or exhausted, to forget (to quote bell hooks) that, as instructors, we have the "power to change the direction of our students' lives."

We have learned much from writing this book together. Because we wrote this during the COVID-19 pandemic and at a distance from each other, we had to learn quickly about what worked and what didn't work, face the gap between high theory and emergency practice, and design creative, useful, easy, and effective ways to teach face-to-face but also online. Our discussion of practical methods was entwined with a continuing debate about the principles behind good teaching. Here's one example: trust that your students want to learn, want to improve their own future, and want to make a difference. Everything becomes a teachable moment if you can ask your students what they think, what they would do. They are a resource and, as soon as you ask them, they are thinking. They are learning—and that's precisely what they came to college to do.

As with all engaged learning, we learn as we teach and teach as we learn. We (instructors and students) begin in one place. We end somewhere better. That should be the goal of all higher education.

In our case, we were inspired by what we read, by professionals in the field of pedagogy, and by instructors in every discipline, teaching everywhere and at every level. Most of all, we are inspired by our own students who "test-drove" and responded to these methods, offering feedback on what worked best for them and what did not.

This book took shape during tumultuous times, featuring both a public health crisis that turned our city, New York, into a disaster area and a ghost town and protests by Black Lives Matter against police violence that stirred our city and the world. Although this book is designed for professors teaching at every kind of institution, we wrote it while teaching at the City University of New York (CUNY), the largest public, urban university in the United States and a model of social mobility through education. Many of our students were valiant health care employees or other essential workers, and they continued their studies even as they and their families experienced the crisis firsthand.

While our university and our city were closed, masked, and socially distanced, we met online twice a week, every week. We wrote every word together, talking through ideas, thinking about the research we were reading, trying the best methods in our courses, and soliciting our students' feedback on what was most effective for their learning. We have distilled what we learned into these pages, including the lived experience of teaching in crisis with little time for lesson prep and a great need to teach the essentials—what will help students thrive in the world they face today.

We brought to *The New College Classroom* extensive research in pedagogy, learning science, cognitive neuroscience, management coaching, and conflict negotiation theory bolstered by interviews and observations with dozens of instructors at every kind of institution and in all disciplines. The two of us also come to this project with very different perspectives at the bookends of a typical academic career: one (Cathy) a senior scholar, one (Christina) a relatively new PhD who has nonetheless taught for over a decade as an adjunct in the harsh world and unforgiving realities of academe today. We've each worked at a range of institutions, including community college, public university, liberal arts college, and elite private and Ivy League universities. From these varied perspectives, we've seen how a successful classroom is less about teaching and more about learning, especially when every participant has a stake and responsibility in learning together. We shared one goal: to produce a concise guide to transformative teaching.

That goal became a through line of our plague years. Amid the tragedy and horror of the global health crisis, we lived our lives and wrote. Christina raised a newborn. She also lost a beloved grandmother. Cathy lost beloved family members and friends during this time. Christina finished and defended a dissertation, earned her doctorate, and started a new job. Together, we worked with our colleagues to start a bold new program at CUNY, Transformative Learning in the Humanities. This program is part of the new cross-disciplinary CUNY Innovative Teaching Academy, which spans twenty-five campuses—two-year colleges, four-year colleges, graduate and honors schools, and professional schools. It is dedicated to exactly the methods and missions of inspiring, effective, and inclusive learning that we describe in *The New College Classroom.*

We despise the "do more with less" refrain often imposed upon faculty, staff, and students at underfunded public universities. We champion the idea that, by thinking through what learning is, we can support caring, independent thinkers—students *and* their instructors—who need not expend energy on time-consuming methods that, the research shows, are unproductive or even counterproductive. Many of the effective teaching strategies we detail in this book take less preparation and offer far deeper, more lasting impacts than the traditional ones we mostly absorbed from those who taught us. We've learned from great instructors everywhere and are humbled by the tremendous work of these colleagues and their students. We are honored to have been able to work through so many of these ideas with such incredible people.

Our goal has been to offer practical answers to a crucial question: how do we teach for *every* student—not only for the ones who most resemble us, their instructors? Our second goal has been to find ways to streamline that process to reduce time spent in unproductive tasks—for both teachers and students. We know all too well how the burdens of high teaching loads and pressure to publish can weigh down our spirits and diminish our energy. We have never forgotten that you, as an instructor, have a life as busy and complicated as any student, a life as busy and complicated as the ones we lived as we wrote this book together.

We have broken down teaching to its constituent parts and, in every situation, have presented effective and efficient methods for planning a first class, creating a syllabus, designing an exam, or trying an alternative to traditional grading.

We hope you will find ideas here that are as invigorating for you as they are for your students.

THE NEW COLLEGE CLASSROOM

We have been raised to fear the yes within ourselves, our deepest cravings.

—AUDRE LORDE

Introduction

Don't you realize that every time you don't answer a question, you're learning something? You're learning how to make do with what you got, and you're learning how not to ask for a raise. . . . You're learning how to take it. That's not good. . . . So, from now on, whenever I ask a question, everybody's got to put their hand up. I don't care whether you know the answer or not. You have to put your hand up. . . . [We] need to teach people they are important enough to say what they have to say.

—SAMUEL DELANY, science fiction writer, educator

The Problem

Fifty people—faculty members and graduate students—sit silently in a department meeting as the chair offers a question, scowls, and tries again. No one answers; no one is happy. The meeting is supposed to be an open forum on the department's collective goals for the next five years, yet no one wants to speak. Tension mounts. Eyes glance at the floor, and some people cross and uncross their arms. Then a graduate student raises a hand and asks the chair if they all might try a short activity. "I think it would be helpful," the student says, "if we could take five minutes to discuss our ideas with a partner first before we share them with the whole room." The chair happily takes up the suggestion. Everyone turns to a colleague, and the room comes alive with excited, purposeful activity. People talk, smile, jot down ideas, discuss and debate them. Even people who seldom speak at department meetings are engaged. When the five minutes are up, the room is so rife with ideas that the chair must ask not once but twice for everyone's attention. The meeting resumes, and people willingly share their groups' brainstorming with the whole department. No one person's big idea dominates the conversation, positively or negatively. The community's collective mission begins to take shape.

We've all been there at one time or another, when a demoralizing silence settles in and suffocates a conversation. It is soul-crushing to talk at a room of seemingly bored people—or at a Zoom screen of black boxes—and equally so to be lectured at. When that full stop occurs in our own classrooms, professors often chide their students for their indifference. Student hesitancy turns into fear of what the teacher will say next: will it be a raking over the coals, a dismissal, another question rephrasing the first? What will the tone be—frustrated or pleading? Or will the instructor just ignore the bruising silence and drone on, lecturing away as if they didn't notice that seemingly no one was listening?

Lecturing seems to be the traditional fallback when a class falls silent. According to an exhaustive study of twelve thousand classrooms, instructors end up talking during 89 percent of class time—even when they insist that they are conducting a seminar or discussion class.[1] We rely on what is, essentially, a highly controlled discussion (a "distributed lecture," we call it) that depends on the two or three students we can always count on to raise their hands. Sociologists Jay R. Howard and Roberta Baird call this "consolidation of responsibility," where students in a class have an implicit pact, delegating the job of participation to a diligent few.[2] Often those conscientious hand-raisers believe they are doing their instructors a service, that they are "saving" the class from that awkward pause. This may seem a solution to what our students term "silence chicken," but it merely masks the central problem and creates a new one.

Both the lecture and the carefully managed discussion reinforce the idea that the instructor is responsible for ideas and that it's okay to leave the majority of the class out of the learning process. When we pause to ask the class a question, we tend to have a "right" answer in mind. Students hesitate—unsure if they have the right answer—or they don't speak at all. As Samuel Delany observes in the epigraph at the start of this introduction, every time students fail to raise a hand, they are learning something about the worth of their education and of themselves: that their participation doesn't matter. As Delany indicates, that's not good.

The Alternative

I (Christina), finishing my doctorate at the time, was the graduate student who spoke up at that stalled department meeting. I suggested a participatory exercise known by active learning educators as "Think-Pair-Share" and by management experts at places like the Harvard Business School as "radical" or "deep" listening. At our department meeting, I made an assumption foundational to active learning: the people sitting in stony silence weren't indifferent, hostile, or stupid. They had been rendered passive by the paralyzing structure (the one we use in our classrooms 89 percent of the time) of one-way communication between a leader standing at a lectern and everyone else sitting in chairs. Because everyone at our meeting was game to try something different, we were able to redesign the meeting.

Think-Pair-Share is one of the handiest devices in the instructor's toolkit known variously as active, participatory, or student-centered learning. These basic, interactive techniques are often used by K–12 teachers, where the focus is on the improvement of each and every student (that is, "student-centered learning") and are commonplace in executive training, management programs, conflict resolution, and other situations where the goal is for everyone to learn how to contribute effectively and equitably. Except for those in Schools of Education, many of us who teach in higher education don't know about these methods or, if we do, it is through the rather backhanded way of trying to figure out how to extrapolate effective, democratic classroom teaching methods from polemical pedagogical theorists such as Paolo Freire or bell hooks.

It doesn't have to be that hard. We now have dozens of books and articles on active learning tactics, mostly designed for K–12 teachers or aimed at professors in professional schools. Equally important, we have over three decades and more than a thousand studies testing and assessing the effectiveness of all of these active learning methods. Over and over, these studies show active learning to be both more effective and more egalitarian than traditional lecture or controlled discussion strategies. In May 2014, several scholars from a variety of STEM disciplines published an exhaustive meta-analysis of 225 separate studies on different ways to teach and learn. In the *Proceedings of the National Academy of Sciences* (*PNAS*), they argue that active learning improved student performance in every way, including when measured by test scores, retention, and applicability (applying classroom learning to new situations).[3] They write, "Students in classes with traditional lecturing were 1.5 times more likely to fail than were students in classes with active learning."[4] Another meta-study, conducted the following year, showed the same results were even more evident if difference, equality, diversity, and inclusion were factored into the analysis.[5] Further research in 2018 showed equally significant improvements in learning and understanding for international students.[6] The authors of the *PNAS* study quipped that if the comparative merits had been this clear-cut in a pharmaceutical study, traditional pedagogy would be taken off the market.[7]

Various innovative programs designed to improve learning in different disciplines (including the arts, the humanities, and the social sciences) have tested active learning in varied settings: middle schools in Chicago, community colleges in New York, a study group at Harvard, an Indigenous program in British Columbia. A growing number of engaged professors around the world report success with these tactics, especially with first-generation college students, students without extensive college preparatory training, and students from low-income and marginalized social groups.[8]

These methods are inclusive and beneficial to students and create interdependent student learning communities, and here's the best-kept secret of all: They aren't difficult for instructors to pick up. They can be adapted to different parts of our teaching and can even take the traditional classroom methods we've relied on for years and, without much effort, transform them into active learning lessons that will make a major difference in what students learn, retain, and know how to apply elsewhere, once the class is over.

And if you lecture to three or four hundred students every semester, fear not! We know quite a few lecturers who have come up with effective and efficient ways of adding an inspiring active learning component to their lectures. Rather than being an additional burden on stressed-out instructors, these methods give insights (before the midterm or final) into what's working for your students and what they are missing. Best of all, they don't require much extra prep time or more grading. I (Cathy) use them in my classes and in virtually every keynote address and public lecture. Several years ago, I even had some six thousand International Baccalaureate (IB) teachers in the Philadelphia 76ers arena thinking-pairing-and-sharing under the Jumbotrons. To this day, I hear back from teachers who insist they still use that tactic in their courses.

In *The New College Classroom,* we show how to put research, theories, and ideas into actual classroom practice. We've learned enormously from those in many different disciplines and educational settings in the United States and around the world.[9] We pass on their wisdom and their methods for offering students—all students—the chance to participate in their own learning. When we use teaching strategies that solicit contributions from the whole class, the burden of teaching is not shouldered by the professor alone. Everyone plays a role in reaching a successful outcome.

Why Change?

In their study *In Search of Deeper Learning: The Quest to Remake the American High School,* Jal Mehta and Sarah Fine reach the depressing conclusion that students become more bored and less interested in learning as they get older. Whereas 75 percent of fifth graders feel engaged by school, that number falls to 32 percent by eleventh grade. When these authors interviewed students even at the very best high schools, the conversations were discouraging: "Most classrooms were spaces to sit passively and listen. Most academic work instructed students to recall, or minimally apply, what they had been told. When we asked students the purpose of what they were doing, the most common responses were 'I dunno—it's in the textbook' and 'maybe it'll help me in college.'"[10] Mehta and Fine discovered the pervasive problem isn't that classes are too hard; it's that they aren't rigorous, engaging, and interesting enough.

What about college? Or let's make this personal: what about *our* classrooms and *yours*? College is voluntary. Students don't have to, by law, attend college, and they don't have to stay there. They do, however, have to fulfill distribution, general education, and major requirements in order to graduate. Are our own students in our classes because they want to learn, because they are excited by the subject matter, because they want to grasp content they know will be important to their lives and their careers? Or, if asked why they are studying a certain topic in a certain course, are they most likely to answer, "I dunno" or "it's required" or "to get a job"? Of course they want a job. But how depressing to think of spending four years of your life bored, going through the motions, checking off course requirements, in the hope that a better job is waiting for you when you graduate. What a wasted opportunity for everyone, including the instructor!

The methods, exercises, and activities in this book are designed to make the learning in our classrooms meaningful, effective, and equitable for every student, and the process of teaching as rewarding and fulfilling as we all hoped it would be when we chose this as a profession. We pass along tactics that anyone can use in their classrooms. We draw from techniques that work, techniques developed by all kinds of instructors, full-time and part-time, graduate student instructors and senior professors. Take this combination of research project and assessment redesign developed by history professor Steven L. Berg's introductory early American history class at Schoolcraft College, a community college in Livonia, Michigan. He gave his students the opportunity to choose their own research projects and used contract grading so that each student could decide which assignments they would do to earn a certain grade. One popular assignment option, for example, was to post a blog on the class website connecting their research on the eighteenth- or nineteenth-century United States to a news event that happened to be unfolding that day. Once students earned enough points in the course for the grade for which they were aiming, they had the option of stopping further work on their projects and assignments. Except they didn't. They were so excited by their research that a whopping 60 percent continued their projects after they had done enough to earn an A. After their grade reached 100 percent, 40 percent submitted assignments. Two students earned more than 120 percent for their final course grade.

As Berg notes, "By giving choices, students completed more work—often significantly more work—than would have been required of them had I not provided options."[11] This example is illustrative in that it connects different aspects of classroom teaching in one assignment that is no more difficult (for student or professor) than its more traditional equivalents. Offering choice, emphasizing peer exchange and collaboration, guiding students through serious self-evaluation, challenging them to solve difficult problems or work through complex ideas, and inviting them to apply their new knowledge beyond the classroom are interconnected, meaningful ways to learn.

These efficient and powerful teaching methods work as well for an adjunct professor with no resources as they do for a full professor with job security and institutional reserves to draw on. We know—because that's the dual experience the two of us bring to this book. In our own teaching, we have both found that when we use strategies to solicit contributions from every member of a class, our students learn more and we enjoy teaching more. Anecdotally, we experience success rates comparable to those in the formal STEM meta-studies. And we do so without having to overprepare for each class session as if it's our thesis defense (a pattern of overachieving but inefficient teaching we have witnessed in several classrooms we've observed).

Teaching should not be solely about *our* performance. It should be about creating the conditions where students perform best. That's a paradigm shift, what Robert B. Barr and John Tagg over two decades ago described as the conceptual shift "from teaching to learning."[12] Although changing the terms of the classroom can seem intimidating at first, it need not be labor-intensive. Once we have a few nearly foolproof activities in our back pockets, they can be pulled out and used on the fly—and instantly change the level of interest and impact in a room.

The majority of activities we offer in *The New College Classroom* are easy to use, understand, and implement. In a few instances, we present exceptionally ambitious projects that instructors, programs, and entire institutions have undertaken to transform how they teach and learn. We applaud these and recognize the profound collective thinking, planning, and execution required for their success. However, most of this book focuses on practical ideas that make a difference and can be implemented easily. Some are, frankly, commonsensical solutions, but some are lifesavers for stressed-out faculty, especially after semester fatigue has set in.

Success for Every Student

We've all heard contemptuous comments about "students today" on campuses or on social media. Such complaints articulate failure—not just the students' failure but that of an educational system that promises inclusion and social mobility but (and we'll look at this research later) too often replicates and even increases inequality.

One common ingredient in almost all of the methods in this book is that they are designed to help every student be better than they were, wherever they started. Learning science experts categorize all of the ways we can structure our classrooms—literally, there are dozens of ways, with advantages and disadvantages to each.[13] Most classroom management techniques for active learning fall into the category of inventory methods. As opposed to the selective methods of picking among a few eagerly raised hands, inventory methods take a literal accounting or inventory of ideas by every student in the room. They are low-stakes, meaning they are not vetted by the professor at the podium or in any fashion graded or judged but are simply put into play as a starting point for developing further ideas or more advanced skills. Students might exchange preliminary thoughts with a partner or in small groups (as they were at Christina's original department meeting) or offer ideas anonymously online on a whiteboard or, in a classroom, scrawled on Post-it notes. There is no shame or premature judgment in a wrong or weak answer. Ideas are put into play and analyzed, debated, defended, deployed, and developed—a practice that allows everyone to improve and bolster their higher-order thinking skills, including problem-solving, collaboration, communication, and persuasion.

Management experts champion inventory methods because they circumvent "groupthink," where everyone ends up with the same idea (typically, the one presumed to be held by the most powerful person in the room). In a classroom, inventory methods allow students to develop essential higher-order thinking skills that help prepare them for their lives beyond college and also, not coincidentally, help them to have a bigger voice in society as a whole. This kind of learning puts students in the driver's seat of their own education.

The social philosophy undergirding much of the theory of active, participatory learning is, unmistakably, democratic and egalitarian.

Progressive educator Alfie Kohn emphasizes the role of community, collaboration, and social justice at the core of true learning from kindergarten to professional school.[14] Many of the learning methods espoused in this book descend from genealogies of progressive education that go back to Italian physician Maria Montessori and American psychologist and philosopher John Dewey, as well as from Paulo Freire's dialogic methods in *Pedagogy of the Oppressed* (1968), Henry Giroux's advocacy of critical, public pedagogy, and bell hooks's emphasis on the intellectual and spiritual goal of "teaching to transgress." We also pass on key egalitarian, antiracist, and decolonial educational ideas from Felicia Rose Chavez, Sandy Grande, Max Liboiron, Bettina Love, Carla Shedd, and Helen Verran, among others dedicated to educational equality, and from "student success" advocates such as Finnish educator Pasi Sahlberg and psychologist Carol Dweck, who designed methods to give each student a chance.[15] Motivating all of these educators is a desire for success for every kind of student. The ultimate social goal is idealistic: for the classroom to model how we can engage and contribute to an inclusive, democratic, and just society that functions better for everyone.

Every student has a right to thrive. We make that success possible when we include our students in the learning process. For example, in one exercise in Part Two we explore how, why, and what changes when we solicit input from each student in developing the learning outcomes for the course they're taking.[16] Active, participatory learning puts into pedagogical practice the values of fairness, inclusion, diversity, equity, and antidiscrimination (racial, gendered, sexual, classist, ageist, and ableist). It reinforces a self-reflective method by engaging students in a process that tasks them with critically examining what they have done—analyzing the learning methods themselves. This process of self-evaluation and self-correction is known by educational psychologists as "metacognition," or thinking about how we think. The process is crucial to students' confidence in their ability to learn and helps them identify the value of what they've learned.

We use these tools in our classrooms to structure equality into our courses because we cannot fight inequality with goodwill alone. As Tressie McMillan Cottom demonstrates in *Lower Ed: The Troubling Rise of For-Profit Colleges in the New Economy* (2017), inequality is as built into higher education as it is in the rest of society. College's promise of social mobility is infrequently and unequally realized. Hard work and dedication are not enough to overcome years of being ranked and rated in primary and secondary schools whose quality depends upon the district's income level and whose policies seem designed to leave multilingual, immigrant, low-income, and minority students behind. Twenty years after writing *Why Are All the Black Kids Sitting Together in the Cafeteria?* (1997), Beverly Daniel Tatum wrote a new introduction to her revised book in 2017, explaining why all the "Black kids" are *still* sitting together.[17] The methods in this book are designed to change the status quo in our classrooms—and even our cafeterias—creating the conditions for all students to flourish in the domains where we instructors have the most control.

We designed *The New College Classroom* so that the transformation can go as deep as you wish, from just the first five minutes of every class meeting to a full course or even department-wide overhaul. Inventory methods achieve what the American Psychological Association calls "Total Participation." They charge not just students but *everyone*—professors, postdocs, administrators, staff, presidents—with bringing anything and everything they know from other contexts into the particular realm of the office or committee meeting, the course subject, the assignment or exercise, or the other task at hand. The methods in this book work for academically savvy students as well as for students who come to college with poor academic preparation.

We offer grab-and-go activities (like Think-Pair-Share) that never fail in turning a dull moment into one rife with engaged learning. When we say "grab-and-go," we mean it: these are activities that we keep on hand and use just about everywhere—in our classrooms, on panels at conferences, and in keynote addresses, both face-to-face and online.

Cathy has also used Think-Pair-Share effectively in numerous management seminars she has conducted with nonprofit and corporate executives all over the United States and abroad.

These methods work. Nobel Prize–winning physicist Carl Wieman, who also holds a position at the Graduate School of Education at Stanford, is one of the most ardent proponents of active learning for science. He compares traditional lecture and one-way discussion methods to "bloodletting," an archaic medical practice that proved to be ineffective and was eventually repudiated and abandoned by the medical profession.[18] In *Improving How Universities Teach Science,* he details his Science Education Initiative, which has transformed physics programs at the University of Colorado and the University of British Columbia and, more recently, is changing how basic science is taught at Stanford University. Wieman laments: "Most students are learning that 'science' is a set of facts and procedures that are unrelated to the workings of the world and are simply to be memorized without understanding. . . . They are leaving classes seeing science as less interesting and relevant than they did when they started."[19] He is an outspoken critic of traditional ways of teaching, especially the lecture, calling it, unambiguously, a "terrible way to learn."[20]

Wieman may overstate the case slightly—a lecture can achieve certain purposes in education. A great lecture, like a splendid sermon, can inspire, motivate, entertain, or stir us—and all of that is good. However, none of those are equivalent to learning, the actual acquisition of a new skill, idea, or body of knowledge in a way that allows us to extrapolate, extend that knowledge and apply it in other situations where it is relevant, and use it to solve problems and make important decisions.

What Is Learning?

I (Cathy) witnessed the crucial difference between being inspired by a lecture and actually learning from one. This was many years ago, when I happened to be hosting a conference in my field at the same convention center in Long Beach, California, as the annual TED Talks. I wandered into the lobby as happy members of the TED audience spilled out of a packed lecture hall exclaiming about "the best talk I've ever heard," calling the recently concluded TED Talk "life-changing" and "unforgettable." Students from a local college happened to be in the lobby conducting research for a class project. They stopped audience members as they were leaving the event and asked them a simple set of survey questions. Student surveyors were shocked that the inspired listeners in the audience were not able to recall even simple, basic, oft-repeated facts from the lecture they were sure they would remember forever. People who had come to the Talks together offered radically different summaries of what was said and what it meant.

The student ethnographers were surprised by the results, but cognitive neuroscientists recognize this well-researched phenomenon. In *Now You See It: How the Brain Science of Attention Will Transform the Way We Live, Work, and Learn* (2011), I wrote about the selective way we attend to certain features of the world around us, including in what we read and hear, and how our brains ignore almost everything else.[21] That's how attention works. Numerous studies using functional magnetic resonance imaging (fMRI) and other neuroimaging devices attest that when listening to lectures (whether in a church, in a classroom, or at a TED Talk) we continuously shift in and out of attention. A great lecture moves us and may trigger associations, memories, past ideas, meaningful recollections, all of which might have significance but can take us far from the actual lecture at hand. By contrast, with active learning, since the learner is also the *agent* and the *source* of the learning, attention is focused. It has to be. A lecture begins and ends whether the student is listening and learning or not. By definition, active learning requires the participation—the agency—of the learner. The learning process is the learning product and vice versa.

In a lecture, the learner does not control the pace—there's no way of backing up to go over a point the learner doesn't understand, no testing to make sure the learner has gotten it right, no adaptation of the idea or method to a new situation to ensure that the principle has been fully absorbed (and is not simply a conclusion memorized). The French philosopher Michel de Certeau uses the term "poaching" to describe the selective, almost greedy way we snatch up things that intrigue us when we are reading or listening, ignoring the rest.[22] Active learning helps us "poach" more effectively, directing our attention through specific exercises and activities that deepen rather than distract us, that engage us in ways that help us learn content, techniques, and ideas. Instead of losing ourselves in our own thoughts during a lecture, active learning requires us to *do something* (that is, "actively") with the content—like the faculty members at my (Christina's) department meeting brainstorming in small, intimate groups, working through their ideas by discussing them with peers, hashing them out, refining them, negotiating across different perspectives or different versions of the same idea, and then offering up the results constructively to others at the meeting. Learning is a process of acquiring new understanding, a proficiency of skills, knowledge, or values. The operative word here is *process*. The faculty members at the department meeting were doing exactly that: processing together.

Sound simple? Philosophically, educationally, and psychologically, it's a revolution. When students study in the traditional way—in order to earn a good grade on a high-stakes test—they forget content very quickly after the exam is over (a subject that has been well researched since the 1880s; we will return to this when we look at grading and assessment). They have little opportunity in a traditional classroom to acquire the higher-order skills that employers insist are most important for both new employees and for professional advancement. These include communication skills (such as interacting across different talents, backgrounds, and levels of authority), critical thinking, collaboration, project management, the ability to move from an idea to implementation, problem-solving, and complex decision making. These skills are fundamental in most occupations and especially in managerial and professional jobs where they are often assumed rather than taught or even explained. Getting ahold of these tools is especially crucial for first-generation college students. They may not know anyone who, in the course of everyday work, has had to negotiate the range of implicit, often unspoken office rules and practices that inform the middle-class workplace.

So if active learning is a more effective way to absorb disciplinary content and methods, is useful for the diverse students in higher education today, and also teaches students a range of essential life skills, why isn't it happening in every college classroom? Why is it called "radical pedagogy" instead of "common sense" or "efficient pedagogy"?

The main reason is that most people who become college teachers have not received much training as teachers.[23] Most of us teach the way we were taught because we have not been exposed to other methods. It's rare even to find an academic outside of education departments who's aware of the extensive learning science research. Most of us have ignored or never been introduced to the benefits of active learning.[24] Graduate students, including those preparing for a lifelong career as instructors, are rarely taught or exposed to any pedagogy at all.

Throughout this book, we offer ways to adapt ideas to your specific needs. For example, when I (Cathy) returned from my conference where the student ethnographers had been interviewing audience members from the TED Talks, I tried an experiment with my class. They were up for the challenge. I delivered to my seminar of a dozen undergraduates and master's students the same formal, keynote lecture I presented at the conference, appropriate since "Digital Media and Learning," the topic of the conference, was relevant to our interdisciplinary information science course. I then gave the students my slides and a transcript of my talk and had them "remix" them in any way they wished. They could amplify my thesis with evidence (or counterevidence) taken more specifically from their majors (computer science, cognitive neuroscience, studio art, history, electrical engineering, education, sociology, political science, film studies, literature). Or they could change the form or the media. They uploaded their remixes to a website, gave one another feedback, and commented on the finished products, which included a short story, a stop-motion claymation video, a digital learning app, a social science survey, and more. Over a decade later, I doubt anyone remembers my original lecture. I'm positive they can still tell you in detail how they conceived and executed their projects.

Active, participatory learning is not a pedagogy of the "oppressed" but a pedagogy of lifelong success for everyone. It is not a competition for rating who is the best in the class or cohort. It is a challenge and an opportunity for each student to be as good as they can be. It offers every student tools they can apply in any aspect of their life when there is no teacher present to support them. It not only teaches to "transgress" but teaches to transform.

Yet change is hard. So, in this book, we marshal the relevant research to explain to colleagues and administrators why active, participatory learning techniques work and where and how they work best. Even college students need to be convinced. If a learner has succeeded in a top-down system and done well enough on grades and on standardized tests to get into college, it can feel like a rug-pull moment to suddenly find oneself in a "flipped classroom." It is hard for students to realize sometimes that active, student-centered, support-based learning really is the most effective. Another *PNAS* study, this one conducted in 2019, looked at large-enrollment introductory college physics courses; it showed that, although students in an active classroom learned more, they felt certain that they'd learned less. Follow-up work showed that apprehension changed when instructors shared the extensive research on the efficacy of active learning with their students, when they showed students the insights of learning scientists on the cognitive and educational benefits of this method.[25] The authors of this study observe: "As the success of active learning crucially depends on student motivation and engagement, it is of paramount importance that students appreciate, early in the semester, the benefits of struggling with the material during active learning." Self-reflection is a crucial part of the participatory learning process. You cannot really engage if you take learning for granted. You have to think about what and how you are learning and for what purpose as part of the learning process.

The New College Classroom

Because we have inherited certain educational traditions does not mean that we, as instructors, have to perpetuate them. *The New College Classroom* sets an ambitious agenda for higher education. In Part I, "Changing Ourselves," we reconsider the assumptions we have inherited on our way to becoming instructors. We examine many of the deepest assumptions embedded in the institutional structures of the modern university and those bad habits that have been passed along, generation after generation, graduate professor to graduate student, and that we then carry out every day in the classes we teach. We need to unlearn much of what we have been taught in order to teach more effectively and equitably.

Part II, "Changing Our Classrooms," is the heart of this book. It puts the theory of active learning into useful and usable form, in any kind of classroom, in any discipline, anywhere. We offer practical, easy-to-follow methods for every part of teaching a class. There are grab-and-go activities for any day of the term. There are virtually foolproof exercises. For those ready to dive in all the way, there are clear lesson plans for flipping classrooms, backwards planning, and codesigning a course with students.

In the Conclusion, "Changing the World," we address the relationship between classroom pedagogy, institutional transformation, and social change. Education's deepest function is to play a role in changing society. In this section, we imagine what would happen if higher education realized this mission.

What's the payoff for all of this? Transformation that answers what Black feminist writer, activist, and critical pedagogy advocate Audre Lorde calls the "yes" within us, "our deepest cravings." The New

College Classroom requires that we learn better and unlearn ruthlessly. It inspires us to find the connections, the through lines, the ways of translating what we love—the content that brought us to this profession—to our students as the single most effective teaching tool we have for helping them toward their own agency and empowerment.

In the following pages, we present tested ways to begin changing ourselves, our classrooms, our institutions, and our society. Whether our courses take place on site or online, we offer ideas that you can adapt to your specific field, institution, and students. But this is only a guide. You are the expert in your own classroom, and you know your students better than anyone. You know who they are and what they are facing right now. Each section of this book is meant to be a starting point in your own mission to transform the classroom into a more effective, inspiring, democratic space.

If learning is a relay race, we see this book as a baton. We hope you will take it and run.

PART I

Changing Ourselves

Engaged pedagogy does not seek simply to empower students. Any classroom that employs a holistic model of learning will also be a place where teachers grow, and are empowered by the process.

—**bell hooks**, *Teaching to Transgress*

CHAPTER 1

Why Change Now?

Where It Started

Before we change our classrooms, we need to look inwards at ourselves and backwards to understand how we got here. We have inherited attitudes, structures, and expectations that are not of our own making. Where did these come from? To embrace the goal of making the classroom a place where every student learns and improves, we need to unlearn some of our most deeply inculcated assumptions about the function of higher education. It's useful to know that there's nothing "natural" about these. Most were invented in the last part of the nineteenth century by educators dedicated to redesigning higher education for the modern world of automation, industrialization, and standardization and needs of the new, modern global corporation. The assembly line, the punch clock, and the Model T were powerful technologies that were reshaping the world. If educators of the time could reshape the Puritan college into the modern research university to prepare students for their future, we can reshape the archaic practices we've inherited, especially in the one realm over which we have the most control, our classroom.

A little bit of history goes a long way to helping us understand the university we've inherited. Charles Eliot, who served as president of Harvard University for forty years (1869–1909), was one of the leaders most responsible for inventing and institutionalizing many of the features of higher education that we now take for granted.[1] He spent an extended time in Germany and France studying the massive changes undertaken in those countries over the course of the nineteenth century to modernize higher education. Eliot took as his model a European system that would train mostly elite men to be the leaders of the industrialized Western world and to influence the countries they colonized. Values of standardization and top-down management hierarchies, influenced by Taylorist ideas of productivity, were key to certifying and credentialing new professions for a growing global managerial class.

Among the changes Eliot adopted for US higher education include such things as college entrance exams, majors, minors, electives, and degree requirements. Along with other colleagues at the nation's elite private institutions, Eliot advocated giving letter and number grades rather than offering students oral and written feedback on their work. He commissioned Pennsylvania executive and engineer Morris Cooke to find a way to align higher education with the industrial workforce, leading to the design of the Carnegie credit hour (now known as "seat time") and the standardized, full-time student course load.[2] Needless to say, not a single feature in that list requires explanation or definition since these are basic structures we all still work within (and sometimes work around).

Interestingly, at the same time that the United States was creating land grant universities throughout the country and developing junior colleges—both ways of spreading and democratizing higher education—Eliot and other peers were formalizing the structures adopted across all of higher education that continue to shape the siloed, discipline-based form of education our twenty-first-century students receive to this day. They created the first American graduate school, for example. They also founded the collegiate law school, nursing school, and business school. They designed tenure, sabbaticals, faculty pensions, peer-reviewed publications, donor-named chairs, and corporate sponsorship of research. They also founded the first accreditation and ranking systems by which all colleges and universities, then and now, are still rated and judged.[3]

As we think about changing how we teach, it's useful to remember that the classroom we've inherited was designed to prepare students for an economy utterly upended by industrialization. Further, the founders of the university we've inherited had a specific kind of elite student in mind and created a system they saw as the best for perpetuating their role in society. Many of the educators of the time, for example, embraced eugenics, a belief in the inherited, biological superiority of white, Anglo-Saxon aristocrats, and they saw elite higher education as a way to support and perpetuate a ruling class. In England, Sir Francis Galton invented modern statistical methods and used his "bean machine" to demonstrate the "bell curve" to Parliament as part of his campaign to have working-class women sterilized and aristocratic women subsidized to bear more children. In the United States, Eliot, like many of his peers, was a dedicated eugenicist and served as the vice president of the First International Eugenics Congress.[4]

As we think about how we can change our own classrooms, it's useful to consider how many features of modern education are rooted in social assumptions about the importance of preserving hierarchy, ranking, and selectivity. We live and work at a great distance from Eliot's time, yet the vestiges of old habits (including the ugly ones) remain. It's no wonder most of the Ivy League schools in the United States, like many of the elite universities of Europe such as Oxford and Cambridge, were all-male schools and had rigidly enforced, albeit informal, rules against admitting too many members of certain ethnic, religious, and minority groups, a practice that continued into the 1960s.[5] That's a long and complicated history for any instructor to shoulder. We can't wind the clock backwards and change the past, but we can, at the very least, recognize it for what it was.

There is one further bit of history that helps us to rethink our own role and practices as instructors. Although Eliot founded the first professional school of education, he explicitly defined its scope as preparing K–12 teachers—and not college professors.[6] As Jonathan Zimmerman notes in *The Amateur Hour: A History of College Teaching in America,* Eliot also followed the European model in believing that the business of a college professor was research. A graduate student determined to pursue a career in academia was supposed to emulate his advisor, carrying forth that professor's research and replicating his teaching methods. Understanding pedagogy—the science of actual learning—was not a job requirement for an academic career.[7]

That is a large inheritance in many directions—social, cultural, philosophical, pedagogical. It would seem that this history is itself a formidable obstacle to change. And yet it is also inspirational to realize that this system isn't very old in the grand scheme of things. It's not fixed, natural, or necessary. If nineteenth-century educators reinvented college, so can we.

We've been saying for decades that higher education is in crisis. The renowned designer Bruce Mau argues that "the biggest problems create the biggest opportunities" for change, for redesign.[8] Further, because of the global pandemic, we now have irrefutable proof that higher education is capable of change. We have all partaken in changes at a dizzying pace and scale. In a matter of weeks, an estimated 1.8 billion students worldwide went online. Entire countries made drastic changes on every level and pooled every resource. Gambia distributed solar-powered radios across communities without electricity, and Morocco's television sports channel became the new school channel. On a worldwide scale, we broke nearly every rule, including changes in break schedule, added flexibility for grades and incompletes, and revision of scholarship rules. We even altered the seemingly sacred Carnegie credit hour.[9]

And here you are, reading this book about how to change. By committing to innovative and inclusive teaching, you are already defying the ingrained habits and biases embedded in the long inheritance of our profession and looking for a better way.

Where We Are Now

We're at exactly the right moment when we can unlearn a system originally designed for standardization, for ranking and rating the elite few. Instead, we can find fair and effective new ways to teach the diverse men and women in our classes today. Along with content, students can learn the higher-order skills they need to thrive in a world upended now by global information technologies—adaptability, cooperation, and innovation.

Today, around 40 percent of US workers live gig to gig. Trillions of dollars are spent and earned globally in the gig economy, where freelancers and independent contractors pick up temporary work. In some countries with extensive nationally funded retirement programs, such as Norway, switching careers late in life is less risky, because the need to save for retirement is lower. In the United States, radically changing career paths late in life can be catastrophic. The more we prepare students to consider problems from multiple positions, using different approaches and strategies, the better adapted they will be to the struggle of keeping up with a fast-paced workforce. That's the least we can do. In the best of worlds, these skills might also help college graduates to organize and fight for better working conditions and equal pay for equal work.

Most of us, however, have not been prepared to teach the students who are actually in our classrooms for the complex future they face. Gail Mellow, president emerita of LaGuardia Community College, says that the requirement of college today should be to reach and teach "the Top 100%." That means understanding the diversity of students today. She notes that of the roughly 18 million undergraduates attending college in the United States, more than 40 percent attend community college, 40 percent work more than thirty hours a week at paying jobs, a quarter are over twenty-five years old, 30 percent are first-generation college students, nearly a quarter come from low-income families, a quarter suffer from food and housing insecurity, nearly 60 percent are female, and almost half are people of color. While those numbers vary greatly in every country, the fact remains that the demographics of students attending college are becoming more diverse.

We have a demographic mismatch between faculty and students. According to a 2017 study by the National Center for Education Statistics, "76 percent of all college and university faculty members were white, compared to 55 percent of undergraduates. By ethnic group, just 5 percent of faculty members were Hispanic, compared to 20 percent of students. Six percent of professors were Black, compared to 14 percent of their students."[10] Part of the mission and project we have undertaken in this book is to encourage all—teachers and students—to identify and resist the imbalances and inequities of our time and to use the classroom as a platform to understand and prepare for that struggle while ensuring that our diverse student body also leads to a new generation of professors who are as diverse as they can be.

Only 0.4 percent of all students in our universities in the United States attend the Ivies, but most books and articles written about higher education and pedagogy seem to assume students from those universities. Perhaps that's not surprising, given that a majority of professors today themselves come from highly selective institutions. As we think about changing ourselves in order to change our classrooms, we need to be aware of that disparity. We need to be introspective about how we were trained and what we were encultured to believe academic "success" looks like. One recent study of college professors revealed that some 80 percent of all faculty at all US colleges were trained at the most elite 25 percent of universities.[11] A study of political science departments revealed that more than half of all tenure-track vacancies were filled by applicants from only eleven graduate political science departments.[12] In short, most professors who have been hired and have achieved tenure do not share the lived experiences of the majority of our students today.[13]

The nineteenth century lingers in another way: educational achievement today correlates closely with wealth. Excellent schools, private tutors for entrance exams, and other costly ways of improving a child's chances of being admitted to college mean that the wealthiest students have a head start. These factors together mean that too much of higher education contributes to, stabilizes, and perpetuates income inequality and all the attendant social inequalities that correlate with income—specifically, racial, ethnic, and gender disparities within and across institutions and fields.

Let's break that down. We have spent the twentieth century and the first decades of the twenty-first developing a system of education that is more likely to select for wealth than for intelligence, motivation, or academic achievement. In countries where a far smaller percentage of students go on to college, the "sort" of who is or isn't college material happens as early as middle school, age eleven or twelve. Inequality and privilege come in many forms—native language, immigration, income—and operate differently in particular countries. In the United States, we take pride in a more democratic system where every student has the opportunity to go to college. Yet, given that school boards and school budgets are determined locally and funded largely through property taxes, the correlation between "college readiness" and wealth is precise. A map of the United States showing SAT score distribution is nearly identical to a map of US income distribution (which correlates with racial segregation and discrimination too).[14]

For the last decade, Harvard economist Raj Chetty and his team of researchers have been analyzing higher education and social mobility. Previously, the most common metric for gauging a school's success was figuring out how much their new graduates earned. Chetty's team looks at the difference between a student's family income upon entering college and a student's earnings when they graduate from college.[15] True, new Princeton graduates earn the most money upon graduation. They also come from families with the highest income levels. By contrast, as of 2021, according to *U.S. News and World Report,* seven colleges from the City University of New York (CUNY), three from the State University of New York, and seven from the University of California rank in the top twenty national and regional universities facilitating social mobility, specifically in moving students from the bottom to the top income quartile.[16] Chetty's research helps us to see our students in a new way, which is crucial if we are going to change ourselves and change our sense of what "works" in a classroom.

Changing ourselves means changing our assumptions about the students we teach. For starters: they aren't "kids." Professor Kandice Chuh uses the phrase "the people in our classrooms who are students" to remind us of the range of people, diverse in every way, in today's classrooms and the different kinds of obligations for work, family, and community that each one might have.[17] It also helps us to rethink "college readiness" as an extrinsic attribute of students and, instead, consider the multiple factors which make it difficult for students to succeed. In the catchphrase of the Association of American Colleges and Universities, this means "becoming a student-ready college."[18] More personally, it means making our own courses student-ready.

We, as instructors, can both pave the way and step out of the way as we help our students transition from lacking insider knowledge to navigating smarter. As we unlearn many of our old habits, we are also helping our students to understand how to learn and how to use that understanding to make better decisions in their lives, both in school and beyond.

CHAPTER 2

Structuring Active Learning

Maria Montessori in Italy, John Dewey in the United States, and Rabindranath Tagore in India were just a few of the Progressive Era educators who opposed the Taylorist structures of education that Charles Eliot and his colleagues were so busy constructing. They developed alternative models for orphanages and preschools as well as for primary and secondary schools and even for universities based on the fundamentals of agency, independence, problem-solving, and collaboration. As some parents reading this book well know, Montessori schools today continue to pride themselves on giving young students independence—toddlers who can prepare their own snacks and invent their own games to play with peers. "Education is a social process; education is growth; education is not preparation for life but is life itself," Dewey famously wrote, making explicit the relationship between education and society.[1] Tagore was even more adamant in his disdain for educational standardization. In his allegory "The Parrot's Training" (1918), a king seeking to educate his priceless bird forces it to eat pages from a standard textbook until it dies.

Active learning insists that college students should be at least as independent as preschoolers and lots freer than Tagore's parrot. Imagine a classroom alive with vibrant activity, where the intrinsic rewards of learning become not just a goal for our course but a lifelong project. Active learning carries forward the vision of teaching with the aim of making a better society and a better world, with students as the architects of the future.

As in all architecture, structure is crucial. Active learning is not "anything goes." Giving students freedom to be curious, to create, and to lead requires planning and organizing activities for them to use that opportunity and autonomy productively. Active learning guides students in taking that leap with us and offers them some structure to buttress their learning even as we give them the flexibility and room to grow.

Before we create the New College Classroom, it's useful to frame some key principles of learning and cognitive science that are foundational to active learning. We have several decades of research supporting us as we make our vision a reality. Literally hundreds of pedagogy theorists and practitioners have addressed the relationship between structure and openness, beginning with intensive study into how we learn and how we learn differently in different situations.

This chapter surveys four key pedagogical approaches that themselves have been studied, tested, revised, debated, expanded, and implemented innumerable times by experts in this field. They are useful in understanding the "why" behind certain redesigns of, say, our syllabus or final exams. These concepts are also useful in explaining active learning to students, parents, and administrators who have inherited traditional values about higher education and might wonder about the learning science undergirding our classroom innovations.

In this chapter:

Scaffolding
Growth Mindset
The Flipped Classroom
Backwards Planning

Scaffolding

Scaffolding is one of the most basic terms associated with active learning. It is based on a progressive idea of learning, that all we learn becomes the support for what we learn next and that the instructor's role is to create the framework for success for the more difficult tasks ahead. In its simplest application, we scaffold by building cumulative assignments, structuring them from easier to more difficult, from "low-stakes" (for instance, little to no impact on a student's evaluation) to "high-stakes." When we scaffold, we break up what we want students to learn into chunks, making the whole process more manageable. When a child learns to read, for example, they might first be introduced to the alphabet, then challenged to sound out short words. You don't teach a child how to read by giving them a copy of *War and Peace.* This principle applies throughout most of education. In college, many fields are structured by implicit scaffolding: you don't learn calculus before precalculus.

The term *scaffolding* was coined in the 1950s by Jerome Bruner, one of the founders of the field of cognitive psychology. Bruner proposed a theory of children's intellectual and emotional maturation, arguing that children are ready to learn certain kinds of content and understand certain concepts at specific points in their lives.[2] In what is called a "spiral" approach, Bruner advocated revisiting important ideas and lessons at different stages in a child's development, when their meaning would become increasingly deep, complex, and difficult. His ideals for complex learning and educational growth have been translated in many ways, including in the stepped approach of the traditional school curriculum. In the United States, physical science is taught in 9th grade, biology in 10th grade, chemistry in 11th, and physics in 12th.[3] The general and empirical principles learned in physical science scaffold increasingly difficult and abstract scientific ideas.

Bruner's principles of scaffolding build on a particular understanding of child development formulated by the Russian psychologist Lev

Vygotsky. Vygotsky coined the term *zone of proximal development* to signal the milestones in a child's life when they are mature enough for certain kinds of insights. Vygotsky added that children can be motivated to learn beyond their limits if guided by an adult or a peer who can support them as they move to the next level.[4] Scaffolding provides that support along the way.

Whether you are a seasoned professor proposing a brand-new course or are yourself new to teaching, thinking about gradual, stepped learning (scaffolding) can be an excellent place to begin implementing active learning. For example, routines that you put in place at the start of the semester can become more student-driven. Say one of your goals in teaching upper-level Spanish is to assign a research project that students complete in groups. Perhaps in the first week you hand out a "to-do" list for each group to get them warmed up—and it ends with a question: "¿Qué más?" ("What else?"). Students add anything else they want to prioritize. As the weeks go by, students begin to keep track of tasks without your prompting, becoming more and more self-directed.

Yet, even as scaffolding is useful, it is crucial, as Bruner himself attested, to expect breakthroughs that disrupt all the progressive learning spirals and instead leap ahead several giant steps. A new Venezuelan roommate moves in with a student in your Spanish class. Or a student takes a semester abroad in Peru. Suddenly, there is no clear step-by-step, but everything happens for that student all at once.

We can scaffold our students' active learning—and, to use a radically different metaphor—we can also structure challenging moments that toss them into the educational deep end. When they have gained confidence in their abilities, they won't sink but instead will learn to swim—and to help one another—when offered new challenges. In their book *Small Teaching Online: Applying Learning Science in Online Classes,* Flower Darby and James M. Lang advocate asking students to solve a problem *before* they are ready. They note, "When we ask people to complete tasks before they learn something new, they will learn it more effectively."[5] The most effective and memorable lessons bring a little real-world chaos into the classroom and demand some creative thinking from students.

Growth Mindset

Beginning in the last decades of the twentieth century, researchers in the areas of decision theory, systems theory, and cognitive psychology have focused on "mindset," the idea that people or groups of people hold assumptions, a worldview, or an evaluation about themselves or others that influences how they act in the world. This mindset, it is argued, governs choices people make and also how willing they are to change—which is to say, how willing they are to learn. In her 2006 best-seller *Mindset: The New Psychology of Success,* Stanford University psychologist Carol Dweck melded the extensive research on motivation and human development that she began in the 1980s with research on the role of socioeconomic conditions on a child's ability to learn, a disciplinary crossing of psychology and sociology. She identified internalized modes by which students judge themselves as having a firm and unchangeable nature ("fixed mindset") or one capable of learning and improving ("growth mindset").

Dweck defines *growth mindset* as "the belief that skills can be improved with time and effort." Practically from infancy, upper- and middle-class parents give their children special lessons, extracurricular classes, and tutors to enhance their abilities and also to demonstrate to young students that, with guidance and feedback centered on their improvement, they are capable of advancing. They go to well-funded schools that pay special attention to subject areas where they are considered "gifted" or provide tutors to help them go from poor work in certain areas to a much better result.

By contrast, many low-income and minority students, in particular, absorb negative social evaluations practically from birth and learn to see themselves in the latter category, "fixed" in failure. In a nationwide empirical study published in 2016 that was conducted on high school students in Chile, Dweck and a team of Chilean researchers found that students from the most impoverished backgrounds were the most likely to have internalized a fixed mindset about their own ability to improve and the least likely to achieve at the highest levels.

Dweck's insights are important in the New College Classroom because they help us, as instructors, to reevaluate our own ideas about "excellence" or "rigor" or "college readiness" as well as ideas about "motivation." They help us to understand that there are deep, underlying social conditions that children can internalize that undercut their confidence in their own ability to learn. Since agency is one of the key values of active learning, it is crucial to understand the ways social bias undermines a student's sense of agency. In Dweck's educational experiment in Chile, the students who were nurtured to develop a growth mindset were "appreciably buffered against the deleterious effects of poverty on achievement: students in the lowest 10th percentile of family income who exhibited a growth mindset showed academic performance as high as that of fixed mindset students from the 80th income percentile."[6] Dweck argues that understanding their own mindset can become a tool for students. In the Chilean study, students were able to use this new self-understanding to counter the debilitating impact of years of traditional school failure.

Growth mindset has become something of a growth industry, with TED Talks, workshops, and multiple millions of dollars in funding from grants and philanthropic foundations—it has also gained plenty of critics.[7] Some have insisted that they have not been able to duplicate Dweck's growth mindset results.[8] Other fault finders think the binary of "fixed" and "growth" is too simplistic. Most of us embody some combination of both, depending on the situation. There are real, tangible factors to consider, too: it can feel too environmentally deterministic to assume that in a global pandemic, for example, a student is underperforming due to a fixed mindset.[9] A growth mindset certainly helps, but without a significant improvement in circumstances, it may not be enough.[10]

Biochemist and science educator Beronda L. Montgomery offers what she calls a "bilateral" approach to mindset theory, emphasizing the importance of "considering the contributions of both the individual and the environment." She insists that we move past any idea that failure to thrive or learn is the student's "fault." Instead, she offers a powerful botanical analogy: "If a plant is not faring well, the caretaker may, as a very last resort, attribute this outcome to a failure to identify how to facilitate the plant in thriving, but not to a failure on the part of the plant itself."[11] The caretaker who finds that their plant isn't flourishing immediately addresses all of the conditions of light, soil, water, and nourishment. They don't assume that the plant is the problem; they work to improve the plant's environmental conditions to optimize its growth. That's a powerful lesson for all of us.

The Flipped Classroom

In the flipped classroom, students watch lectures, read assignments, or do problem sets outside of class and then, in class, answer challenges or problems presented to them by the instructor, typically working with partners. This is not the same as a discussion format ("raise your hand if you know the answer") but is an inventory method where *everyone* proposes an answer at the same time. Often answers are demonstrated in a low-stakes, preliminary way.

In a large lecture, a professor can poll students and have them use electronic clickers (remote control keypads that communicate student answers to a central computer) to offer an answer. There are equivalent polling affordances for online classes. Their aggregate poll results are then projected on a screen. The professor might highlight the distribution of the answers and solicit a few student opinions about which answer is right but typically does not confirm or refute the results.

Instead, in the New College Classroom, students work in groups or with a partner to think through the alternative answers and argue the case within their group about which is best. The professor then takes another poll. When it goes well, students learn by correcting one another, arguing viewpoints, and observing the different ways classmates arrive at their answers. Optimally, everyone eventually develops the thinking and knowledge to arrive at the correct answer.

The flipped classroom frees the instructor from lecturing and allows them to devote more time to mentoring and pushing students toward greater depth and insights. Professors Donna McGregor and Pamela Mills flipped their chemistry classes at Lehman College so that all content is explained outside of their class meetings. Students study at home through audio or video instruction, which affords the instructors the opportunity to use active, participatory learning strategies in class. They invite students to apply real-world examples to their lessons.[12]

Physics professor Eric Mazur at Harvard University is one of the nation's most eminent proponents of the flipped classroom method.[13] He uses clickers to poll students on the answers and also to find out which areas from the homework students either do not understand or that may hold little interest beyond the classroom. Students come to his class having explored key physics principles, and then, in real time, he asks students to apply the content to a real-world problem, such as, "What if a gamma ray burst hit the Earth?"

Similarly, in a business law class, Craig Cameron and Jennifer Dickfos, professors at the Griffith Business School at Griffith University in South East Queensland, Australia, ask students which legal principles addressed early in the course have relevance to their own businesses. The typical business student never takes another law course beyond "Introduction to Business Law," a class that is often mandatory but is rarely esteemed by most students. Rather than lecture, Cameron and Dickfos structure their class to present the course's key legal principles early and then ask students to contribute ways that the principles had applications to the product, consumer relations, management situations, or business plans in their own industries.[14] They then use the students' own examples to restructure the second half of the course, turning legal theory into business practice.

Most importantly, the model works. It prioritizes practice, mentoring, and coaching. As reported in a 2017 *Inside Higher Ed* article by Jennifer Goodman, the flipped classroom model "boosts passing rates to 80+ percent."[15] The flipped classroom helps students at every stage of learning, whether they need individual attention or want to delve deeper into information.[16] Right answers aren't the point. The process of acquiring and sharpening the tools needed for gaining expertise and finding the best ways to learn together are all embedded in the flipped classroom and are useful to different forms of engaged, effective teaching and learning.

Backwards Planning

The term *backwards planning* comes from outcomes-based forms of learning where instructors or programs decide in advance which learning outcomes are most important for students. It allows students to know "why" from the beginning. The course or curriculum is then constructed "backwards" with the intention of arriving, in the end, at the intended goals. Backwards planning requires breaking down each part of the learning into a specific module or skill set directly related to the final task. Anyone who takes a Lamaze class knows this pedagogical technique: the end result is, if all goes well, exactly what you're practicing for.

Advocates of backwards planning often focus on it as an efficient method of moving toward the learning goals, with fewer disruptions and less time spent in tangents and byways. In active learning adaptations of backwards planning, we avoid rigidity and use the cognitive pay off of the "why" as inspiration, not as a narrowing of purpose to a solitary goal. In Part II, we show ways that students can be included in designing the learning outcomes for a course—to contribute more meaningful "whys" and goals based on their biggest questions and deepest interests. We especially like asking students how a course might change their lives and what skills they hope to develop during the term to be successful in the next semester, in the next year, and in the next five or ten years.

CHAPTER 3

Teaching Is Mentoring

What makes a good mentor? "Mentor" is the name the goddess Athena assumed when she appeared in human form to serve as the trusted adviser to the twenty-year-old Telemachus while his father, Odysseus, the Greek king, was at sea. Mentor intervenes in the youth's chaotic life—and not by telling him exactly what to do. Instead, Mentor instills Telemachus with the mental fortitude he needs to be the hero of his own story.[1] That's a big role, and Homer had it right. A mentor is a trustworthy guide with good intentions who advises someone else's child (no matter how old). In the dire case of Telemachus, the stakes were very high, necessitating Athena's wise intervention. Fortunately, no one expects any of us to be a goddess.

That heroic tale underscores the crucial role of mentoring in a person's life, and it's a good reminder of the best gifts we can pass on to our students: skills to help them become self-directed learners, such as sound reasoning, resourcefulness, critical thinking, and time management. Mentoring is not just what happens in office hours: the best teachers mentor in the classroom by modeling best practices for students, sharing strategies for success—how we would approach an assignment or how former students have done it and how much time it took them. Likewise, teaching extends beyond the classroom, and we can be good mentors to our students by encouraging them to study together and go to one another with questions before they come to us professors. Forming networks of peer-to-peer support bolsters student learning because learning is social—and students may make the friendships of a lifetime in the process.

Mentoring can sometimes feel overwhelming to mere mortals. Every student has their own unique needs, and we only have so much time and advice to give. That seemingly insurmountable problem—one of us; hundreds of students—is also the solution.[2] We cannot be everything to our students. Instead, we can give them a little bit of our humanity, our honesty, our limited perspective, our understanding, and guide them to collect strategies and skills from a wide range of people—advisers, bosses, coaches, and peers—with different experiences and perspectives, not just one. Mentoring is a form of caring for others—caring for the souls of our students, as bell hooks aptly phrased it in *Teaching to Transgress*—to ensure that they are given their best chance to learn and to make the most of their time with us.[3] Professor Maha Bali at the American University of Cairo refers to this as "a pedagogy of care."[4]

Yusef Waghid, Distinguished Professor of Philosophy of Education at Stellenbosch University, South Africa, proposes using the *ubuntu* practice as a model of caring for our students.[5] The *ubuntu* practice involves (1) showing moral respect to all; (2) considering all humans worthy of our acknowledgment and engagement, even those we resent; and (3) prioritizing the humanity of all, recognizing that all are equal and that no person should undermine or disrespect another's right of belonging to humanity.

The *ubuntu* pedagogies of care imply that the care must be mutual, applying equally to instructors and students alike. As mentors, we are often in difficult situations, trying to advise students who are themselves also in difficult situations. A good mentor establishes healthy boundaries to prioritize care for themselves and also model appropriate self-care in the workplace for our students by ending office hours on time, not answering emails on weekends to respect time off, and so on.

Finally, the best mentor (and here again, Homer is a good guide) helps the mentee to mentor themselves and, ideally, others too. Even worse than not having a good adviser is having one who infantilizes you, makes you feel dependent on them. In very simple, practical terms, we ask our mentees to bring a written agenda when they meet with us, where they write out their own priorities and what they hope we can discuss together. As in other instances throughout this book, we know that, as soon as they write out their priorities, they are already learning how to be more self-directed and to apply "self-care" to their studies. They are already practicing agency, empowerment, and a sense of self—even as we are pledging to help them on their journey.

This chapter focuses on ways to translate best practices of active learning into our mentorship in order to create an engaged and equitable learning community for all.

In this chapter:

What Do I Want Students to Call Me?
Prioritizing Student Wellness
How Can I Be Personable Without Getting Too Personal?
Office Hours That Empower Students
What Happens If a Student Tells Me About Sexual Harassment?
How Do I Address Racial and Other Forms of Discrimination?
How Do I Support Students with Cognitive and Physical Disabilities?
How Can I Be a Good Mentor to Returning Students?

What Do I Want Students to Call Me?

It may seem unusual to begin a section on mentoring by talking about how we want our students to address us, yet, as in all active learning, respect is a great place to begin, and titles are part of that. In some

How To Be a Good Mentor: The 3-Minute Manifesto

This 3-minute exercise by acclaimed designer Bruce Mau helps anyone facing a complex task to greater self-knowledge on the way to designing a workable solution. Mau notes that a designer's job is to accept the biggest challenges we face today as the beginning, not the end of a process. This includes learning how to be a good mentor. He keeps the exercise short to spark ideas and emotions. Three minutes is enough, he insists, because people know what future they want—all we need to do is ask them.*

Choose one of these prompts to get started. If you finish before time's up, then go to another, and another:

- **What kind of mentor do you hope to be?**
- **What special talents do you have to offer?**
- **What can you give?**
- **What are your boundaries?**
- **Who are your students?**
- **What kind of students do you work with best?**
- **Where can you improve?**
- **If you were your own ideal mentor, how would you mentor the student you?**

* Bruce Mau, *MC24: Bruce Mau's 24 Principles for Designing Massive Change in Your Life and Work* (New York: Phaidon Press, 2020), 65.

places, this is straightforward. In German-speaking universities the title "Professor" is reserved for those with full professor status. In Japanese culture you would never call someone who was not an immediate family member by their first name—and certainly not one of your professors.

In the United States and some other countries, the question of titles is a more vexing issue with no right answer but with lots to think about.

Just as we deride any faculty member who refers to their students as "kids," we are aware that titles carry much more than denotative meaning. When Dr. Jill Biden fiercely defended her title (and her doctor of education degree) to her critics, many of us cheered, including other community college professors too long denied status because of the hierarchical nature of higher education.

Every institution has its own explicit or implicit ways of showing respect or disrespect, and what we expect from our students in part depends on what is considered the norm. I (Cathy) know a woman administrator at a famous school of medicine who once showed me the minutes of a meeting in which she was listed by first name only on a roster of male doctors who were all labeled as "Dr. So and So."

There is no right answer to this question, but there are plenty of things you don't want to be called. I (Cathy) know another distinguished scientist who has received every imaginable award short of a Nobel Prize, yet, because she is less than five feet tall, is often addressed by a diminutive nickname she doesn't use herself. For this reason, she asks students, lab assistants, and junior colleagues to call her "Dr." or "Professor" in order to remind them not to diminish her professional stature. Many of my graduate students who did their undergraduate training at historically Black colleges and universities (HBCUs) continued to call me "Dr. Davidson" even after they became distinguished professors in their own right. In response to our country's long history of racism, their undergraduate professors at HBCUs insisted that their students use their titles when addressing them, even in contexts where other schools might have encouraged the students to use first names when addressing their professors.

What we expect from our students in part depends on what is considered the norm. As an adjunct, I (Christina) struggled with this question each time I began teaching at a new institution. I taught for ten years before I earned my doctorate, so "Dr." was not an option, and, as an adjunct, "Professor" wasn't right, either. When I taught in Florida, students conditioned to respond to authority with southern manners automatically called me "Mrs.," much to my offense (I wasn't married) and despite my repeated requests that they call me anything but that. When I taught in New York City, I met many students who were the first in their families to go to college, and it was an honor for them to be able to call their instructors "Professor," so I gave up resisting that, too. In general, I prefer my students to call me "Christina" because I want to earn their respect, not demand it. At the end of the day, what I've learned is that everyone shows respect in their own way, and allowing students to honor you in the way that is most meaningful to them also honors their hard-won admittance to college.

Prioritizing Student Wellness

Good mentoring includes cultivating resourcefulness in students as well as thinking about how students' lives outside the classroom impact their learning. One of the best ways to do both things at once is to help students find all the tools and support that an academic institution affords them. Sometimes the last page of the syllabus furnishes information about accommodations as well as helpful details about where to find tutoring. Take a moment to do some digging and offer students more, particularly for those students who face food and housing insecurity. Often, more students can benefit from this information than you might think, and it is a hundred times more challenging to learn course material when their basic needs are not regularly being met.

Adashima Oyo, who teaches health care courses as an adjunct at Brooklyn College and New York University, spends extra time updating that page of her syllabus every year to include information about campus offices with resources on internships, jobs, and writing help as well as "social determinants of academic success." She shares that she's not a social worker or a therapist, but she still wants students to know where they can find what they need to thrive, such as the campus health clinic, the mental health center, and the social service center. These resources can be a lifeline to students who are navigating college for the first time, managing language and cultural or disability barriers. In addition, as she reminds us, "There are also many students who need to know where and how to access a food pantry, health insurance, emergency housing, legal support, or other urgent issues like referrals for those students dealing with domestic violence or substance abuse. I remind students that these services are confidential, shame-free, and free of charge."[6] We cannot be experts in all these things, but we can learn where these offices are located and share that information with students to help them be resourceful and gain access to what they need.

Whole institutions can help here as well. At Purdue University, the first-year Cornerstone program offers integrated general education courses to some four thousand students a year.[7] Taught by full-time faculty, this program integrates reading, writing, and listening skills with content that addresses some of the biggest problems in the world today, such as sustainable solutions to environmental disasters, medicine and health care, and human rights and conflict resolution. Equally important—and integral to the program itself—Cornerstone assigns faculty mentors to the first-year students, building counseling into the learning experience. This means that faculty too are trained to offer advice on everything from mental health to study abroad. Rather than mentoring being an "add-on" assigned elsewhere, it is designed into the most foundational learning experiences of Purdue students—and, not incidentally, of Purdue faculty too.

How Can I Be Personable Without Getting Too Personal?

It's daunting, especially at the start of your career, to assume that you know how to balance being *personable* while maintaining professionalism. We care deeply about our students, and we genuinely want to help them. Setting healthy boundaries *is* a form of caring. Modeling a healthy work-life balance is as good for our students as it is for us.

There are easy ways to support the sociality of learning and encourage students to form bonds with their peers. Community-building within a course is personable and generous, and it keeps the focus on students' lifelong learning through sound pedagogy. An effective and fun way to do this on the first day of class is to create a student "yearbook." Sam Arsenio, a third-year student at the John Jay College of Criminal Justice in New York City, introduced this idea in an interdisciplinary CUNY Peer Leaders program in 2021. He asked all of the returning and new peer leaders to introduce themselves in their Zoom meeting by creating an autobiographical slide. Their slides instantly allowed students to feel a sense of community and engagement while also setting their own personal parameters for privacy and sharing. Inspired by this student, Professor Shelly Eversley, Interim Chair of Black and Latino Studies at Baruch College, adapted the method for the first meeting in her online class a few weeks later. Eversley created a blank template of a yearbook using Google Slides and asked her students to spend five minutes filling in a slide of their own to introduce themselves to their peers. Each student added their name, pronouns, and a few pictures or things about themselves that they wanted their peers to know.

Community-building activities like these thoughtfully invest time in centering students' lives and prompt students to get to know one another's names and not just that of the professor. In addition to laying the foundations for a healthy and respectful learning environment, this activity shows students that they are not alone, that they have a support network they can go to before they come to you with questions—and that takes off a bit of the pressure on us professors, too.

Remembering that we're neither goddesses nor therapists is freeing and can aid us in determining who really needs our help and who needs help from a professional with a skill set we do not possess. Once you decide where your boundaries lie—including ones involving time—set them in place. If you know yourself to be poor at setting those, err on the side of making stronger boundaries. Then consider ways that the whole learning community might be structured to support students' learning beyond one-on-one help from you.

This is where student-centered learning helps everyone, especially the professor. Students can go to one another (via an email list or Slack channel) for support and answers, becoming more independent and developing their own ability to network in addition to having us to guide them. That's how we care for our students while also guarding against faculty burnout.

Office Hours That Empower Students

On his YouTube and TikTok advice channels, "First Gen Prof," Tom Mulaney, a professor of Chinese history at Stanford University, offers students insights into "How Academia Works." He frequently provides viewers with information he wishes he had when he was the first member of his own family to go to college. "When I was an undergrad, I *never* went to office hours. I assumed that unless I had a burning question or a brilliant idea, that I was wasting the professor's time. Then I became a professor and no one was coming to office hours, and I realized maybe this is a systemic problem, maybe everyone has the same assumptions. So let me say, you do not need a good excuse to go to office hours. Your professor wants to meet you. Trust me."[8] Since his TikTok video received over thirty-eight thousand likes and a thousand comments on the first day it was posted, it's safe to say that, yes, not going to office hours is a widespread concern.

In addition to encouraging students to come to office hours, there are ways to make office hours more welcoming or to highlight their importance to student success. Even the term *office hours* is intimidating and alienating to many students because it carries many of the resonances of failure: being sent to the office for detention or counseling in grade school or high school. Recently, some institutions have renamed them "student hours" or redesigned "course centers," blocks of time set aside in empty classrooms where students can come together to work outside of class with peers and with the instructor present to give advice or feedback. Sometimes faculty from different programs supplement traditional office hours by holding joint course centers. At one college, instructors in an Introduction to Symbolic Logic and an Introduction to Physics course held joint sessions with instructors and teaching assistants moving between the rooms to offer advice to those studying for exams or writing research papers.[9] Some professors require them: they build attending at least one or two one-on-one meetings or collective office hours into their course requirements.

What Happens If a Student Tells Me About Sexual Harassment?

In an urgent and immediate situation like this, you can be compassionate but should also facilitate a formal introduction to the best and most trustworthy people at your institution who are responsible professionals trained to address these issues. It is far too serious, on every level, for an amateur, no matter how well-meaning you may be. In addition, as Sara Ahmed warns in her starkly compelling book *Complaint!* (2021), bureaucratic structures for complaint can often end up harming the person making the complaint.[10] Given this turn in institutional defensiveness, it is crucial to help a student, first, remove themselves from potential harm and, second, make sure they are aware of and follow procedures if they wish to offer a formal complaint.

Not knowing how to proceed might cause you to exacerbate what is already a terrible situation. It's your responsibility to have this contact information on hand and to familiarize yourself with your college's health and wellness center and security department, and to know what the next steps would be if a student came to you with a problem beyond your area of expertise.

There are things we all can do at our various institutions to be proactive and create networks of support for ourselves. After all, students are not the only ones who experience harassment. After hearing numerous complaints from female and gender-nonconforming adjuncts about sexual harassment—from advisers, peers, and students—I (Christina) formed an advocacy group for adjuncts called "Better to Speak" with my colleagues Destry Sibley, a Fulbright National Geographic scholar, and Alicia Andrzejewski, then a graduate student and now an assistant professor at the College of William and Mary. Named after a poem by Audre Lorde, our group adopted the mission to "create spaces in which women and gender nonconforming graduate students and adjunct faculty members share experiences and support." The group provided a space for colleagues to exchange advice on the best ways to handle delicate or even aggressive situations. As with in-class peer-to-peer collaborative groups, this mentoring network helped us to turn to one another and ask "Am I right that this does not feel right?" Once validated, we used one another to help address the issues we were facing.

How Do I Address Racial and Other Forms of Discrimination?

The same cautions for gender and sexual harassment apply to racial discrimination. Before you even encounter such a situation, it's important to know your university's policies and, even better, to educate yourself and establish your own zero-tolerance policies for your classroom (for instance: "We do not tolerate racist, sexist, transphobic, and other kinds of aggressive comments directed at any group of people"). In addition, it's helpful to be an informed participant in your campus community and to know where students might seek friendship and support, such as your local Hillel group, PRIDE group, and organizations for Asian American, Black, Indigenous, Latinx students as well as any other group. If you want to become even more familiar with managing or participating in difficult discussions in your classroom, department, or campus, a book that deftly addresses this question from multiple perspectives is *Difficult Subjects: Insights and Strategies for Teaching About Race, Sexuality, and Gender,* edited by Badia

Ahad-Legardy and OiYan A. Poon. For a more theoretical approach that offers an Indigenous or decolonial perspective, you might consult the excellent essays in Sandy Grande's *Red Pedagogy: Native American Social and Political Thought.*[11] Beyond that, you might also seek bystander intervention training, which will prepare you to address racial and other forms of discrimination when they arise. Depending on the situation, you might intervene, or you might realize that the best thing you can do is to ask someone for help—before you do, we advocate being thoughtful about whom you approach and how you approach someone for help. People of color are not responsible for educating everyone else about racism.

Faculty of color spend far more time mentoring students of color, including offering advice about how to proceed in situations where they face tacit bias or overt discrimination.[12] We believe universities should be aware of what Nicole Truesdell calls "cultural taxation," the ways primarily white institutions often assume that faculty of color will become mentors to students of color, without offering credit or compensation for this "invisible labor."[13] Similarly, part-time or adjunct faculty often are overburdened with mentoring duties that they are not compensated for in their salaries or in other reward systems. Universities need to find ways to address these glaring inequities—and some of them are doing so. Examples include the Hope Center for College, Community, and Justice at Temple University; the Percy Ellis Sutton Search for Education, Elevation, and Knowledge (SEEK) program; and the Accelerated Study in Associate Programs (ASAP), which began at the City University of New York (CUNY) and now exists at ten other colleges in five states. Students in ASAP (where mentoring is a key part of the program) are twice as likely to graduate in three years compared to similar students not in the program.[14]

What should you do in a case where a student accuses you or someone in your class of being insensitive to their particular identity or experience? Self-education and a little bit of role playing can do a lot of good to prepare you for moments like this. We highly recommend Melissa

Schieble, Amy Vetter, and Kahdeidra Monét Martin's *Classroom Talk for Social Change,* a book filled with examples of various scenarios in which professors become mediators to difficult and highly charged conversations.

Sometimes, deep listening is the answer. Dr. Jade E. Davis, director of educational technology and learning management at the University of Pennsylvania Library System and a rare African American in her technology field, once suggested to a seminar of mostly white participants: "If a person of color overcomes their own inhibitions and takes the time to point out that something you (a white person) are doing that feels racist, you should have one response: listen! Most people won't even tell you." Her point is generalizable to many different situations. However uncomfortable the experience, listening without defensiveness is an act of trust (on all sides), a learning experience, and a precious opportunity for unlearning and relearning that will serve you well in the future.

How Do I Support Students with Cognitive and Physical Disabilities?

At the Spring 2021 workshop "Is Universal Design Enough? Learning from the Neurodiversity Movement How to Engage Diverse Learners," Kristen Gillespie-Lynch, a psychology professor at the College of Staten Island, noted that no design, no matter how well intentioned, is actually "universal."[15] What works for the abilities of one student might be crushing and confusing for another. She argues that "universal design is an iterative process," a constantly changing and adaptive response to whatever situation presents itself. Universal design requires understanding, explaining, adaptation, and, most fundamentally, a willingness to observe and to be flexible in all the ways that define the New College Classroom.

To make this point, she showed a video clip by Stephen Shore, a professor of special education at Adelphi University who is himself autistic. In one assignment, he had his students write about the workings of a new electronic sound device.[16] One student in the class was stymied by poor penmanship and an inability to write rapidly and asked if, instead of writing about the device, he could draw a map. Professor Shore was stunned when the student produced an elegant map on the spot, but what stood out to him was how easy it would have been for him—an autistic professor teaching students with disabilities about disability—to have missed this student's contribution. "The exercise was supposed to be about mastery of content, not handwriting," he noted.

Sometimes, however, we aren't as flexible as Shore, and we simply fail to give each student the opportunity and support they deserve. If a student reports a problem, we should address issues of accessibility in the same way that we do other complaints. There should be an official at your institution charged with maintaining standards of compliance and access for your students. As with racism, we all have much to learn when addressing those who have different perspectives, identities, points of view, and abilities than our own. In the case of cognitive difference, it is important to remember that part of mentoring is helping students make their case—for themselves and with their professors, in their communities, and with future employers. "Camouflaging" is commonplace among those with invisible or cognitive disabilities, so inviting students to talk about the best ways of representing and presenting themselves can be especially helpful to their academic success.

How Can I Be a Good Mentor to Returning Students?

In college today, over a quarter of all students are "nontraditional" or "returning" students—over the age of twenty-five, working full-time, with family and other personal obligations, and typically commuting to campus. All too often, older students are not offered mentoring and advice at institutions that cater to students of "traditional" age.

Todd McCullough, president of Adults Belong in College, a nonprofit advocacy organization, argues that every returning student needs five kinds of support from institutions: financial aid specialists (to help with the complex rules around part-time and transfer students); transition advisers (to help returning students acclimate to a new campus and to find out what services are available); supportive student organizations for returning students; mentors and counselors; and an institutional and classroom atmosphere of inclusion.[17]

In addition to these ways of mentoring, it is also crucial to help our returning students be aware of all the ways their institution offers credit for prior work and life experiences. More and more institutions offer credit for prior learning (CPL) or Prior Learning Assessment (PLA), which are two names for the same thing: a means whereby institutions assess and give college credit for students' training and workforce experience outside of college. These include military training, standardized exams, industry credentials such as licenses and certifications, and community service. A good discussion to have with older students would include evaluating prior work and life experiences combined with advising them on which prerequisites are worth retaking at this stage in their careers so that they can benefit the most from their time to graduation.

Finally, and this will come as no surprise, we advocate organizing peer mentoring groups for nontraditional, returning students. Most colleges and universities aren't equipped to address all of the varied issues nontraditional students face—from childcare to carpools, health insurance to veterans' benefits. Returning students can often be the best sources for information and support for their peers, because most resources on campus are geared for traditional students between eighteen and twenty-two years old. This is not to exempt schools from providing services for the nontraditional students they accept but to acknowledge that peer mentoring, in most places, has proven to be extremely successful in addressing the complex educational and life challenges faced by returning students. Programs such as Pioneer Connections, a peer mentoring program for adult and nontraditional students at Volunteer State Community College, a public, comprehensive community college in Gallatin, Tennessee, are a promising feature in the higher education landscape. Once a year, the college seeks out successful adult learners with leadership potential and offers them professional development to enhance their own leadership skills as well as a scholarship and stipend so that, during their tenure as students, they can also earn money teaching other adult learners to be peer mentors for incoming and returning students.[18]

Teaching is mentoring, and mentoring is teaching. As with other forms of active learning, sometimes the single greatest gift we can offer is knowing when to support students, when to advise them, when to help them take their skills to the next level, and when to honor the knowledge and experience they bring and then step out of their way.

PART II

Changing Our Classrooms

In our classrooms, we have the opportunity to create communities that can serve as models for what the larger world can become. What's more, we have direct influence on what our students will be able to anticipate as acceptable and what they will be able to begin to imagine as possible.

—ERICA CHU, "The Least We Can Do," in *Difficult Subjects*

CHAPTER 4

Before the First Class

In a typical classroom, planning is assumed to be the province of the instructor. When students come to class on the first day, they usually receive a syllabus that sets out the basic structure, rules, outcomes, and regulations of the classroom, all predetermined. The timeline, requirements, assignments, goals, exams, and assessment methods are decided in advance. They are a "given."

In participatory classrooms, there are challenges, not "givens." Questioning the traditional features of a class becomes part of the learning / unlearning process for students and the foundation for transforming a classroom for instructors. Some components might be left open or flexible so that students can participate in rethinking the assumptions of the educational system they have inherited. Even when the course content seems fixed by your institution or departmentally mandated, there are ways to center students so that they can take ownership of their own education.

This chapter focuses on each aspect of planning a class and offers ideas and models that make room for students to contribute and alter the inherited dynamics, the givens. If one goal of education is to provide students with the tools to shape their (and our) future, inviting their participation is a first step toward imagining what is possible—in the class and beyond.

In this chapter:

Crafting a Syllabus That Works for Every Student
Cocreating a Syllabus with Students
Estimating Student Workload
Innovative Textbook Design and Online Resources
Establishing the Goals of the Course
Building Midterm Reflection into the Course Design
Making Class Time Count
Bridging Distance Online

Crafting a Syllabus That Works for Every Student

It may seem like the first order of business for our classrooms is designing the syllabus. But, as we know, in a traditional course, we aren't so much designing a *new* syllabus as modifying one that has been handed down to us—officially by our program or department, unofficially by our own professors in the courses we took from them—and too often we teach very much the way they taught. A syllabus is a genre, a format, a template, a set of expectations, an implicit guarantee of "quality," "rigor," and "coverage." It exists as a "thing" before we begin to create our own and often lives on in class after class we teach, constantly adapted, modified, appended, and, inevitably, growing.

Where does the modern syllabus come from? Although its history goes back to the fourteenth century, the syllabus we see most often is a compendium of past assumptions and contemporary legal ("risk management") practices.[1] In other words, it's a hot mess. Given all the requirements of the contemporary syllabus, it is hard to balance our desire to make the course and its content inviting while at the same time conveying requirements.[2] Instead of innovating, we add more and more content until a syllabus becomes a tome. When students ask us questions about the mechanics of a course, the common refrain goes something like: *It's on the syllabus.* Typically, a syllabus is as dry as a terms of service agreement, which seems to be written expressly for the purpose of having the user *not* read it.

By contrast, a participatory syllabus invites students to contribute to its making. Ideally, it conveys the essentials in a manner that is visually attractive and to the point.[3] White space and maybe a few flourishes (intellectual or artistic, challenging or even humorous) show students that you are attempting to do something different—to educate, not dictate. And then it also leaves strategic openings where students can contribute their own content and ideas.

The required parts of a syllabus are familiar to anyone who has ever been a student: course title and number, meeting time and place, instructor's name, contact info, and office hours; a reading schedule; and the required exams, projects, or papers. It might also include teaching philosophy and learning outcomes. Two pages may be a good rule of thumb for these basics. Everything else can go in an addendum or on a course website or learning management system (LMS), such as Blackboard, Canvas, Moodle, or whatever your institution employs. The addendum might include a supplementary schedule of assignments and readings, legal and quasi-legal material an institution requires as well as helpful content about mental and physical health services or other student wellness resources. Given the tab structure of a website as well as search functions, these supplementary materials are more easily seen and retrieved online than on a conventional, long, linear (typed) paper syllabus.

Although most of us hand out a syllabus that looks pretty much the way the genre has looked for decades, some professors have taken the daring step of reimagining how they will represent their courses in an inviting, unconventional, genre-disrupting format. An adage of human-computer interaction design is "you get what you design for." That's also true of the syllabus. Starting with a bold and student-centered syllabus sets the tone for the course. Even as students prepare to contribute something bold and new, they know that they are in good hands. We all know that an exciting ride is more enjoyable when we are sure the seat belt is fastened and secure.

Revamping a syllabus is no small task. Fortunately, several instructors, at various institutions and in different disciplines, offer us inspiring models for where we might begin. Kathy Klein, associate professor of occupational therapy at Stockton University in Galloway, New Jersey, champions accessibility in her revamped syllabus. Klein realized that the previous version—a more traditional, black-and-white syllabus—didn't leverage the features of document creation available in programs like Microsoft Word. For example, the tables could not easily be read using a screen reader or other accessibility devices. Now she uses a Microsoft Word newsletter template to design her Clinical Neuroscience syllabus. She provides alternative text for images, and the whole document can be read by screen readers. Her revamped syllabus is colorful, features engaging graphics, and is accessible.[4]

Professor Tona Hangen, who teaches Introductory US History at Worcester State University, gave her syllabus what she calls an "extreme makeover," transforming it visually and conceptually. She allows students to participate in the course material at different levels of prior knowledge and interest.[5] Her pre-makeover syllabus is fairly standard: it includes long blocks of text and lots of rules. She made her new syllabus visually inviting and accessible with high-contrast graphics to help organize information for easy usage. Her redesign came from time spent outside the classroom on professional development; it was inspired by digital humanities scholars who had revamped their CVs.

Along with her syllabus, Professor Hangen has remodeled her teaching to invite students to approach her course in different ways: "Waders," perhaps new to US history, explore *what* happened. "Snorkelers," who already have a grasp of the basics, study *how* and *why* events happened and may be ready to have a more wide-ranging conversation about history. Finally, "Divers" are aware of historical controversies, understand the stakes, "alternate between wonder and rage," and are ready to *critique* and *make* historical knowledge.[6] According to Hangen, introducing students to these learning modes helps them to be more intentional about their studies.

Many educators have been inspired by Hangen's work to redesign their own syllabi. Professor Angela Jenks has developed an interactive syllabus for her Medical Anthropology course at the University of California, Irvine. Students earn credit toward their grades for taking a survey about the course syllabus using the learning management system Canvas. She learns a little more about the students as well as their first impressions and concerns about the course. Meanwhile, students learn something about constructing a survey, which is a standard methodology in the field. In the first week of class, she responds to questions they raise in this survey, lessening the need to repeat the old refrain—*It's on the syllabus!*—later on.[7]

In each of these cases, an instructor redesigns a syllabus to convey something unique about the way the course will be offered. Kim Holder, who teaches basic finance and accounting courses at the University of West Georgia, and Daniel Kuester, who teaches economics at Kansas State University, practice what they are about to preach by adding a simple "grade calculator" to the first page of their syllabi. Nick Sousanis, who has created a master's program in comics at San Francisco State University, presents his syllabus as a beautiful comic that would inspire any student to aim high.

We can borrow ideas from all of these inventive instructors and create syllabi that invite the degree of interaction we want in our courses. And for those confident enough to place trust in their students, why not show them several of these examples and challenge them to go wild and redesign the syllabus for the course? We guarantee there will be far fewer questions that need to be answered when students are the ones in charge.

Scintillating Syllabi

Kim Holder, Director of the Center for Economic Education and Financial Literacy, Senior Lecturer of Economics, University of West Georgia

Kim Holder has redesigned her macroeconomics syllabi to be lively and readable, including a relevant cartoon and a banner that states "Your Future Is Created by What You Do Today ~~Not Tomorrow~~." Her redesign was inspired by a talk given by Eric Chiang and Jose Vasquez at the 2014 Conference of Teaching and Research in Economics Education. If students are concerned about what they need to do for a grade, they can use a "Calculate Grade" table at the top of the syllabus that helps get grade anxiety out of the way and visually minimizes its role in the exciting content learning and skill building about to take place. Holder has worked with colleagues in the field who have implemented this method in their syllabi as well. Holder also provides contact information to make herself accessible to students, announcing the "Best" (class group text), "Better" (email), and "Good" (telephone or office hours) ways to reach out.

Nick Sousanis, Associate Professor of Humanities and Liberal Arts, San Francisco State University

Nick Sousanis, an Eisner-winning comics author, designs syllabi for his courses as comic books. He also shares creative, detailed, and engaging images of his syllabi on his public website, spinweaveandcut.com/education-home/, offering both course requirements and inspiration for students who are themselves aspiring comics authors. Unsurprisingly, one book Sousanis often includes on his syllabi is the brilliant book *Syllabus,* by comics artist Lynda Barry, as well as his own stunning *Unflattening,* a theory of how we read the world in more complex, multidimensional ways with comics, including by analyzing and building connections in the white spaces between the images and the words.*

* Lynda Barry, *Syllabus: Notes from an Accidental Professor* (Montreal: Drawn and Quarterly, 2014); Nick Sousanis, *Unflattening* (Cambridge, MA: Harvard University Press, 2015).

Cocreating a Syllabus with Students

Warning: This Section Contains Extreme Teaching Methods

Cocreating a syllabus means literally inviting your students to choose a problem or question of their own design to focus on for a class, a segment of a course, or a whole term. Cocreation means embracing choice in the classroom and asking students to make choices about the content you cover or the policies that influence their grades (for example, what is a fair participation policy that works for every student, including extroverts *and* introverts?). This method, done with a whole class and integrated into the course of study, can be more inclusive than other models.[8] Most of us are more comfortable giving control and responsibility in increments. Perhaps after successfully having students design a course unit, you might ask them to think about assessments, research topics, and other projects.

How radical or cautious an approach you take to having students contribute to building a syllabus depends partly on your comfort level but also, realistically, on the institution at which you teach. If you teach at an institution where syllabi must be approved in advance or must conform to a departmental or school template, there are still ways to individualize a class. Letting students know what those limits are gives them an understanding of how to be innovative within constraints. Students learn an essential life skill by understanding how one finds ways to act responsibly and creatively, even within limits.

No matter the scale of student intervention and no matter the class size or level, the steps are the same: the trick is to start with a structured activity or conversation in which students identify what is most meaningful for them to learn. Students then develop and tailor their ideas with course requirements and learning goals in mind, drawing from your guidance as needed to make better choices. Students can be invited to submit proposals asynchronously online or present them orally in person. Then, by consensus or majority voting (if you teach political science, this could in itself be a productive and meaningful lesson) students reach a final, collective decision. This process can be used in a class of any size, at any level, synchronously or asynchronously, in person or online. It might take one or two homework assignments or a class period, depending on the scope of the changes. What we know from active learning research is that planning part of a course is itself an effective and efficient way for students to begin learning the course content and goals. In essence, it's a participatory version of backwards planning.

If you've never done this before, we suggest having students contribute to a unit or project that will come later in the term. You might give students a heads-up that a time for voting on a part of the syllabus is coming down the road. Trust is crucial to giving students a say and cocreating a syllabus successfully. When the day comes for students to propose a topic and vote, organize a low-stakes activity where all students play a role in choosing the material or topic for one class period. A deep listening activity (such as Think-Pair-Share) works well for this.

You might give students a prompt. For example, in a general education course such as Introduction to World Art, you might ask: "What one artist do you find relevant to this class, who we haven't yet covered, and whose work you would like to recommend we all examine together?" Or, in an Algebra and Trigonometry class, you might give students a choice: "On the last day of class, would you rather: (1) talk about the hardest math problem in the world that requires algebra to solve; or (2) talk about some of the most important and famous algebra and trigonometry equations that impact your daily life?"

Students can share their ideas in pairs or small groups before deciding what one or two suggestions to propose to the entire class. This activity could be designed to suit the field or methodology of a course. In a law, nursing, premed, or language learning class, you might challenge students to practice communication skills in 1-minute oral presentations answering the question, "What is the central skill you hope to have command of by the end of this class?"

Using paper ballots or some other polling tool, students can rank the top three suggestions by their peers. Narrowing the scope in this structured way is important. Sometimes, when we hand students the wheel and ask them to take part in planning a class, we have to help set realistic expectations.

One common misconception about students is that they will do the least amount of work if they are given the freedom. More often than not, we've found the opposite to be true when we have given students the opportunity to set goals for the course. Lisl Walsh, an associate professor of classics at Beloit College in Wisconsin, has designed a system that helps students think about what decisions most benefit the class as a whole. Students decide if an assignment they propose is "good for you," "good for your peers (including your instructor)," or "encourages long-lasting learning from the course."[9] Every part of this exercise prepares students for deeper engagement with the course material and helps them form a learning community, which is especially valuable for remote instruction.

A few words of caution from experience: once you give students autonomy, you cannot take it back without breaking trust. If you suddenly realize that something isn't working and you need to "redo" a step or change direction, let students into the revision process. There is no shame in modeling the "essential skill" of responding constructively to tough feedback from students. In fact, watching you accept feedback and make a self-correction may turn out to be the most lasting and invaluable lesson students take from the course.

The key to making cocreation work is being transparent from the beginning, informing students why and how this process will benefit them, and being clear about the goal of having them involved in the process of constructing their own course. Students should not feel that they have to become subject matter experts in an instant. At Portland State University, Professor Robert Biswas-Diener builds in some onboarding time in his course on positive psychology: he ensures that his course covers the core topics and lets students choose from an array of optional topics to fill out the course syllabus (in some cases, he allows students to choose from a variety of potential assessment methods).[10] Biswas-Diener's "class-sourced" syllabus achieves a middle ground: students learn the core concepts *and* tailor a course to meet their greatest interests and biggest learning goals.

There are many variations of this crowdsourced, student-centered approach to cocreating a syllabus.[11] Robert Kilgore, an associate professor of English at the University of South Carolina-Beaufort, asked his students to choose a class theme and help construct the kinds of assignments they would be doing for a sophomore-level survey of early British literature. Their participation in this process, and the conversations Kilgore encouraged about how power typically operates in classrooms and in class discussions, proved useful when the class needed to discuss the power dynamics in the medieval romances and early modern love poetry that fit in the class's chosen theme of love. Over the course of the semester, students engaged in deep and insightful conversations about feminism, sexual assault, and consent in difficult texts by writers as various as Marie de France, Katherine Philips, and Lady Gaga. As a final project, students collaboratively wrote a newspaper in which they reported on the texts covered in the course and offered an "Agony Aunt" column written by Christine de Pizan where they revised Andreas Capellanus's rules of courtly love to better reflect the class's more feminist understandings of healthy romantic relationships.

At Stanford University, Howard Rheingold, the distinguished artist, digital designer, and early contributor to the modern Internet, taught Digital Journalism to his "colearners" (a term he prefers over "teachers" and "students").[12] Along with the required readings, Rheingold had students choose a "beat" that they would pursue for the term. The digital journalism they produced became part of the content that other students analyzed in the course. Each student chose a topic (as general as environmental journalism or as specific as environmental policy at

Sunnyvale City Hall). While studying the varieties, tools, and affordances of digital journalism, they reported using these media and an array of methods: writing or video or audio in blogs, wikis, op-eds, tweets, news stories, podcasts, micro-documentaries, reviews or micro-analyses of events, texts, or web resources. Each week, they posted some form of a digital story, read one another's work, and posted one "cogent comment" about all the work by the other colearners, noting such features as the use of RSS feeds, social bookmarking, and other tools then available.[13]

Cocreation is colearning. Both require students to invest more in a class and offer students practice in deep, transferable higher-order skills that can last a lifetime. Understanding the nuts and bolts of an institution—studying an org chart, best practices, and policies—is an ideal way to learn and plan how to move up to the next level, set goals for promotion, and take on more leadership responsibilities. We know this because we have done it. Our students learn this when they take tools like a syllabus into their own hands. Once involved in the planning process, students know a class inside and out and are equipped to critique and change it for the better.

Estimating Student Workload

One of the biggest problems in building or cocreating a syllabus is overestimating how much work to require outside of class and underestimating how much time it actually takes students to read, write, or do the other assigned work (data sets, problems, term papers, research).

There are lots of reasons we might slide into overassigning work, beginning with a (typically unexamined) assumption that quantity equals "rigor" and "coverage." If we love a topic and everything about it feels dear to us, we often want to pass that love on to our students. Or if we want to show that our field is important and relevant, we struggle to cover everything, giving our syllabi depth and breadth without a realistic hope of getting to it all. In addition, we sometimes simply forget how long it takes to read, solve, or work through a new and complicated text, concept, or problem.

Unfortunately, there are also institutional factors that encourage overassigning. Certain rules or practices of rigor come down to us from the founding of the research university in the late nineteenth century. One "given" of that Taylorist historical period was that quantity equals quality. Agencies were set up to determine if an institution should be accredited with measurements and outcomes. This productivity measure extends to the present day. Take New York state, for example. The Higher Education Act (1965), reauthorized in 2008—stay with us here—charges the Middle States Commission on Higher Education to monitor a standard set by the New York State Education Department (NYSED) for all New York State institutes of higher learning (IHLs). It gets worse: "Semester hour means a credit, point, or other unit granted for the satisfactory completion of a course which requires at least 15 hours (of 50 minutes each) of instruction and at least 30 hours of supplementary assignments, except as otherwise provided pursuant to section 52.2(c)(4) of this Subchapter."[14] Note that there is nothing here about the quality or depth of learning, only seat time.

Many opinion articles claim that rules are necessary because "students today" simply don't work as hard now as they did before; they are lazy or distracted by technology. Perhaps. But it is also true that one of the justifications for mandating seat time in 1910, when the Carnegie credit hour was first proposed, is that many professors *back then* felt that "students today" didn't work as hard as they once had, were lazy and distracted by all the fancy new technologies emerging in the Age of the Telegraph and Telephone.

The larger sociological issue involved here is that the typical student at the time the Carnegie credit hour was invented was from America's upper crust, likely lived on campus, and did not hold down a paying job during the course of studies. Perhaps forty-five hours a week devoted to academic work was feasible under those conditions. Even in a traditional, residential college (attended by less than 20 percent of today's students), extracurricular student life is an important complement to classwork and can be demanding in its own right.

Consider student athletes. They spend an average of forty hours per week practicing. In a lawsuit against the University of North Carolina-Chapel Hill and the NCAA, two former UNC student athletes claimed that their duties representing UNC on the field of play deprived them of a "meaningful education."[15] There was simply no way for them to accomplish the work assigned in their courses and also be engaged and competitive scholastic athletes. Nevertheless, judging by a small sampling from over seven million syllabi (in English alone) on the Open Syllabus Project, most instructors implicitly assume the Carnegie rules in their course planning, as if students have no other work or family obligations in their lives.[16]

Our overstuffed syllabi are a legacy from this time, and today they sound like defensive maneuvering. Decreasing workloads in a thoughtful way is not a dumbing down of education but a move closer to a future where, in bell hooks's phrase, "learning can most deeply and intimately begin."[17] Assigning a manageable workload means choosing an attainable goal: students' proficiency in a method, skill, or subject. That serves students better in the long run than encouraging skimming and cramming, which clearly do not carry the same weight and credibility. If we assign Thomas Piketty's 817-page *Capital,* we are tacitly assuming that most of our students will actually be reading the Instaread summary that clocks in at a lean 34 pages or the 4,900-word Wikipedia entry or the 500-word exam study sheet prepared by another student that is available online. Skimming and summarizing well are skills to be learned in themselves but, if that's what we're deliberately training students to do, then we need to say that and also mentor them on how to read an introduction and use indexes wisely—not to read thoroughly or for proficiency but to read quickly.

Given the realities of our students' lives, it is time to admit that when we overassign, we are really rewarding the skim, the quick summary, and the cheat. That's the opposite of rigor.

As with everything about our classrooms, the seemingly simple act of assigning homework is fraught with a host of cultural assumptions and biases. Students who come from affluent college preparatory backgrounds are enculturated to the packed syllabus. They are the stuff of AP courses nationwide. Students from college prep schools come into our classes with prior reading to draw on as well as the cultural knowledge and confidence to be able to separate what is important from busywork. They have learned what to skip, how to skim, and where to bluff. For those without such cultural capital, a daunting workload on a syllabus can signal failure.

In a webinar on the economics and social norms of higher education, a professor noted that, when they taught at Harvard, they found that students came to the classroom with enough cultural expertise and prior training that they could talk boldly and assuredly about works they hadn't actually read. When teaching the exact same texts to first-generation college students at the University of Massachusetts at Boston, this professor noticed that students would invariably answer questions with a polite apology, "I only had time to read the introduction, so this might not be right." When we over assign, we need to think about whether we are being rigorous or if we are implicitly rewarding those students with the cultural cache to "fake it." Is quantity really synonymous with rigor? Are we trying to benefit the students in our classes or impress our colleagues (or even some fictional ideal of the professors we tried to impress when we were students)? What if an unreasonable workload actually discourages the majority of students—including smart ones who don't have cultural expertise and middle-class backgrounds—from pursuing majors in our field?

Rather than assign students wheelbarrows of intellectual pig iron, we can give them an inspiring syllabus with attainable learning goals. The Teaching and Learning Center at Rice University has developed a helpful tool to help us estimate the time it takes for students to accomplish what we assign. The "Course Workload Estimator" (https://cte.rice.edu/workload) allows instructors or students to enter the required reading and to specify the goal of the reading (to survey, to understand, or to engage). The tool then provides an estimate of how much time it would take a typical student to read the material. The tool also allows users to estimate writing and research time as well as exam preparation.[18] It does not solve the problem of overassigning but it helps professors estimate how long work might take to complete. Once we arrive at a reasonable workload, the "heavy lifting," so to speak, will be in the critical thinking, creative problem-solving, and active application of new ideas and knowledge we ask of our students—exactly what society will ask them to do after graduation.

Innovative Textbook Design and Online Resources

Few things are as intimidating as holding a large, heavy, and dense textbook in one's hands in the first week of class. There are ways to make course materials more inviting and more accessible.[19] If you are able to design your own course materials, you might add some prefatory materials such as a welcome letter to make the content more engaging and personal and to assist students' learning, offering various suggestions for approaching the course content. You can also have students work in groups—say in the second half of the course—to research topics and propose their own readings for the course. Needless to say, the work they do in proposing an evolving textbook or collection of readings for their peers is some of the most vital, engaged learning they will do in the course as a whole.

The same holds for truly ambitious professors who embark on creating their own textbooks geared to their own students. Professors Joan Petersen and Susan McLaughlin decided to create their own online, open-source, free textbook for their Microbiology course at Queensborough Community College to help students with both the form of learning and the content they are learning. Their text opens with a welcome letter. The title page is speckled with line drawings of cells and insects that introduce a textbook filled with illustrations to help students comprehend instructions for experiments, making even a black-and-white syllabus come alive with microbial activity. Throughout their instructions, they offer expertise and guidance for getting unstuck: "If you 'get lost,'" while using the microscope, they advise, "it's better (and faster) to go back to low power and refocus, then switch back to 100X." They make clear in their joyful preface that the field of learning is already familiar, reminding students, "Always remember—you are never alone because your microbes are always with you!" This inviting approach encourages introspection and application of lessons learned from the very beginning of the course.[20]

Math professor Ke Xin and a team of educators, web and YouTube developers, and over one hundred volunteers at Borough of Manhattan Community College, developed and now coordinates an online math center to help students study. "Help Your Math" is an open educational resource with over 250 videos and hundreds of quizzes in algebra, nursing math, statistics, and trigonometry.[21] The team built the site from scratch under a Creative Commons license. The site reiterates course requirements and homework assignments commonly found on syllabi and college handbooks to make the information easily available in a single place. The videos can be watched in Chinese, English, Korean, Russian, and Spanish. In addition, the website offers students ways to find part-time paid jobs as tutors or "leaders" in some courses.

Professors of physical and mathematical sciences at the Universidad de Chile went so far as to create a mobile app designed to motivate students to learn about probability. A multidisciplinary team from the Mathematical Education Lab of the Center for Mathematical Modeling (CMM) at Universidad de Chile developed the book and accompanying mobile app, *Alice in Randomland: A Mathematical Adventure,* as part of an initiative to contribute to school mathematics education. Readers of the book can experiment and analyze the situations described in the story by playing interactive games after scanning QR codes found throughout the book. The graphic designs are beautiful, imaginative, and fantastical, making the whole experience a true adventure. While the book caters to students 11–15 years of age, it showcases just how far participatory learning can go to engage students.[22]

Establishing the Goals of the Course

Thinking about the purpose of learning and teaching should be a thrilling and purposeful component of education. Too often, it becomes the opposite: empty requirements, red tape, and hoops to jump through. At some institutions, instructors are required to conform their syllabi to meet formal "learning outcomes" in advance. Syllabi for existing courses and course proposals have to be submitted to a department chair or dean or, more likely, a committee for approval. Many of us copy and paste required learning outcomes into our syllabi as if they were meaningless—and they can seem so to our students as well.

Something magical happens when we invite students to contribute their own learning goals for a course, when we listen to students give voice to their fondest dreams for their education. The best workaround we have found in cases where institutions require preapproval of syllabi is to cover the approved outcomes on the syllabus and then plan a brief exercise in which students supplement those outcomes with their highest aspirations for the course. Students may need coaxing and reassurance that their own learning goals are valid and valued.

Working individually and collectively with a method such as Think-Pair-Share, students can be invited to propose learning outcomes for the course. These too, once voted upon, can be imported into the syllabus. In an activity on the first day, try prompts such as: "What do you want to learn in this class that you will take with you for the rest of your life?" Instead of asking students why they are taking the class (maybe it's required, maybe not), ask where they find value in the topic. It's especially valuable if you collect these original comments and hand them back to students midway through the course or at the end and offer them the opportunity to revise their expectations, an ideal "meta" way for students to reflect on how much they are learning and an invaluable tool for professors. Their comments are formative feedback that professors can use to improve courses. The process signals a serious investment in learning, namely, yours.

Taking time to think hard about our goals for learning helps ensure that our courses are fair and effective for all students. Offer students, as an example, some learning goals that discourage discrimination and foster trust, like this one: "Learning to collaborate with, respect, and be respected by others from different backgrounds and with different perspectives than my own." We can emphasize the importance of neurodiversity as well, as in this learning goal: "A commitment to and understanding of how to approach problems in more than one way." By setting difference as a learning outcome, we invite students to break through the "echo chamber" of the traditional classroom.

In my (Cathy's) class Introduction to Transformative Teaching and Learning in the Humanities and Social Sciences, co-taught with Eduardo Vianna, a psychology professor at LaGuardia Community College, we began the discussion of learning goals by having students search for notably dry, standard-issue "accountability" guidelines online. For example: "Incorporate a professional expression of cultural competence." We then compared these with the "ground rules" for meaningful dialogue established in Ilarion (Larry) Merculieff and Libby Roderick's *Stop Talking: Indigenous Ways of Teaching and Learning and Difficult Dialogues in Higher Education.* Merculieff, who was born on the Pribilof Island of St. Paul, Alaska, and raised in a traditional Aleut community, lists the "Ways of Real Human Being":

- Listen
- Experience the world without words
- Revere all life

- Respect all others
- Affirm all others
- Observe closely
- Feel the connection to All That Is[23]

These Indigenous principles inspired us to aim high and think deeply about the learning outcomes for our course, to consider both individual and community goals, and to link personal achievements to community success.

Here are some learning outcomes students have recently created in courses we (Cathy and Christina) have taught:

- Learn to respect one's intellectual life and education as a precious gift that no one can steal from you;
- Be challenged by a scholar of impeccable standards to succeed educationally to one's own very highest standards in any endeavor;
- Learn to absorb and transfer wisdom from lectures, class discussion, and scholarship into one's own cogent thinking and writing;
- Gain the highest respect for intellectual rigor, including self-respect;
- Come to understand how everyday incidents—the small victories and constant abrasions of life and politics—are deeply grounded in histories and cultural practices, including those of racism or other inherited and structural forms of discrimination that are sometimes so widely practiced they are invisible to those who perpetuate them;
- Be able to assert the validity of my own ideas, reality, and identity even when I am in the minority and learn to listen to others who express minority views;
- Stay alert to surprise.

Building Midterm Reflection into the Course Design

Teaching at the John Jay College of Criminal Justice in the early 1970s, Audre Lorde shocked many of her academic peers not only by asking students to evaluate her performance as their professor but also by building a midterm student evaluation into her syllabus.[24] She asked her students, "How do you feel about the class—are you satisfied—where do you think we are going?" She designed her course around this student-led, mid-course correction. By letting her students know she wanted their opinion early, she allowed them to experience the benefits of offering sound and careful feedback. This requires flexible course design and planning in advance both to carve out time to respond to students' input and to show students our sincere commitment to listening. This activity works best when scheduled during a week in which we aren't grading and know we will have more capacity.

Like Lorde, Anne Gulick, an associate professor of English at the University of South Carolina, plans for midterm feedback to be incorporated into her course. She has students in her classes write her a letter at the beginning of the term in which they articulate their personal goals for the course. At midterm, they write a self-evaluation in which they review their own letter of introduction, reflect on their progress toward those goals, and state their ambitions for the rest of the semester. Gulick then responds to those midterm self-evaluations, often inviting students to help change the syllabus for the remainder of the course.[25]

The questions we ask midterm should be as carefully worded as the prompts for exams. We might ask for some qualitative feedback about the teaching and pacing of the course. For example, students could share their input on how class time is allocated:

- "Do lectures need slowing down? Do students need more time for questions?"
- "How is group work going?"
- "Is everyone clear about expectations for the final?"

Other questions might dig deeper into how students are engaging with the course content:

- "What has been the most meaningful or interesting content in our course?"
- "What haven't we covered that we need to address before the end of term?"
- "What problem sets are still a problem?"
- "Which topics have been the least appealing? Is there something we can do to increase their relevance, or should we jettison the topic altogether? If the latter, what alternatives would you suggest?"

Specific, contextualized questions that ask for more than a simple "yes" or "no" answer lead to better and more productive responses, more accurate mid-course corrections, and greater student satisfaction. With enough prior planning, you might even include these questions in the addendum to your syllabus—that way, students know they are coming and can reflect in real time and give you better, more thoughtful responses. As educators we also have a responsibility to our students to explain why and how this feedback, and the tools used to collect it, will be used. It is crucial to inform students about how their data will be used, whether it is anonymous or not, and who will have access to their responses. This, too, shows students that we genuinely want to listen and respond to them, and will help to establish trust from day one, the moment they read about this planned process in the syllabus.

The more invested we are in soliciting student response, the more students respond. By building in opportunities for students to communicate feedback, even before the first day of class, we teach them how to give and receive constructive (not punitive) feedback. As we implement and apply it going forward, we model how to accept and act on constructive feedback.

Making Class Time Count

Why do college professors need lesson plans? For K–12, sure. But higher education? Surely *we* don't need them.

Or do we?

We expect our students to come prepared for class. Are *we* prepared?

Building a lesson plan is like planting seeds: there are ideas we plant that might stick and grow, some early and some late in season, and there are ideas that never find soil. For those who have planned many lessons, we know just how easily even the "best-laid plans go awry." For those who have never planned a class period before, it's a daunting task to imagine how much time it takes for a class to settle in, to take attendance, to cover the material, and to set expectations for the next meeting. When we plan, we imagine covering enormous ground. How often have we reported that a class flew by and we didn't even have a chance to scratch the surface of the topic we'd planned for that day? And the ultimate question for active learning: how do we plan a class *and* create the conditions for student-centered and student-led learning, allowing questions to flow, encouraging digressions that are productive, and in all ways supporting openness?

It's important to be realistic, to plan for everything to take longer than we expect. It's also useful to expect the unexpected. An ideal lesson plan manages both.

Warming Up the Room

Even before we manage the class business (attendance, announcements, and the like), a quick participatory exercise changes everything. During the first five minutes, as students are getting settled, filing in late, setting up their laptops, and other preliminaries, we like to engage every student in a low-stakes intellectual exercise that involves everyone and, in practical terms, has the effect of focusing everyone's attention on the class material. An "idea sprint" (sometimes called an "entry ticket") offers everyone a chance to weigh in and be present. Even the stragglers tend to hurry up and settle down in order to be part of the easy, transitional group activity. It's like a warm-up stretch in participatory learning before the heavy lifting begins.

Dr. Kristina West used fruit to begin a discussion in her critical theory class at the University of Reading in the United Kingdom. She challenged her class by bringing an apple, a lime, and a banana into the room and asking students what each was, asking how they know it's an "apple," a "lime," and a "banana," and questioning their answers. Students began grinning, catching on to the purpose of the activity by the time they got to the banana. The point was to encourage students to consider language and categories carefully, to question everything, to take nothing for granted, and to consider the relationship between language and what we deem as reality.

An entry ticket prompt can begin at the official class time, as soon as students begin to arrive. No need to wait until everyone arrives: write the question on the board or in the chat or repeat it verbally as new faces enter the room. "How do you know this is a banana?" You already have their attention, their participation. You've energized the room. At the same time, it's best to set a limit. As every designer knows, setting a constraint inspires rather than limits creativity. We like to set a timer to enhance the game-like quality of a warm-up exercise. In the lesson plan you've charted for the day, you might note, "Warm Up: 5 minutes."

Rather than being a waste of time, this exercise transforms the normally wasted time it takes for students to settle down into an inspiring learning opportunity. If you collect students' responses on note cards or pieces of paper or with clickers in a large lecture hall or in the "chat" in remote learning, this also doubles as an efficient way to take attendance. As a byproduct, it also lets students know the precious first minutes of class time are important.

Entry tickets give you extremely useful information as a teacher. If you encourage students to communicate their triumphs as well as their difficulties with you, they might write, "I struggled with Problem #14 and I still don't have an answer." This activity affords you a low-stakes way to gauge how each and every student is doing, to discover what kinds of questions they are asking or not asking on their own, before the actual class period begins. It gives you a quick temperature read on how well students are comprehending the material and helps you see the areas you will need to give more attention.

Class warm-ups were especially creative during the COVID-19 pandemic. Some instructors took "warm-up" literally, with yoga, stretches, mindful meditation exercises, or even dance parties to rejuvenate students (and themselves) after hours of sitting on chairs and staring at screens. To combat Zoom burnout, some professors opened synchronous class meetings with games or wellness check-ins. Some instructors who recognized that their students were falling behind on homework provided students brief moments to catch up and read their peers' posts on an online discussion forum; then class would begin with students sharing their reflections on what peers had written.

So Much Content, So Little Time

When there is a lot of material to cover, time in class often seems to melt away, especially when teaching intro and survey courses where it's impossible to dig deep enough into the material before we have to move on to the next major event, problem, experiment, or concept. How do you squeeze a century's worth of content into fifty minutes?

Lesson plans don't solve the problem of "so much content, so little time." However, even a loose lesson plan helps safeguard the essentials as the hour whizzes by and can help us keep our own unrealistic expectations (and overplanning) in check. A lesson plan can be as free as a few bullet points or planned down to five-minute increments. The important thing is to ensure that no matter how long the period lasts—whether it's a fifty-minute class that meets three times a week or a three-hour class that meets once or twice a week—we get to the most important points before the bell. If not, we can decide (including as a group) which items are worth bringing back at the beginning of the next class, and that discussion then becomes a form of review.

Setting an agenda with time stamps can be useful. Not every instructor will want to have a class planned out this carefully. Ironically, we find students relax more and contribute more constructively if they see there's a structure and know their professor is respectful of their busy lives and doesn't intend to drone on for another ten minutes after time's up. Structuring segments is also a great attention device, helping students to focus. An agenda might look like this:

1:45–1:50 Warm-up (interactive exercise)
1:50–2:00 Lecture / Presentation (by instructor or student)
2:00–2:10 Group Work or Participatory Activity
2:10–2:30 Discussion
2:30–2:35 Reflection / Review

Since an agenda with time slots requires keeping an eye on the clock, we like to ask for volunteers to serve as timekeepers. We've had students gamify the process and lighten the mood by setting timers with hokey, hip, or humorous playlists (Cher's "If I Could Turn Back Time" or Talib Kweli and Hi-Tek's "Memories Live" or Chopin's "Minute Waltz"). Rotating the designated timekeeper each class teaches students to value one another's time and helps create an atmosphere where the success of the class is everyone's responsibility.

When everyone participates in the same goal of staying on time, everyone respects one another's busy lives. Anyone who has attended a panel at a conference and seen one or two people hog all the time, leaving the final speaker with nothing, knows how debilitating it is when the timekeeper fails to do the important task of keeping everyone on time.[26] Surveys of who speaks in rooms—classrooms and boardrooms—repeatedly demonstrate that men tend to speak 25 percent more on average in meetings where both men and women are present.[27] There are also racial disparities in who speaks. Setting up equitable practices early on supports democratic participation in the classroom and, ideally, creates better habits when students go into the workforce after school.

Building in Time for Review and Reflection

Reviewing and reflecting on what we have learned—what neuroscientists call "metacognition" or thinking about how we think—is key to deep learning that we can remember and apply in other situations. In reviewing what we have learned and reflecting on how we learned it and for what purpose, we give ourselves a tool for applying that learning in other situations beyond the classroom.

When Professor Dina Limandri teaches continuing education courses in nursing and health care sciences at Kingsborough Community College in Brooklyn, New York, she includes slides on "Active Listening: Developing Skills for Patient Advocacy in Health Care" for her adult learners. Throughout her lecture, she embeds questions designed to elicit self-reflection from her students. She begins with an "Active Listening Quiz" and then, after reviewing standard health practices and principles, she leads students in activities where they apply those principles to hypothetical situations, actual case studies, and incidents the students themselves have experienced. She emphasizes that students haven't just learned content but have learned how to extrapolate from that content to a practical application in the real world. In each case, students not only apply nursing content but also a range of soft skills—careful listening, analysis, synthesis, communication, empathy. At the end of her lesson, she makes room for a discussion of how these skills will serve students in future employment.[28]

Even saving five minutes for review and reflection at the end of class can make an entire lesson more memorable. Before everyone leaves, ask students a question parallel to the opening warm-up. It can be very effective to repeat the same question with which the class began. Other prompts might include: "What is one real-world application of the statistical method we discussed today?" Or, "What is one way you would use what you learned today in your ideal profession?" Or even, "How would you explain the importance of something we did today to a friend?"

Setting the Agenda Together

Getting students involved in contributing to the agenda for a day's class is an effective way to share the responsibility for learning. We typically think of one person leading a meeting and setting the agenda. The best managers ask people who report to them to set the agenda and lead the meeting. Business schools often call this "managing from below." There's no reason this can't be done together, collaboratively, in the classroom. Collaborative agenda-setting boosts everyone's attention and participation.

Instead of the teacher / supervisor / boss circulating their agenda, the leader facilitates a more democratic meeting where all participants contribute. Just as you could ask students to add learning goals to a syllabus, a single class period could be shaped by starting with the question: "What do *you* want to talk about today?" In a classroom, the instructor offers students the chance to determine the course of the day's discussion (for instance, what problem sets or questions they would like to prioritize).

In our courses, students write down one or two things they want to cover that day, either on slips of paper or on the board. We keep a tally, either by circling keywords on the board or by projecting our live notetaking in an editable document on a screen at the front of the room. The point is that everyone contributes to the agenda taking shape and has a chance to vote topics up or down.

If the class is small, it's easy to simply go around the room and have everyone share at least one topic they would like to discuss. A notetaker can keep track of repetitions—shared concerns, curiosities, and interests. Keep a tally and set the agenda with the most popular idea first, working down until the class ends. By taking inventory and then organizing proposed agenda items by the number of votes, the collaborative agenda mirrors the priorities of the community.

Collaborative agendas can pique the attention of other students who had never even considered those matters before and also make the material new and relevant again, even to longtime professors. Showing students how to design a collaborative agenda also helps them in their own group projects and study groups as well as in school clubs, sports, and other areas of life. The skill of collaboratively deciding on topics also translates to a diverse range of situations in the working world: a meeting agenda, a project management tool, a way to map workflow and to make sure items don't fall off the radar.

Planning an Unplanned Day

Students will be surprised by—and enjoy—a syllabus that has one day that has no homework, no quiz, no test, no lesson plan, no agenda. This could be a day for review, open office hours in which students can "ask anything," a field trip of choice, student team meetings, or a floating "snow day" with a digital attendance option in the event of a real snow day or another disruptive event or emergency. If you are at an institution that insists on a specific topic or learning goal for every class meeting, you might call this class a "Review Day." That should work just fine.

While this might seem to reduce the rigor of the class or of this particular class period, it requires your expertise to adapt to the needs of a particular class on a dime. To respond to what students are most curious about, you must rely on your knowledge of the topic or your skills as a researcher if students want to know more about something outside your coverage area. That's not easy, but it really is a thrilling prospect for a scholar who loves a good challenge, and the creativity it inspires in professors can also motivate student learning.

Bridging Distance Online

Virtually everything we're advocating in this book becomes even more critical when teaching remotely. Building a community in a virtual environment takes extra preparation and extra care. Applying participatory learning techniques with some key adaptations can ensure equity and accessibility in remote learning while also making the experience lively and joyful.

In online classes, it is crucial to build in an opportunity to solicit feedback as early as possible—before the first day of class, if there is a mechanism for doing so. Before the course begins, it's important to determine what forms of access students have. Key questions include:

- "Do you have the right tools for meeting the course requirements?"
- "Are you working from home or from a library or computer lab?"
- "Do you have your own work space?"
- "Are you sharing bandwidth at home? If so, who else has priority to be online and what impact does that have on your participation?"
- "What other obstacles to learning are you finding online?"

Although these questions may seem mechanical, they are designed to remove the shame students might feel coming forward to admit they are not as connected as we might hope. They allow us to gauge students' comfort levels with the online learning tools, methods, and resources for the class and to address and ease difficulties early on. Also, quite fundamentally, we cannot have community if our students are, literally, disconnected.

Once we know how students are participating, we can then think about ways to promote community even in remote classes. At Sultan Qaboos University in Muscat, Oman, Professors Abdelrahman Mohamed Ahmed and Mohamed Eltahir Osman have studied the effects of collaborative visualization, whiteboard, web conferencing, polling, and other digital technologies, assessing their ability to promote better learning, community, and collaboration. From extensive quantitative and qualitative research, they have found that, although learners were "more engaged in their learning when provided with collaborative learning environments," these environments alone were not enough. Success requires "a deeper level of social interaction that engages learners in active knowledge acquisition and knowledge construction."[29]

This study underscores that the fanciest interactive technology cannot compensate for passive, one-way learning. Interactive technology works when it supports and inspires creative human interaction. No matter how elaborate the technology, how expensive or lavish the setup, the best way to inject life into the zombie experience of staring at a Zoom screen all day is to sprinkle in engaging activities.

Disrupting the one-way information flow requires designing exercises that solicit contribution.[30] There's room to inspire student creativity, from tasking students with virtual scavenger hunts to designing miniature digital projects and uploading them to an online repository.

There's also room for building and maintaining a community of support. During the COVID-19 pandemic, instructors did this in various ways, from show-and-tell sessions with pets to dance parties at the start of class. Professor Roberto Rozenberg, who teaches biosciences at the University of São Paulo, Brazil, enlivened his course on Genetics and Human Evolution by hosting post-class jam sessions. He played piano for them and then another twenty or so students sang, read poetry, played guitar and violin and improvised hip-hop. On-the-spot innovations like this proved to us in 2020, and prove to us still now, that we have communities right at our fingertips, even when they are remote.

Adashima Oyo is a doctoral candidate and adjunct professor at Brooklyn College who teaches the gateway course for students in health professions, including nurses, physician's assistants, home health care workers, and premed students. To create community amid disaster, she changed quizzes to journals. Her prompts began with: "How is the

Coronavirus affecting your life?" and included such complex questions (key to principles in health science) as "NYC is the epicenter of the COVID-19 outbreak in America, there is a shortage of ventilators and personal protective equipment (PPE) for health care workers, and we haven't 'flattened the curve' yet? What lessons can we learn from these problems?" Her prompts also included complex policy questions: "The Coronavirus Aid, Relief, and Economic Security Act, known as the CARES Act, was passed last month. Many individuals will receive up to $1,200, some small businesses and nonprofits are eligible for aid and larger companies like airlines will also receive federal relief funding. Is the CARES Act enough? What would you change about it?" Students offered their own prompts too, pairing issues in their lives with the course content. The course covered the material of a basic health science course in ways that had direct relevance to students' lives and with lessons that are likely to last a lifetime.

A more political model of community building arose in May and June of 2020 as the Black Lives Matter movement became an international phenomenon. Groups such as Academics for Black Lives joined with community-based activist groups to organize young people worldwide via online networks, both academic and civic, inspiring political knowledge, interaction, and activism in the midst of national pandemic shutdowns.[31] A series of connected, international working groups, "do tanks" (think tanks with an activist component), and reading groups were created, enhanced and promoted and connected by the 18 million students whose courses the COVID-19 pandemic had moved online. In a sense, the online courses became the inadvertent infrastructure for an international student political movement.

Online Learning Preliminaries: Asynchronous and Synchronous Participation

During the pandemic, 1.2 billion students went online globally in an emergency, most with no warning and with instructors with no training. However, professional online instructors with decades of collective experience have much advice to offer us on what works and doesn't work. We learned a lot from Flower Darby and James M. Lang's *Small Teaching Online* and many other titles.

One rule of thumb with which every online instructor seems to agree: keep the one-way lessons as short as possible. If you are relying on pretaped video lectures for your students, think about everything we know about the ineffectiveness of face-to-face lectures and multiply that exponentially to account for the remote learning context. For an asynchronous course, instead of posting a 45-minute video of a full lecture, plan to post a few short videos in modules. Keeping each to 6–12 minutes is ideal; even 20 minutes is probably too long. A study of student habits at edX, one of the purveyors of massive open online courses (MOOCs), found that "certificate-earning students generally stop watching videos longer than 6 to 9 minutes. They viewed the first 4.4 minutes (median) of 12- to 15-minute videos."[32]

When we consider how much screen time students have outside our own classes, it's no wonder they fade so fast. Authors of a global study, including experts from Brussels, Geneva, and Silicon Valley, conclude: "The best virtual schools limit live video conferencing sessions to 30 or 45 minutes and follow up with independent work to reduce fatigue and free up teachers to provide small-group and one-on-one coaching."[33] This puts the maximum length of synchronous sessions into perspective as well.

In addition to concentrating on length, online lectures can be made to be more engaging if each short segment includes an accompanying challenge, quiz, recap, or other interactive study guide. Is this a good way to learn? Sometimes. It depends. We all have had to take online training sessions of one kind or another (for example, to be certified by an institutional review board to be allowed to run an experiment or to understand an institution's anti-harassment policies). How much we learn from them varies. The same is true for your students and the courses they take.

To supplement the asynchronous video lecture, we might design an interactive online discussion forum, sometimes asynchronous and other times during established office hours where students can ask any questions. Engaging students doesn't require real-time presence. It does, however, require interaction. For those who are able to supplement the asynchronous with some synchronous component, the remote "facetime" can be dedicated to creating a vital sense of community. Whiteboards, Jamboards, and other tools that allow students to respond visibly and personally (including with doodles and so forth) foster engagement while diminishing the boredom and physical depletion of staring passively at a screen.

For a synchronous class, it is important to be clear about what will be required of students during the session. Consider these questions: are they expected to listen, to unmute themselves, to show their faces, to talk? Will they be visible to their classmates, and how much multitasking (kids, pets, and so forth) is or is not appropriate?

In a seminar or smaller class, rather than open class by taking attendance with a simple "present" or "here" response and maybe a wave hello, consider using an icebreaker. Many instructors teaching under duress in the COVID-19 crisis invited their students to share, in the first few minutes of a synchronous class, what challenges they were facing with the technology or to do a version of "show and tell" with household objects and pets. Our favorite video conferencing icebreaker is to ask all participants to unmute themselves and to briefly share their local soundscapes while everyone listens.

Many of the tactics for on-site learning can also be very effective in remote or hybrid courses. Professors Susan Greene and Buck Goldstein revamped their Introduction to Entrepreneurship course at the University of North Carolina-Chapel Hill to make it a more impactful, engaging, and applied learning experience. The class is one of the largest in the school, with over four hundred students enrolled in the course. It involves, among other things, approximately eighty-five teams working on developing an entrepreneurial venture throughout the semester. Goldstein and Greene had a goal of using more progressive and innovative approaches to teaching and learning, with an emphasis on seeking to derive the benefits of a large lecture class, but at the same time make a class of four hundred feel like a class of twenty.

The team partnered with PBS North Carolina, formerly UNC-TV, to create virtual sessions that enabled them to create a blended classroom learning experience. The virtual sessions they developed essentially serve as the textbook for the course. Students are expected to complete the assigned virtual session, including taking a quiz on the content, before each class. So instead of spending the bulk of class time in a lecture format, students spend in-class time completing challenges and activities that foster a deeper grasp and application of concepts. Greene and Goldstein are able to get into more of the details on a particular topic, do much more applied and experiential learning through in-class exercises and group work, as well as bring in a multitude of speakers that provide real-world insights on the different topics they are covering around entrepreneurship.

The blended model also has enabled a special component to the class—thirty volunteer entrepreneurs are paired with four student teams that they work with during six different classroom sessions over the course of the semester. These entrepreneur-coaches work with the student teams as they navigate developing their venture ideas. Enabling a smaller environment allows more personal interaction to reinforce the content they are learning, both the technical tools and skills, as well as how to navigate working to be a high-performing team.

While there is a virtual component to the learning experience, attendance in class is critical for this learning model to work. Greene and Goldstein argue that teamwork is one of the most important skills students can practice in college. In the workforce, we have to collaborate with people who have different perspectives and different needs. Learning to balance and embrace these differences should be central to student success in college. Students periodically fill out peer-to-peer feedback and learn how to professionally and productively give and receive feedback.

All the work that Goldstein and Greene put into the revamp of the class has resulted in strong positive feedback from students. In 2020, Goldstein shifted roles at UNC. With such a robust and innovative curriculum in place, it made it seamless for the newest professor, Jiayi Bao, to step in and work with Greene to teach the class and continue refining and enhancing the learning experience.

Applying a Tool from Your Toolbox to Remote Learning

Entry tickets work especially well for synchronous experiences. Students might do the readings, watch the lectures, and do the homework any time (asynchronously) but then could be engaged in an online forum together once a week. One simple entry ticket technique is to have students write out, in a way that is public to the entire class, one question they think will engage their classmates. You could do this in a Blackboard (or other CMS) discussion forum, in a Slack channel, a shared Google Doc, or even on Twitter using a hashtag unique to your class.

Whichever tool you use, the question students ask should not be a "yes" or "no" question or one with a simple answer. The point is to provoke deep and diverse responses. Even better, to give the conversation a boost so it really takes off, ask students to do more than post and sign off: for an entry ticket or discussion board to inspire a community to gel together, students ought to respond to one another as well. Some of the most exciting responses we've seen have included memes and gifs as well as thoughtful contributions in words.

Prioritizing Community Makes a Difference

Professor Farrah Jasmine Griffin at Columbia University had never taught online before March 2020 when her university sent students home in the face of the COVID-19 health crisis. She found herself having to redesign her Introduction to African American Literature course during a crisis that exposed the racial and economic disparities of who lived and who died in the crisis. She did what every great participatory instructor does: she considered her course in ways relevant to the students taking it. The pandemic highlighted the particular urgency of designing a student-centered course.

Her on-the-fly makeover first meant changing some of the assignments, thinking about what literature means at certain times of crisis. She reduced the number of pages being read since her students were experiencing the trauma of sudden dislocation on every level. She also gave her students a "creative option" instead of a term paper, and she asked them deep and personal questions suitable to the subject of the course and the historical moment.

Most importantly, she asked her students what *they* felt they needed in this emergency and did so in ways designed to make the actual experience of an online class a community even as the world was playing havoc with their sense of community. She turned the pandemic itself into a profound educational experience. On her digital platform, she asked students: "As we pass through this portal, let's think about what we might take to the other side, and what we want to leave behind. One or two sentences per question. No more," she instructed. Then, she posed four questions:

- "What one book from class would you want to take with you?"
- "What, if anything, from your old life do you want to leave behind?"
- "What do you appreciate that you would like to take with you?"
- "What change, if any, would you like to see, and commit to bring about, on the other side?"

Griffin notes Toni Morrison's famous insight that, in moments of crisis, "artists go to work. . . . That is how civilizations heal."

What we see from Griffin's exercise is that "online" and "on-site" matter less than creating an equitable community where students recognize themselves and one another. Taking Toni Morrison's injunction to heart, she asked her own students to become healing artists. They did not disappoint her. "In this season of unimaginable death," she writes, "especially black and brown death, these young people rose to the occasion. With careful consideration of the books and for each other, with a strong desire to help heal the world in which we live, they went to work."[34]

They went to work. That is the best, most intimate practice—remote or in our physical classrooms—that we can offer and the very best way to think about preparing for the course we are about to teach and the students from whom we are ready and willing to learn.

CHAPTER 5

The First Class

Who hasn't handed out a conventional syllabus and watched the collective life drain from the class? The longer and more intimidating the syllabus, the greater the distance between you and your students. For first-time teachers, this might feel like the safest option: the syllabus becomes a buffer, a display of expertise and authority. For overworked teachers, this gives us a quick lesson plan for Day 1: we review the syllabus, answer questions, all (including ourselves) are made to feel sufficiently anxious and overloaded, and then we're done. The experience is enervating, for students and instructors alike. And when students ask about subsequent assignments and deadlines, the weary teacher can respond, predictably, *"It's on the syllabus!"*

We can do better. There are more engaging and inspiring ways to begin a class and more effective methods to guide students through even a daunting syllabus.

In this chapter, you will find a variety of activities designed to get your class off to a great start. Needless to say, you will need to plan these activities in advance, but there's no need to overplan. The magic happens when students are presented with an alternative to the deadening march through the syllabus—every requirement, the laborious rules and institutional policies, all of those features of higher education that are more about risk management than learning.

In this chapter:

Activities for Engaging Students with the Syllabus
Introduce Yourselves as Cocreators
The First Assignment: An Evolving Résumé
Critical Reflection
Transform Institutional Policies into a Class Constitution

Activities for Engaging Students with the Syllabus

Scavenger Hunt (Prep Time: 5–10 Minutes)

An easy way to engage students is to ask them light-hearted, trivia-style quiz questions about the syllabus. Make it a game. These questions should challenge students to find key information in the syllabus or in the course Dropbox folder, LMS, or website, if you've spent time building one. This need not be taxing, either for the instructor or for the student. Ask them, "When is the midterm due?" Or, "What assignment is due the week before Spring Break?" The point is to give students a memorable way to focus on the key points in the syllabus. You can have students record their answers using a variety of tools, such as a popular survey platform, a polling device, or clicker. If all else fails, simply have them shout out the responses.

An alternative is to divide the class into groups, assign each group a section of the syllabus, and have them ask the rest of the class questions about their section, in the manner of the questions suggested above. This method not only breaks up the monotony and overload but sets up an active learning method that saves you time and deepens your students' learning experience. You'll use it many times throughout the term, when you let students take the lead.

Mapping the Syllabus (Prep Time: 5–10 Minutes)

With a little advance planning to collect supplies and bring them to class, this is another welcoming activity. If your class is meeting in person, distribute blank sheets of paper and drawing devices (markers, pencils) and ask students to visually represent the syllabus through a timeline, a concept map, a comic, or some other graphic form. Give students a few minutes for reading and drawing and then ask them to tape their maps to the board or surrounding walls. You can allocate different parts of the room to different page numbers or parts of the syllabus. Give everyone 5–10 minutes to walk around the room and look at the maps. Finally, ask students to explain their drawings to the class.

Students can engage in this activity online as well, no matter whether yours is a course in art history or data visualization, geography or GIS mapping. If meeting online, use the whiteboard feature on Zoom or Google Jamboard for collaborative or parallel drawing time. Students can work on the same white space or on separate sheets, each with a prompt to get things started. Each sheet can be devoted to particular sections of the syllabus or "You Are Here" points on the map. Then take screenshots of the final product(s) and ask students to talk through what they did and why.

Collaborative Annotation (Prep Time: 15–20 Minutes)

This technique, which is frequently used in executive leadership workshops, can work in a seminar of ten or a lecture of three hundred. Group students into teams of up to four or whatever the physical architecture of your classroom allows. Divide up your syllabus (including any addenda at the end) into sections and assign one section to each team. For a large class, different teams can work on the same section. Let them read together, annotate, ask questions, and do whatever they want in their teams, including choosing one person who will be the spokesperson and another who will be the transcriber.

It is especially satisfying to adapt this collaborative annotation method to remote teaching. As a primer, show students how *you* annotate a digital text, sharing your screen to demo the tools and techniques you use as you explain why you highlight particular things. Then simply assign different parts of the syllabus to students by number, have them work independently for a short time on their given section, and then, if working asynchronously, ask students to share what they did and why in a group chat, text, or video.

Go through each section, and have the relevant individuals or groups present their annotations and raise questions. The annotations can be made in the digital document itself using a proprietary collaborative tool such as Google Docs or an open-source one like GitHub, Manifold, or Hypothes.is. If none of these is familiar, in a pinch you might project a Microsoft Word document at the front of the room (or share your screen on Zoom) and comment on the document live with Track Changes to show students how the function works, then ask them to come back next class with their own annotated syllabi. When students report back, you may find that some of the language can be edited for clarity, so carve out some time after class to sort, edit, compile, and compose a revised syllabus. The revised syllabus becomes the official class document.

Peer-to-Peer Syllabus Learning (Prep Time: 30–60 Minutes)

Give students the task of teaching parts of the syllabus to one another. Assign different parts of the syllabus to small groups of 2–3 people. Each group will need time to absorb and interpret their section; then, in the second half of class, flip it around and have those groups present their section to another group or to the whole class.

In remote learning, assign parts of the syllabus to groups of students who then create an FAQ to that section for the other students and respond to questions from other students in the chat. The FAQ can be added to your learning management system (Blackboard, Canvas,

Moodle, etc.) for the course, or it can be made into a page on your course website. As the instructor, of course, you will be watching this activity unfold and adding explanations, making changes, fixing mistakes. They will find all of these mistakes—and that's a good thing for them and for you. In the world of co-learning, finding and assessing, receiving feedback and correcting mistakes are essential skills, in the classroom and beyond.

Interactive Syllabus Project (Prep Time: 2–3 Hours)

The Interactive Syllabus Project was developed by Guy McHendry, associate professor of communications at Creighton University in Omaha, Nebraska.[1] It goes like this: build your syllabus as a survey that delivers a portion of the content, then asks the students questions related to the content before they move on to the next section (similar to a conditional release of content in some learning management systems). This functions like a training session to ensure that students acknowledge and understand what they have read. Importantly, short-answer questions also should be directed to students themselves so that you can gather information about their learning goals, their concerns, and their highest aspirations. For example, after reading the instructor's name and contact information, the survey might ask students for their pronouns and the best ways for the professor to get in touch with them. After reading the course learning goals, the survey can prompt students to pick which goal is most important to them. This format is an effective method to get to know your students and to gauge student reactions to course policies and requirements.

The interactive syllabus uses a Qualtrics tool, but you can use any popular survey platform or Microsoft Forms (which has an accessible screen reading feature) to walk students through each part of the syllabus and ask them questions every step of the way. Better yet, give students credit for completing the survey so that they are rewarded for careful reading and engagement. McHendry recommends sending the syllabus to students before the first day of class to give yourself time to read their answers in advance. This will also give you time to prepare to correct any misconceptions or misreadings and empower you to know your students and engage with them in meaningful ways on day one. Their answers might even alter the way you teach the course.

Introduce Yourselves as Cocreators

We like to start on day one with interviews and introductions to emphasize that learning does not come only from the instructor but also works student to student, peer to peer. Ideally, this introduction exercise should be conducted in pairs, with one student interviewing another and then introducing their partner, verbally, to the class. We encourage students to talk about the skills they possess that could be of value to everyone in the class.

To ensure privacy, we offer students a template with a list of categories for discussing skills. These later will become "tags" (for instance, "public speaker," "great editor and proofreader") so that, when students later do group projects, they can assign themselves tasks that match their tags and work to ensure the group has a range of different skills and perspectives. We also make sure to say, explicitly, that this is purposeful, in the way a job résumé is purposeful. Whether in job letters, interviews, professional bios, personal statements, or everyday work and life situations, we are called upon to "introduce ourselves" all the time. But we are all complicated, and we choose which aspects of ourselves we want to be known in a given situation.

We set a timer for this exercise. Three to five minutes tends to be ideal for a focused and relevant interview session. Here is a sample template, adaptable to any course or field:

- Name, nickname, pronouns
- Major, minor, certificates
- Job experiences

- Cross-disciplinary interests (Example 1: Black studies, Indigenous studies, feminism, accessibility, other culturally relevant topics; Example 2: Visual studies, sound studies, digital humanities, ethnography, quantitative social science, case studies, psychometrics)
- Practical skills (with obvious relevance to collaborative projects): Statistics, digital skills, PowerPoint skills, oral presentation skills, graphic design, photographer for group recap, professional writer, proofreader / copyeditor)
- Fun facts / superpowers (skills one is proud of that might not at first seem relevant: avid Minecrafter, comics artist, rapper, amateur magician, poet, stand-up comedian, incurable optimist, etc.)

The First Assignment: An Evolving Résumé

One practical reflective technique is to ask or require students to build the skills portion of their résumés throughout a class. This can follow naturally from the "introduce yourself" exercise or can be independent of it. We like to start the process as an assignment after the first day of class, especially in introductory or general education courses. We ask them to upload an online, editable résumé (with the appropriate privacy settings) to our course website. Each week, we ask students to reflect on the specific higher-order skills they developed in a given participatory activity, and we discuss wording that might be used on their professional résumés. For example, in an exercise where they read and collaboratively annotate the syllabus, they develop critical reading, interpretive, and collaborative skills. In a more radical participatory model, where the students actually build the syllabus together, they also develop project management skills, attention to detail, an ability to communicate with others, leadership, and adaptability.

We recommend tasking students with finding examples of professional résumés online and collectively developing a list of higher-order skills. This practical exercise in metacognition helps them to think about everything they are learning besides content in, say, an organic chemistry, statistics, or Spanish course that uses participatory techniques. It helps them to see how their engagement in class (individually and in groups) builds management skills that they will be able to rely on long after they have forgotten specific formulas or equations or syntax rules.

As the semester goes on and students acquire more essential skills, we take a few minutes to review these "evolving résumés" and have students add to them each month. In one of the final class periods, it's powerful to remind students that a good résumé for a first job is typically one page long and to invite them to prune their résumés. It's a practical way of showing them how much they have accomplished and how their new skills will serve them in the world beyond.

Critical Reflection

Critical reflection is an exercise to help students understand how they learn best. The many benefits of participatory learning, for example, are maximized by student comprehension of . . . the many benefits of participatory learning.[2] Without frequent and repeated critical reflection about *how* and *why* we are learning something (what learning scientists call "metacognition"), students lose the opportunity to absorb the full value of the problem-solving strategies they are acquiring.

In general, people aren't very skilled at identifying when we're learning something new except in extreme cases, typically "aha!" moments of trauma or epiphany. When we think carefully about our own thought processes, we gain confidence in knowing *how* and *why* a particular lesson is relevant to us and applicable to our immediate, everyday lives.

Reflection is also how we learn from failure. Any situation can become a "teachable moment," an experience to learn from, if we set aside time to examine what happened, how it happened, and what we could have done better or differently. Activities that help students think deeply about the ways in which they learn best can be among the most valuable in the entire college experience.

We want to give our students more opportunities to lead in the classroom, but that requires some unlearning on their part. Without the benefit of understanding decades of research on active learning, most students (especially the most successful ones) believe that the best way to learn is by listening passively to a lecture in the sage-on-the-stage model. Take a moment—even five minutes—to explain *why* you are flipping your classroom. Or briefly share the research behind the limitations of the lecture for learning. When we share our own reflections on how and why a lesson or assignment is structured this way, not that way, students begin to trust that there is a purpose to using these methods. They are tried and tested and have been proven effective.

In explaining the importance of metacognition to our students (as well as to our colleagues and administrators), it is useful to note how extensively educational and occupational psychologists have studied the tactic. It has been found to improve a learner's decision-making and their ability to modulate and revise opinions and prejudices. It increases memory retrieval, problem solving, project management, and both short- and long-range planning.[3]

Developmental psychologist Marilyn Price-Mitchell teaches at the Institute for Social Innovation at Fielding Graduate University, a private university in Santa Barbara, California, designed for midcareer professionals specializing in the fields of psychology and counseling. She argues that students develop a sense of independence by taking an inventory of which subjects or methods are easy for them and which are most challenging. They learn to identify their own strengths, gaining enough confidence in their own competence to feel ready to ask others for advice in areas where they are less skilled. She lists seven basic questions any student can ask themselves:

- "What was easiest for me to learn this week? Why?"
- "What was most challenging for me to learn this week? Why?"

- "What study strategies worked well as I prepared for my exam?"
- "What strategies for exam preparation didn't work well? What will I do differently next time?"
- "What study habits worked best for me? How?"
- "What study habit will I try or improve upon next week?"[4]

Having students ask themselves questions like this reinforces the idea that *every* student can learn, grow, and improve. This is true of all students and especially first-generation college students and students of color in majority-white institutions. Effective learning isn't magic—and it's not the same for everyone. When our students learn what works best *for them,* they gain an essential skill that will serve them throughout their lives.

Transform Institutional Policies into a Class Constitution

What if we had students transform all of the dreary, deadening, legalistic, and policing policies of a syllabus into their own class constitution, a set of principles that all members of the class agreed to abide by? Their constitution might include a preamble, some amendments, and some rules. We encourage our students to think less in legalistic or punitive terms and to aim for maximal inclusiveness: how community guidelines can be modified to support every learner. Instead of a top-down set of mandates, collaborative creation of a constitution is key to forming an effective, respectful learning community whether meeting on site or online.

Designing a collaborative class constitution makes an excellent first assignment in any class of any size. In disciplines where this kind of social or pedagogical activity may seem "irrelevant" or a "waste of time" (let's say, Chemistry 101), yielding one class period where students rearrange the syllabus into a constitution might be considered "front-loading" against the time we often waste at the end of a semester arguing with students about plagiarism, grades, attendance, and other policies (areas that a class constitution would address). In more advanced, research-based classes, the skills students acquire in dividing labor and setting expectations for a class constitution lay the groundwork for later collaborative work, such as a coauthored research paper (for example, "Authors on this paper must contribute X.").

Any nation's constitution can serve as a good launching point for your students' critical examination. Dr. Urvashi Sahni, founder and chief executive of the Study Hall Educational Foundation in India, advocates training students to be democratic citizens using India's constitution to help students think of themselves as "We, the People . . ." That is: *we the people with the power to change laws and society.* Sahni asserts that educators can explain the constitution and also apply a critical lens to it so that students recognize their responsibility to participate in the democratic process. She emphasizes that enabling and encouraging students to bring themselves—their interests, their concerns, and their lives—into the classroom teaches them to become problem-solvers in society.[5]

The goal of creating a constitution is to envision the classroom as a small nation—a community—with a set of rules that guides its most responsible participants and protects against the most serious abuses of its members. In the United States, students will be familiar with the three main parts of the Constitution:

- The Preamble
- The Articles
- The Amendments

As an exercise, we suggest dividing the class into three groups, each of which focuses on one of these parts. For larger classes, the parts themselves can be subdivided. A preamble sets the values; the articles establish rules and responsibilities; and the amendments allow for a range of additional second thoughts, exceptions, and inclusions.

The students working on the Preamble to the US Constitution might begin by looking at the preamble as a rhetorical model—an exercise in

"We the People" Activity

We don't advocate adopting national constitutions wholesale, because each of these documents has its own unique and often turbulent context and history of amendment and revision. When teaching the US Constitution, I (Christina) led an activity with students on the first day of class to determine who in the class would be included in "We the People." First, I asked everyone in the room to stand up, and I stood up too. Then, I said: "If you do not identify as 'male,' please sit down." At this point, I was sitting down with approximately half the class. "If you rent or do not own your house, apartment, or wherever you live, please sit down." In New York City, where I taught this course, most students rented apartments, so by this time only a few students, if any, were left standing. Finally, I said: "If you have any student loans or any debt whatsoever, please sit down." Given the extraordinary cost of a college education in the United States, there is seldom a single student left standing in the room by this stage. Why go through all of that? Because it means that no one in the class would be included in "We the People" nor, in 1789, would they have been considered deserving of the right to "life, liberty, and the pursuit of happiness."

This irony—that to go to college they must accrue debt, a condition that would prevent them from being considered citizens with voting rights in the original US Constitution—is not lost on students. This injustice informs and transforms the discussion about what we mean by "democracy," then and now.

Anyone reading this might wonder why race and the three-fifths status of enslaved people are not included in this exercise. That is intentional. As a white instructor teaching majority nonwhite and immigrant students of every imaginable background (Hunter College boasts over a hundred first languages spoken by its student body), I wanted to start with the idea of exclusion more generally and ensure that I was in the first excluded group. Once we all were sitting down, it seemed the right time to talk about race and the most heated, common ways of talking about elitism, privilege, exclusion, inclusion, and citizenship. Students immediately noted that enslaved people could not vote anywhere, while free Black men could vote in only four Northern states. A quick internet search will inevitably turn up that Indigenous people were prohibited from voting until 1924. And anyone looking more seriously would discover the anomaly that, in New Jersey, women could vote until 1807 and then had voting privileges retracted until 1919, with the passing of women's suffrage in the Nineteenth Amendment.

principles stated briefly. It's not the time to argue whether the United States has lived up to these principles but rather to see what elements pertain or do not pertain to, say, Chemistry 101. Here is the Preamble to our country's Constitution:

> We the People of the United States, in Order to form a more perfect Union, establish Justice, insure domestic Tranquility, provide for the common defense, promote the general Welfare, and secure the Blessings of Liberty to ourselves and our Posterity, do ordain and establish this Constitution for the United States of America.

And here is how it might be written in today's language (this revision is courtesy of an Adult Basic Education Class at Southwestern Illinois College):

> We the people of the United States want to form a better country, create a fair and just legal system, have peace inside the country, defend our country from other countries, help everyone live a better life, and make sure these things last during our lifetimes and our children's lifetimes. Therefore, we make and authorize this plan of government for the United States of America.[6]

Now, think about what elements work for Chemistry 101 (or Creative Writing, Introduction to Medical Anthropology, or any other course).

> We the students in Chemistry 101 at Our College want to learn the basics of chemistry, under a fair and just evaluation system, in a classroom that is equitable, free of antagonism, in order to help every student learn better. Therefore we make and authorize the following guidelines and principles for Chemistry 101.

The students working on "articles" should focus on relatively clear and simple instructional matters. They should read and either accept or rewrite in their own constitutional language all of the institution's policies that pertain to the class: plagiarism, attendance, deadlines, course requirements, and so on. They might also include a resources section that addresses online archives and other tools available to the class. What learning management system will be used? Will there be blogs required, and, if so, on what platform? Will students be required to register, or will there be an alternative? What kinds of information will they be required to share? Will this be public or private, anonymous or not?

In my (Christina's) early American literature survey class, students first accepted the basic goals for the course but then took exception to a uniform policy for homework. They modified homework policies to match their learning goals. For example, they wanted more "or" options in the syllabus (for instance, *either* write bi-weekly reading reflections *or* a midterm paper).[7] In the end, this policy adapted to different kinds of learners and workers, both those who prefer smaller assignments and continuing feedback as well as those who simply want one assignment and one deadline.

Some policies on a syllabus are even more complex and nuanced. Students might want to "amend" traditional classroom dynamics and practices, for example. The students working on "amendments" could tackle such difficult matters as accessibility, inclusion, pronoun usage, and respectful disagreement. They could reassess institutional procedures that seem bureaucratic and find ways to make them comprehensible and even humane.

One group might interpret the university's honor code (if there is one) and break down its key points, while another reevaluates plagiarism policies. Any way that students can move from a mentality of punishment to one of understanding and respect is a net good for learning in your course.

Take plagiarism. In the business world, sharing isn't cheating—until it is, and then you're fired. A collectively agreed-to plagiarism policy provides students the opportunity to discuss and understand the difference between sharing and stealing—and the potential negative consequences for intellectual theft, not just in the classroom but well beyond.

In every part of this exercise, students are negotiating across competing values and agendas. The whole class has an opportunity to discuss what it means to move from differences to agreement. This is also an excellent opportunity to discuss the difference between majority and consensus voting. In majority voting, it's easy to follow the herd and ignore the minority, but then the community misses a potential opportunity to improve upon the policies and make them more broadly applicable to all participants, including those who objected and offered alternatives. Consensus voting requires a general agreement of all voting parties, so by its very nature it gives every student and perspective a chance to be heard. In my (Christina's) class, this discussion—including the decision to vote by consensus—was pivotal to devising an "or" option that catered to different student work needs.

More often than (usually white) educators will admit, the dissenting vote is supplied by a student of color or another underrepresented minority student who is working to make their particular perspective and position visible. The classic book in this area is Beverly Daniel Tatum's *Why Are All the Black Kids Sitting Together in the Cafeteria?* (1997). Two decades later, the problem has not been solved by any means, as described eloquently by Anthony Abraham Jack in his personal and sociological study of implicit ostracization, *The Privileged Poor: How Elite Colleges Are Failing Disadvantaged Students* (2019). A simple vote is further erasure of the dissenter's point of view. In cases where a dissenter's opinion is harmful to another learner (for example, when the dissenter is from a majority group and feels strongly that one should be free to say whatever they want, including harmful things about minority groups), this is a teachable moment for all. In cases like these, we revert back to Professor Yusef Waghid's *ubuntu* practice, which, once again, includes: (1) showing moral respect to all; (2) considering all humans worthy of our acknowledgment and engagement, even those we resent; and (3) prioritizing the humanity of all, recognizing that all are equal and no person should undermine or disrespect another's right to belong to humanity. Respect is that simple, straightforward, and nonnegotiable.

An ability to collaborate across different perspectives is an essential skill that will serve every student well in the workplace, in communities, and in everyday life. As the professor / president of this small

A Useful Way to Present Intellectual Property / Plagiarism

Professor Anne Balsamo, Inaugural Dean of Arts, Technology and Emerging Communications, University of Texas, Dallas

In her large introductory lecture course on Technoculture, an offering in the core curriculum of this STEM university, Balsamo hands her two hundred students a readable, inviting booklet instead of a conventional, densely packed syllabus (see https://dox.utdallas.edu/syl69167). The booklet outlines course content and explains why and how skills such as researching, analyzing, and synthesizing are important in and outside the class. On facing pages, Balsamo includes the official (sometimes punitive) university policies and then, on the other side, a constructive framing of the same principle.

To address plagiarism, Balsamo includes the university's policies on "Academic Honesty" across from three "Basic Tips" on "How to Protect Your Intellectual Credibility." Rather than simply assume students know what plagiarism is, she advises students on research basics such as making notes of where they find things as they are doing their research, learning to love citations, and reading Wikipedia critically. Some famous professional historians have gotten in trouble for not being careful in their citation practices. Additionally, other countries have different norms for quotation and citation. Listing useful preventative measures is far more valuable than simply listing the punishments.

"nation," you will need to make final decisions, including about consensus versus majority positions. In our experience, however, opposition is rare, and the document the students decide on is less bureaucratic than a typical syllabus while still being remarkably fair and comprehensive. Because everyone has participated, it serves as an invaluable document to guide your course, including if things go wrong later on.

CHAPTER 6

Activities for Any Day of the Term

It's Monday morning. You are rushing to your class, which begins, it seems, before the crack of dawn. You haven't figured out a brilliant, thoughtful way to engage your students and change their lives. Creatively and equitably structuring a brilliantly effective classroom experiment is the last thing on your mind. Thank goodness for those lecture notes from the last time you taught this class! Sure, they're a little rusty, but hey, it's 8 A.M., and class is about to start.

Been there, done that! Too often when we are hurried and harried, we simply fall back on what we already know, on well-rehearsed habits that have served us (for better or worse) in the past, on lectures that have worked well enough once before. For many who are teaching a heavy load or working as adjuncts at a number of different institutions at once, originality is not easy. Even those who have supposedly "cushy" lives can feel beaten down by a relentless expectation to publish, childcare or eldercare responsibilities, a terrible department chair, or any number of other personal, institutional, or national events (such as a student death or censorship or a natural disaster). If teaching is not rewarded and respected within academic hierarchies, often it is our teaching that goes first as we juggle other requirements of life.

Have no fear! This chapter offers a range of activities that can work in every classroom, any day of the term. They can be adapted to all subjects or can be re-adapted with a different focus, a different question, a different setup. One thing they all have in common is active, participatory learning.

Participatory learning has at least four clear benefits:

- Participatory learning is an efficient way for students to learn
- Participatory learning can help your students advance in their careers
- Participatory learning can improve society
- Participatory learning supports *you* as an instructor

Importantly, the first three in many ways "add up to" the fourth. The overworked, overprepared, constantly lecturing, always-knowing-the-answers professor is a bad model of pedagogy. It is extractive, and it exhausts you, and it undermines your students' learning.

This chapter offers specific, tried-and-true activities to keep in your back pocket at all times. They work in any situation (including department meetings) that calls for total participation. We show you how to do them, how to vary them, and how to explain them to your students, their parents, your administrators. Next to each activity listed below, we have included an estimate of how much class time each activity takes. Some activities take literally no extra time—they are continuous with the class—yet transform the class dynamics, engage all students, and enhance learning. We promise these activities will turn even a sleepy-eyed Monday morning class into a lively experience.

In this chapter:

Universal Tools for All Subjects and Class Sizes, Everywhere
Total Participation
Essential Skills

Universal Tools for All Subjects and Class Sizes, Everywhere

Think-Pair-Share (5 Minutes)

Think-Pair-Share is the Swiss Army knife of the participatory teaching toolkit. It can be adapted to just about any situation. Most instructors doing it for the first time are self-conscious or are certain it won't work.

It will work. As we discussed in our introduction, it can even work to save a faculty meeting that has fallen desperately into the shoals.

We like to do Think-Pair-Share with index cards, pencils, and a timer, and it works equally well online if you follow the same guiding principles. We like to use index cards in part because they have no significance in the paraphernalia of education. They aren't bluebooks, and they do not have circles to fill in like the SATs. Recycled or scrap paper works well too. The pencil works because it's very obviously *not* a laptop (although for some students a laptop may be helpful and more accessible). The timer ensures that this exercise remains quick and low in stakes. All of these features promote spontaneity and offer possibilities for creative, honest, engaged, unfiltered contribution.

Online, we've maintained the same principle by having results be disposable, low-stakes, fun, and never graded. In large lecture classes, students have tweeted responses or used Slack or some similar medium to pair; in smaller breakout rooms the chat function works just as well.

Here's how to Think-Pair-Share:

Think: Ask students a question that can't be answered with a simple "yes" or "no." This might be a general question such as "What was the biggest challenge you faced in this week's assignment?" It can also be something specifically related to the week's reading assignment. In a political science, management, or human relations course, for example, you might ask students to jot down one political or personal event from their week that would have benefited from using a conflict resolution strategy or tool like the Thomas-Kilmann Conflict Mode Instrument, a standard method developed in the 1970s and still used by both conflict managers and human resource departments.

Give students 90 seconds (maximum) to write out an answer on their card. Depending on the subject, they might write about getting past problem set #4, arriving at different results from the same experiment, or confronting personal biases. The 90-second rule is important. If they plead for more time, that's a pedagogical win—after all, they're engaged! Offer another 30 seconds. More than that, and this becomes a pop quiz or even an exam and may begin to feel like another way the professor is testing rather than an occasion for self-improvement.

Pair: Have each student turn to a partner sitting nearby, ideally not someone they walked in with. A group of three is fine if there's an odd number of students in the room. Give students 90 seconds to take turns sharing what they wrote down. Student A reads their card while Student B listens, and then Student B reads their card while Student A listens. We like to underscore the importance of listening silently, with no interrupting. For some students, it's a rare chance to speak and an even rarer chance to be heard. For introverted students and students with cognitive disabilities, reading off a notecard, without fear of interruption, is often far easier than speaking spontaneously. After they've read to one another, the pair then decides what they will share with the class as a whole. They might merge their responses, revise them, or choose one of the two responses (Student A or Student B). When the timer sounds, they must have a synthesized comment to share with the whole class and have come to an agreement as to who will read what's on their card.

Share: Go around the room (if less than 40 students) and have one person from each pair read / share their comment with the group (again, without interruption or explanation—simple, quick reading).

If you have more than 40 students, you can create a Google Doc or another collaborative tool where students write out what they had written on their card. If you have projection equipment in your class, you can display everyone's answers on screen. They can be anonymous.

If you are teaching remotely, you might use the chat function or another online collaborative tool for everyone to record their comment.

When students come to expect a Think-Pair-Share activity as part of a class, they know they will be contributing every time. When our students sense a discussion is reaching an impasse, or a few students or a few ideas are dominating, they will often shout out "Think-Pair-Share!". The results never disappoint.

This Swiss Army knife of a method also offers you instant insights into how the class is going. From collecting and reading the cards, you gain a sense of what the students know, what is important to them, what they are missing, and what you need to spend more time on (either because they have not understood it or because they are passionately invested in it).

Think-Pair-Share gives you a sense of the learning patterns for the whole class. In addition, reading all the comments helps you structure the next discussion or assignment. In a smaller class, you might pick cards randomly to read aloud and then address students' points, answer questions, and add your own expertise. This is another way to cut down on time spent lesson prepping while also making the knowledge transfer more relevant and engaged. You can also have students sign their cards—not for a grade but for roll, another way of saving class time. Think-Pair-Share is a perfect pedagogical inventory at a glance, and one as helpful for you as it is for the students.

Entry and Exit Tickets (5 Minutes)

Entry and exit tickets are based on some of the same principles as Think-Pair-Share. As we have seen, the entry tickets work well while latecomers are still settling in, whether in a face-to-face class or remotely, to gain a quick sense of what students have on their minds. The exit tickets, using the same method, reveal what worked or didn't in a class. Simply hand out cards or slips of paper on which all students jot down ungraded, spontaneous responses to a prompt. A few minutes is plenty of time before collecting the responses.

In any kind of class you can ask an open-ended question such as: "What was the most difficult part of this week's assignment?" Or, "What did you read this week that you're still thinking about—because you liked it, hated it, or didn't understand it?" Or in many kinds of classes (from Sociology 101 to Introduction to Biology) you might ask: "What did you learn recently in this class that helped explain something that happened this week—in the news, on TV, on social media, in your life?" Some years ago, a student came up with, "Write out one sentence from this week's reading assignment that interests you (good, bad, or ugly)." I (Cathy) like to ask: "Invent a prompt of your own. 90 seconds."

In a virtual classroom, an entry ticket might be a way of making community across distance. For example, you can ask each student to say how they're doing in a small class or even to offer one word (or maybe two) to indicate how they feel on a given day. In smaller, virtual sessions, you might do this in "popcorn" fashion: after one student responds, they randomly choose another student and ask how they are doing, then they "popcorn" the mic to the next person, and so on. This helps connect you to your students, and it helps students connect with each other.[1]

When students share their responses, either by reading out loud or putting answers in a collaborative online document, they not only get off to a great start, but they also see all the different ways they can respond to the same material—another life lesson. A side benefit to the busy professor: This is another easy way of taking roll; we've also found that if students come to expect entry tickets, they make it a point to arrive on time. Rather than taking up valuable class time, entry tickets can get things started promptly without the usual shuffling (or tedious roll taking).

Exit Tickets: You can do this with all class sizes, even in a lecture for six hundred students or more, as happened in the participatory massive open online course (MOOC) that I (Cathy) led with over eighteen thousand people online. It also works as a substitute for pop quizzes or taking attendance. At the end of class, have students write down one idea from the class that they can't stop thinking about or a lingering, burning question that they would like to discuss further, that will keep them up at night, and the like. If students protest that nothing memorable happened, invite them to write down what they think would make an unforgettable class topic. You can begin your next class by drawing from some of these reflections or by handing students' responses back with your written comments. If teaching online, you can do this via email or using a discussion board in whatever learning management system your institution uses. You can save student responses and hand them back at the end of the semester when students are studying for their final exam.

Total Participation

Everybody Raise Your Hand (0 Minutes)

This is the method used by the self-taught speculative fiction writer, polymath, and former Temple University professor Samuel Delany. Whenever you ask a question, have every student literally, physically raise a hand. You call on anyone. They can either answer or say, "I don't understand the question" (in which case you can ask "why?" and start a discussion about that) or say, "I don't know the answer—but I bet [Student A] does." This simple technique asserts that "I don't know" is a starting place, not a source of shame. Delany explicitly states that it does not matter whether or not a student knows the answer. He wants them to be present even if they are uncertain. We know from cognitive neuroscience that the very act of physical engagement—raising your hand—already activates attention. In class, it serves the symbolic function of saying, "I'm here, I belong—even if I don't know the answer today."

In an online class, a useful technique in synchronous situations is to call on students randomly, by a student number chosen at random or alphabetically. You can frame this as a fun and thrilling game rather than allowing, at worst, the dreaded feelings of "please don't pick me" to surface as students wait to be called on. To make it truly random and also a bit of a game, use a basic random number generator, coin flip, dice roll, or even a wheel spin online (a basic search in Google produces all kinds of options).

The "Everybody Raise Your Hand" exercise is not an opportunity for humiliating students who don't know the answer. On the contrary—the value that needs to be reinforced is twofold: everyone is learning, so everyone is allowed to "not know." If someone feels completely flummoxed, as if they have nothing to contribute, then it is important to make sure they know it is their right (this has to be established with clarity and even performative gusto from the beginning) to pass the question on to the next person—again, chosen either randomly or alphabetically. Not knowing is the *ideal condition for learning*—at all levels.

Name Cards and Green, Yellow, and Red Dots (3 Minutes)

Sociologists of education report that many students leave even a relatively small class knowing only the name of their instructor and not that of the other students with whom they've shared space for several weeks.[2] A basic principle of active, participatory, student-centered learning is that everyone else in the room is important too, a source of learning, community, networking, and crucial collaborative potential. Name cards are an easy way to underscore the importance of all class members while also helping students (and you) with names.

We like to provide cardboard and colorful markers on the first day and have everyone make a name card. We like to include full name, nickname (if students have one they prefer), and pronouns. We typically keep these cards, collecting them at the end of each class. For subsequent classes, students simply pick up their own name card and place it in front of them on their desk or table. As with many participatory methods, this one makes it easy to take attendance—simply by noting which name cards have not been picked up. In a larger class where collecting name cards becomes burdensome, students can be responsible for keeping these cards on their persons and bringing them to class each meeting (although in all candor, neither of us has had much success with this method).

We also provide a sheet of red, yellow, and green stickers alongside the name cards. If a student does not feel up to participating on a given day, they can attach a red dot to their name card. This exempts them from the day's in-class participation. Are you introverted? Ill? Weighed down by family or work problems? Cognitive issues? Feeling alienated from the class? These are all issues an instructor should address privately if they recur. For the student who does not wish to participate orally at any time in the term, instructor and student can come up with an alternative method of participation, such as a contribution to the class blog, either in class time or later.

Fishbowl (10–30 Minutes)

Fishbowl is an effective strategy for organizing small, medium, or large discussions while also developing equitable and constructive group discussion skills. It is also a method for helping students improve their listening skills. Participants are organized in an inner and outer circle. The smaller inner circle or "fishbowl" should have a minimum of five students. They are the only ones allowed to talk for the duration of the discussion. Students in the outer circle practice listening: they observe the discussion and take notes, examining not only content but also the form and efficacy of the discussion itself (who speaks, who doesn't, the role of body language, *how* they are speaking or are not speaking, and so on). Participants inside the fishbowl focus on responding to different viewpoints voiced by peers in the circle and sharing their own. Observers who make up the outer ring of the "bowl" see and hear patterns of response and interaction that those active "fish," mid-discussion, may not notice or take in. By asking students to be keenly observant, the goal is to prepare them, by the discussion's end, to share their critical insights into what makes a group discussion effective.

In order for students to gain the most from the fishbowl, they ought to experience sitting in both circles. Your role is to facilitate the discussion by providing a question to get the fishbowl started or a set of questions to keep things going longer. Don't forget to set a timer for how long you would like this to go on (anywhere from 10 to 30 minutes, depending on the size of the class).[3] Finally, after all students have rotated through both roles, facilitate a class-wide discussion or smaller discussions in breakout groups where students comment on the dynamics of the discussion itself. In a class where participants speak multiple native languages, you might ask students to share what verbal communication felt like knowing that others were listening, and, when observing, what nonverbal cues helped them understand the conversation. By giving everyone a turn in both roles as well as an opportunity for metacognition—to reflect on how the discussion went—fishbowl helps to build an inclusive and supportive environment and discourages bias in the classroom by making everyone more aware of membership, identity, and belonging.

60 Seconds (1 Minute per Participant)

This activity works well in smaller classes (up to 30 students). Begin by notifying everyone in the room that they each will have 60 seconds to speak and that they must use up all of that 60 seconds—no more, and no less. If they run out of things to say, they can start singing a song or use the remaining time to talk about whatever else they like. The order can be random, or you might go alphabetically, or around the room, or ask students to volunteer knowing that there are benefits and drawbacks to going earlier or later. In introductory writing courses, I (Christina) use this activity to assess and improve reading comprehension in my classroom: students summarize the major plot points of a novel, filling in the gaps as they volunteer to go next. Students who don't finish the reading assignment might volunteer to go first, whereas students struggling to remember details might volunteer to speak when the class gets closer to the part they remember best. Students control when they participate, and the whole activity is an exercise in recall and reflection, which also makes for a rigorous, class-wide review session before an exam.

Raising the Stakes (30–60 minutes)

At the College Preparatory School, a private, urban school in Oakland, California, enrolling students from eighty different high schools in the San Francisco Bay Area, teachers stress dialogue as a key component of all learning in all subjects. In math class, teachers assign students a relatively straightforward math problem designed to be solved in no more than fifteen or twenty minutes. In class, students work in groups, exchange their homework with a partner in the group, and evaluate it, giving credit if the peer has done the problem correctly. They then explain to the person and the group why they evaluated as they did. The teacher circulates around the groups, listening in to see how everyone is doing. Before moving on to the next group, the teacher then presents the whole group with a new problem to solve. This one is, by design, significantly more difficult than the work each student did for class. Together, the group then tries to tackle this new problem or concept. Before the class period is over, each group presents their solution to the day's in-class problem to the rest of the class, and then the teacher gives students a new problem to solve for homework, based on the group solutions.[4]

The key part of this assignment is that homework is kept to a minimum and yet its impact is maximized. In class, students not only discuss how each of them arrived at a solution but evaluate one another's solutions and then collectively use their knowledge from their discussions to tackle the more complex problem. The teacher is constantly raising the stakes in the context of collaboration, the class environment, and collective problem solving.

Essential Skills

Interview (15 minutes)

Interviewing and being interviewed are two essential skills that students can use both in and outside the classroom. "What questions do you have for us?" is the final question that interviewers typically ask job applicants, and, as every good job candidate knows, the question really is about the applicant: how curious are you, how serious, how much prior research have you done, how able are you to connect with others, how successful are you at initiating a conversation, not simply at answering questions?

This activity is a highly effective way to warm up a class, especially when we make clear that students are becoming proficient in skills that will serve them for the rest of their lives. Students work in pairs to interview one another. In a few minutes, one student asks the other a series of questions (interview questions can be relevant to the course, or, say, on the first day of class, they can be icebreaker questions to get to know one another). For example, medical students can ask each other questions they might expect in residency interviews, such as "Why did you choose this program?" or "Why would you like to pursue Internal Medicine [or another specialty]?" At the halfway mark, reverse the roles such that the interviewer becomes the interviewee. Discretion and privacy should be discussed in advance, as always. Then each student introduces their partner to the class as a whole. Ultimately, students learn three essential skills: they practice interviewing, close listening, and introducing a colleague in a social context. In a small class, this is done orally; in a larger one or in a remote situation, it can be done in a collaborative digital document, LMS discussion board, Slack team, or the like.

Listening Dyad (2 Minutes)

We learned this technique from Frances Tran, assistant professor of English at Florida State University. Students work in pairs and take turns speaking / listening for one minute: one partner speaks for exactly one minute (get your timer ready!) while the other partner listens—without interrupting—for the full minute. When the timer sounds, partners reverse roles, and the timer is set again for one minute. Now the person who spoke first gets the chance to practice listening, and the person who listened first has the opportunity to speak (and to respond to what their partner said, if they so desire). In a listening dyad, the objective is to practice being a good listener and for speakers to realize how long a minute lasts. A lot can be said in a minute, so we don't need to take much longer than that to speak in class. Instead, we can practice sharing our time and learn to be respectful speakers. The hardest part about this activity is that the person listening cannot, under any circumstances, interrupt the person speaking—not even to say, "Yes!" in agreement or to ask a follow-up question. The purpose is to practice being respectful listeners.[5]

What is discussed in the dyad is *not* shared with the class. The shared privacy is a defining feature of the exercise. The purpose of the listening dyad is for each student to have a chance to state ideas and opinions without censorship and then to have an opportunity to listen to another student's thoughts in the same open way. For example, one student might ask why their peer chose a specific topic for their dissertation. One fascinating feature of listening dyads is how difficult it can be at first. Two minutes can seem like an eternity. Then, over time, the activity becomes expected, even welcomed. Tran notes that it improves the levels of trust, community, and participation that students bring to general, more traditional class discussions.

Collaborative Note-Taking (0 Minutes)

Participation doesn't have to be verbal. As an alternative to verbal participation, students can contribute thoughts, ideas, resources, and summaries to collaborative notes that everyone shares. Set up a shared digital documentation tool or social network channel for each class period and have students take notes together in your class meeting. This activity is most effective when students are able to use a back channel for conversation during class (for instance, comments in Google Docs, or comments in a video conferencing chat for remote classes). Any digital space where they can add links they find in relevant web searches would work. This puts a twist on the "laptop or no laptop" question. To keep everyone focused, you can create extra credit reward systems for those who contribute the most, require that everyone contribute something, have students vote ideas up and down, or find another way to make laptops instruments of learning and not modes of diversion and escape.

If you're using a Google Doc or another tool that does not automatically track who contributed what (for instance, Padlet, Slack, WhatsApp), ask students to put their names next to their ideas as well as those of their peers, embedded in the text itself. This helps to combat video conferencing fatigue that makes it harder to remember who said what.[6] There is value in learning names, in echoing what someone said, so all have time to reflect and absorb it, contributing to higher-order thinking and processing information. Learning names and echoing the voices of others are good first steps to building a community of trust and care.

Collaborative notes are one way for absent students to catch up on what they missed and a good place for students to add their thoughts on homework as their way of participating remotely and showing their engagement with the material. The upside is that everyone benefits from these contributions—and someone who wasn't privy to the class discussion might seek out additional resources or outside information to add to the notes, offering everyone valuable insights that went unexplored in the class meeting.

Given what we know about gender bias and who typically takes notes in a meeting, it is important to structure this responsibility so that it does not fall on only one student or one group of students—such as the women in the group. Deborah M. Kolb, Deloitte Ellen Gabriel Professor for Women in Leadership (Emerita) and a cofounder of the Center for Gender in Organizations at Simmons College School of Management in Boston, notes that women shortchange themselves in the business world by spending too much time "tidying" the workplace—essentially assuming a secretarial rather than managerial role. This is a practice we must nip in the bud in our classrooms.[7]

One method to democratize the taking of notes is to rotate the editor of the day. They might be called the class "editor" or "annotator" who signs the day's collaborative notes in that capacity. Made into a rotating role, this can be part of a participation or effort category in a student's final evaluation and provide opportunities to discuss workforce readiness.

This activity also can be structured as directed group work. For example, in a social work class where students are reading different case studies, the collaborative notes can be broken up into three sections for each study: (1) summary, (2) analysis, and (3) class discussion. For the first case study, in the collaborative notes document, Group 1 summarizes it, Group 2 analyzes it, and Group 3 develops discussion questions for the class. For the next case study, groups rotate roles: Group 2 summarizes, Group 3 analyses, and so on.

Collaborative Research (15–25 Minutes)

Set up three columns on the board (or using a collaborative space online) with these headings: "Know," "Think We Know," and "Don't Know," leaving plenty of space between each of the three columns. You can do all of this together as a class to start out. Ask students to list what we know about X; for example, the historical context of a book. You, or a volunteer student, can keep track of this list under the "Know" column. As students run out of facts they *definitely* know, the conversation will naturally drift into things that should probably be fact-checked. Put those under the list "Think We Know." Eventually the conversation will get closer to what you *know* you don't know.

Set a timer for 10 minutes for groups to do research on any device they have with them as well as drawing from one another's knowledge. Each group is responsible for distilling that research into salient points to share with the class. Once time is up, go around and share. Doing this activity online makes it even easier to share links to useful resources. In ten minutes, students can develop a bibliography for the class. They might spend an extra ten minutes annotating that bibliography in a reflective activity that will give you an opportunity to talk about the authority or credibility of the sources.

How to Write an Email (Homework Assignment)

Steven L. Berg, professor of history and English at Schoolcraft College, is baffled by instructors who complain that their students don't know how to write a proper email. "Teach them!" he insists. At the beginning of a new course, Berg has his students write him an email. As he notes in his book *Promoting Student Transformation at the Community College,* some of his students simply do not have experience writing professional letters or emails.[8] Many are not from middle-class backgrounds and have not been in situations where an inability to write proper business correspondence can destroy their chances, at school or at work. Or (what you might not have considered) for some, email is an archaic form that they just do not use very much.

Berg tasks them with reading the syllabus carefully and then writing him a business email in which they ask one good, thoughtful question about the syllabus. Of course, this also means they have a structure for reading the syllabus carefully. Berg responds to every email, editing it into the proper form for a business email. For instance, "Hey" or "Hi" are not how one starts a formal correspondence. "Dear Professor Berg" is much better. Berg demonstrates that he will not judge them or talk dismissively about their class or educational deficiencies. Rather, he explains that the email exercise is a tool to help students build a portfolio of skills that they can use to advance in the world.

This activity can also be used in the middle of term, as a means for students to present a final project proposal to you. For example, this email could be a cover letter to a first draft, a précis for a paper or a working thesis with a prospective title as if they were pitching it to an editor for consideration.

CHAPTER 7

Democratic and Antiracist Pedagogy

It can come as a shock when incidents of racism, transphobia, Islamophobia, antisemitism or other forms of prejudice erupt in our classrooms. As instructors, we don't always feel qualified, prepared, or well trained to address these moments—but it's our classroom, and sometimes tensions arise. In such situations, we need to address them. Overtly discriminatory, prejudiced, biased, or racist remarks are not "free speech." They are analogous to crying "Fire!" in a crowded theater because of the disastrous pedagogical effects they have on everyone in the room.

Because we want all students to have a voice and be heard, learning how to navigate complex classroom dynamics is essential. In a short class period, time is too precious for any one person or group to dominate the discussion, and the activities below help to distribute participation time equally. Ideally, we want to aim for unity, not sameness, to bring all students into respectful conversation without glossing over or even reconciling differences and without maintaining false perceptions, adopting what Eve Tuck and K. Wayne Yang call "an ethic of incommensurability."[1] Not all questions may be answered which can feel unsettling to us and our students—and that's a good thing. There are effective ways to make some of that discomfort more welcome than it is stressful, and more manageable too. The following methods help ensure that everyone has a vote and a voice and that everyone speaks within the community guidelines for participation that the class has already established through collective learning outcomes, a collaborative class constitution, or other participatory activities.

Democracy, though, is not the same as equality. As bell hooks reminds us, the classroom is the most radical space of possibility within the academy. If we are not careful, the open, engaged classroom can all too easily replicate larger social patterns, allowing some voices to predominate, especially when students of color are the minority in the classroom. It's also easy, in predominantly white institutions, to fall into glib sanctimony, kneejerk phrases boasting egalitarianism, or the opposite, an accusation that antiracism is equivalent to antiwhiteness. It's delicate, often tricky, and the stakes could not be higher. How we orchestrate participation in the classroom contributes to who will become future leaders, including future instructors and future university deans and provosts and presidents.

Given the intensity of the debate, we offer here a portfolio of experts who use an array of antiracist teaching methods. While the examples we offer mostly focus on the United States, we underscore the international importance of this issue. Black Lives Matter (BLM) has increased awareness around the world of tacit biases, police violence, histories of colonialism, and discrimination against Indigenous peoples, migrants, and refugees. Reporting in July 2020 from Singapore, Shashi Jayakumar argues that the common ground is a "struggle for equality against the backdrop of societal indifference and apathy, and a not-so-distant history of racial segregation."[2] Jayakumar, who is head of the Centre of Excellence for National Security at Nanyang Technological University in Singapore, cites the impact of the BLM movement in that nation and around the world, including in the streets of Taipei and Tokyo, the emergence of #PapuanLivesMatter in Indonesia, and the protests against police violence in the context of President Rodrigo Duterte's so-called War on Drugs in the Philippines.[3]

In higher education, BLM has sparked numerous conferences, panels, coalitions, ad hoc committees, reading groups, and "Diversity, Equity, and Inclusion" training sessions to shepherd eager educators ready to bring antiracist teaching practices into their classes. Academics for Black Survival and Wellness (sometimes called Academics for Black Lives or A4BL) has hosted massive, free, virtual antiracist trainings for non-Black academics "to honor the toll that anti-Black racism has on the Black community and their colleagues."[4] At the same time, right-wing, racist populism has also spread globally. Hate crimes are on the rise the world over, and aggression against minority populations is rampant, including that initiated by governments, from Israel to Colombia and many points in between. In the United States, several states have launched campaigns to limit teaching concepts such as racial equity or white privilege.

In any classroom where the professor is a member of a minority group within the general population of that institution in particular, they should proceed with caution. There is ample documentation that a person who is considered a "minority" (however defined in the given situation) faces more scrutiny, higher stakes, and greater consequences than colleagues whose identity mirrors that of the majority of their administrators, colleagues, and students. Since I (Cathy) have spent much of my career among computer scientists and technology designers, I know from decades of experience that my voice "sounds" different when I am the only woman in the room.

Structuring equality in the participatory classroom has a different ring—and is heard differently—when the authority figure shares a gender, racial, religious, or ability identity with the majority of their students and peers. All of the methods and models offered in this chapter can be heard, received, and responded to differently depending upon those real-world circumstances. Working to "balance" a classroom does not change social inequality in the world at large, nor even how those efforts will be judged by one's students, peers, and administrators.

Entering into controversial subjects now is not, in other words, for the faint of heart. Yet it isn't avoidable. As the lifelong antiracist educator Beverly Daniel Tatum notes, because of residential segregation in the U.S., "a lot of young White people don't start thinking about racial issues until they get to college, because college is often the most diverse learning environment they've been in."[5] If the college classroom is often a place where race becomes an issue, it is part of thoughtful, inclusive pedagogy to think of race as a key factor in learning design.

The methods discussed in this chapter can do a world of good for structuring equity into our classrooms. We offer these ideas as resources for you to try, accept, reject, or modify. Some have been in use for decades. Others are new ideas and strategies developed by inspiring educators who are experts in antiracist teaching practices. All are designed to turn conflicts and tensions into teachable moments.

In this chapter:

Popsicle Sticks
Question Stacking
The "Oops"/"Ouch" Method
Modeling Repair by Identifying Common Needs
Facilitating Recovery Through Deep Listening
The Antiracist Creative Workshop: Discovery-Based Crit
Critical Race Theory and Antiracist Futurism

Popsicle Sticks

This popsicle activity is not new. It was designed several decades ago by feminists who noted the gender disparity in group interactions. They developed a method of structuring discussions to be more egalitarian without having to constantly scold some participants for contributing too much or too often. Research shows that male students speak more than female students in class (1.6 times more, according to one study), and white students speak more often than students of color, especially when the professor is also white.[6] In meetings, male instructors and administrators dominate, by a wide margin, over female counterpoints.[7] Race exacerbates this gender inequality. The popsicle stick activity works to ensure all forms of balance—gender, racial, and ethnic—and also to ensure equity where there are cognitive and physical disabilities as well. It ensures that no one person or one group dominates class discussion.

The method is simple. Each student is given two popsicle sticks. In any class period, they use up a popsicle stick each time they speak, placing it on their desk or the table in front of them. This means that everyone gets two turns to speak each class (the number resets with every new class period). Knowing they get two turns to speak, students must decide if what they have to say is important enough to "burn" a stick, which represents a turn speaking. This is adaptable to different class sizes and situations. For example, in a smaller class you might give students three popsicle sticks, or in a large lecture, everyone gets one popsicle stick. Another way to adapt this activity is to keep track of participation, asking each student to write their name on their popsicle sticks and to deposit them in a shoe box or tin can or whatever receptacle you wish to use to collect them each time a student speaks. This allows us to observe and even quantify who speaks, and, if needed, we can speak privately to those who are taking up too much class time, as confirmed by all their popsicle sticks. Learning to listen and not speak at every opportunity can be as important a part of our education as finding our voice.

The key component to making this work is to do this joyfully, not censoriously. Following an activity like the listening dyad mentioned in the last chapter, the popsicle method values the privilege of speaking and makes room for *all* participants to speak; its purpose is not to shut conversation down. To help students understand this, you might require that everyone use *at least one* popsicle stick every class. If some are intimidated, you can lower the stakes by asking a direct or simple question (equivalent to one popsicle stick) such as: "What assignments are due next week?" Lowering the stakes somewhat makes this method accessible to language learners and introverted students alike, allowing them room to develop and to gain confidence in their ability to speak.

This activity need not be branded in any particular political way. We've all been in situations (department meetings, sessions at professional conferences) where we know which person is going to dominate the discussion. Popsicle sticks are a way of helping everyone be more thoughtful and self-aware about their roles as participants. The purpose of this activity is to not just show but also *act* on the fact that every member of the group deserves airtime.

Question Stacking

Question stacking—also known as "progressive stack"—is designed to allow those who are "typically silenced" in a classroom to speak first. Question stacking or progressive stack can be adapted as a good pedagogical method to give all students equal opportunity to participate in a classroom environment.[8]

Here's how it works: ask students to raise their hands in response to a question and write down the name (or make a mental note) of everyone with a hand up. If you're using Zoom, the hand-raising function can do this for you automatically. If you're teaching in person, have everyone put their hand down and call on people in *progressive* order, meaning typically marginalized voices get to speak first. The stack prioritizes the voices of those who you have observed are not speaking up in your class, especially if you have noticed a general pattern in the silence. Who is in the minority may change given the context. For example, in a computer science class where there are only two Latina women in the room, if either or both of them raise a hand, they would be stacked first.[9] In a Queer Poetry course where the majority of students are from the LGBTQ+ community, the minority voice might be the straight Catholic student who ventures an answer, despite being new to queer theory. There's tremendous value in allowing nonexperts to speak first because they often have original contributions to make that the majority hadn't considered before. No one has a right to ask a second question until each person in the stack has had a turn. Anyone who wishes may withdraw a question in the "stack" if they feel someone else answered it already.

Why is this important? A 2019 study led by professor of educational sciences Klara Sedova of Masaryk University in Brno in the Czech Republic charted the success of some seven hundred middle school students. Researchers in the study documented a direct and significant correlation between how much students talk in a class and how much they learn. Regardless of socioeconomic background, they found "classroom talk" and "talk time" correlated with and contributed to overall success in other forms of writing, reading, and literacy.[10]

Ideally, as educators, we want all of our students to succeed, not just some of them, and this is true both inside the classroom and beyond. We've all seen Q&A sessions at conferences in which only men are called on even though several women scholars have their hands raised. Using question stacking works to bolster "talk time" for *all* participants, whether in department meetings, community meetings, or the classroom. Conversation in groups—a notably difficult and fraught form of public speaking—is a high art. It's stressful for most of us. Adding a timer to keep questions from becoming longer comments helps remove some of the burden of responsibility. One friend brings in a gigantic and goofy red alarm clock to keep timekeeping lighthearted (while still keeping time).[11]

The "Oops" / "Ouch" Method

When a class is suddenly interrupted by a racist, sexist, or otherwise offensive remark made by a student or professor, it is often hard to get the class back on track. How do we acknowledge the offensiveness of the speech without shaming that person, without interrupting and shutting down the conversation, without doing even more damage?

Jesús Treviño, vice provost for inclusive excellence at Arizona State University, advocates what he calls the "Oops" / "Ouch" method.[12] This method needs to be explained at the beginning of a class, workshop, or meeting. When someone is hurt or offended by something that is said, they have the right to say "Ouch," and the offender has the right to say "Oops." These intentionally comical words allow both participants to acknowledge the offense and then swiftly move on. If it happens again, or if the incident was particularly striking, the class can always circle back to the oops / ouch incident later and discuss it, not as a source of shame but as something all can learn from.[13]

Like the timer that helps to train us to limit how much discussion time we take, the "Oops" / "Ouch" method helps us to learn the pain speech inflicts and the difficulty of apology. Imagine, for example, that someone in a theater class accidentally uses the "dead name" or the old pronoun of a classmate who is gender transitioning. Another student notices this mistake and says "Ouch," giving the speaker a quick way to acknowledge the error by saying "Oops" and correct themselves. Then, room is made in the conversation to talk about *how* to talk about transgender, transitioning, and gender identity more broadly.

Modeling Repair by Identifying Common Needs

In *Classroom Talk for Social Change,* Melissa Schieble, Amy Vetter, and Kahdeidra Monét Martin advocate negotiating tension by modeling repair. When tensions rise—a White male student says something offensive about affirmative action and a Black female student is quick to shut him down with an insult—instead of saying, "Let's move on," Schieble, Vetter, and Martin recommend pausing to ease tensions immediately by identifying students' common emotional needs.[14] Feelings demand answers and can be incredibly useful in propelling learning in the classroom and beyond. They intensify inquiry, drive us to double down on research to support our convictions, and inspire us to critically examine and cross-check assumptions, hypotheses, and theories. In the words of Dian Million, "we *feel* our histories as well as think them"; feelings are "culturally mediated knowledges, never solely individual," which means it's crucial to bear witness to them.[15]

Instead of sidestepping around the tension, we can model repair by confronting the feelings of both parties and reflecting their emotions back to them. You might recast the situation by observing the feelings you notice bubbling to the surface: "It sounds like you feel some resentment about affirmative action and feel that it's unfair," and "When you hear claims about 'reverse racism,' does that make you feel angry and exhausted?" Or, for Asian American students, "Do you feel frustrated being cast in the role of the 'model minority'?" Chances are, the authors counsel, "that if you have accurately reflected back student emotions, you will receive affirmative responses, which is the beginning of diffusing tensions in order to move forward." If there's time, you can engage the whole class in what they call a "Think-Write-Pair-Share" activity, the purpose of which is to give all students an opportunity to listen and an opportunity to be heard. They suggest prompts such as, "In order to feel safe and respected continuing this conversation, I need . . ." and "Above all, I care most that my peers . . ." Prompts like these help students to understand that some speech can be thoughtless and even harmful to others, hindering students' right, as Barbara Applebaum phrases it, "to be educated in a safe environment free from overt and covert forms of discrimination."[16]

Finally, if you have time within that class or at the start of the next meeting, you can reframe the conversation to center the focus on the learning community's common needs. Importantly, Schieble, Vetter, and Martin note the importance of seeking advice from your institution's counselors who are trained in these matters and may be better prepared in these areas, especially if you are new to antiracist teaching practices.

Facilitating Recovery Through Deep Listening

Adriana Estill teaches at Carleton College, a historically white small liberal arts college in Minnesota. Professor Estill uses a class contract in all her courses. Students develop guidelines they all agree to, and while these vary course to course, contracts usually contain these three items (and when students don't bring these up themselves, Estill makes sure to get them in): "some articulation of the need to share space / time; some recognition of our promise to keep our discussions confidential (the Vegas rule); some statement of our desire to assume best intentions." Over the years, what constituted "best intentions" largely went unexamined until the day a student confidentially reported that the Vegas rule had been broken outside of class. This student overheard peers talking about the class, disclosing specific students' names in a mocking tone. When Estill later informed the class that their contract had been broken, it became apparent that although everyone wanted to assume best intentions, "when listening to others, we didn't always know what that meant."[17]

For the next class, Estill organized a fishbowl activity, where 4–6 students sat in the center of the room to address this difficult topic and the rest of the 30-person class sat in a circle around them, listening and bearing witness. Estill required all students to "tap in" to the inner circle at least once: someone sitting in the outside "listening" circle would tap a peer sitting in the inside "speaking" circle and they would trade places. Estill's discussion prompts worked to move the conversation away from feelings of guilt or shame and toward an understanding of how and why the contract was fragile and easily broken:

- "What does it *feel like* to assume best intentions? How do you notice and pause your intellectual and emotional reflexes as you make deliberate moves toward best intentions?"
- "What are your *best practices* for how you engage in this class with best intentions? What has that looked like? Why has it been challenging?"

Students had the floor entirely and they spoke honestly and vulnerably, engaging in deep self-reflection. This method can work in any similar situation to begin healing the community after trust has been violated. However, Estill gently details the specific racial dimensions of this particular incident. Multiple white students owned up to the fact that they had broken the contract; "these admissions became opportunities for students to consider why and how they had been unthoughtful and what it might feel like to recognize the 'betrayal' of classmates." The productive result of this activity shows the immediate rewards and benefits of "not looking away" from conflict.

Conflict may happen in many circumstances; in this one the focus was the "neutrality of Whiteness." By extension, the discussion had to address the definition and inflection of anyone not "white" as "other." What is the relationship, for example, of "American," "African American," "Asian American," "Asian," and "African"? Those terms are not simply descriptors but categories that come bundled with unexamined and unequal hierarchies, blurrings, confusions, and assumptions.

"Not looking away," Estill writes, and "making a commitment to remembering" were crucial to repairing a painful situation and moving forward to begin to rebuild trust that had been violated. The discussion evolved to include practical suggestions about how to listen when you feel yourself getting angry and, equally, how to listen when you feel yourself getting defensive. By the end, students arrived at the recognition that it takes effort to listen well, to extend emotional awareness ("to listen for impact and to not hide behind intent"), and to recognize the humanity of each individual student.

The Antiracist Creative Workshop: Discovery-Based Crit

Professor Felicia Rose Chavez, author of *The Anti-Racist Writing Workshop: How to Decolonize the Creative Classroom,* is herself a scholar of color, and she does not assume her audiences will only be white. Chavez, the Creativity and Innovation Scholar-in-Residence at Colorado College, focuses on ways to be "culturally attuned, twenty-first century educators" and works to "create healthy, sustainable, and empowering classroom communities." She offers specific exercises, examples, and principles for designing a "democratic teaching model" that allows each and every student a place for "creative concentration," a way to powerfully "exercise voice," and to "self-advocate as responsible citizens of a globalized community."

Chavez reexamines the most basic terms of how a creative workshop functions. As she writes, "The traditional model assumes that workshop participants share an identical knowledge of craft, and wields academic vocabulary as a badge of authority."[18] By contrast, in the antiracist model, participants collectively define the workshop vocabulary.

This exercise can be adapted to any course, in any field. For example, there are innumerable new terms and concepts for students to learn in college (for instance, "area" in math; "epistemology" in philosophy; "hermeneutics" in religion; "decolonial" in anthropology; "neoliberal" in critical university studies, etc.). To make these terms more approachable and easier to grasp, students can be tasked with defining them using their own words (e.g., "the space something takes up," "how we know what we know," "interpretation," etc.). They find a common language, one that has more meaning to them. This makes the essential vocabulary for any course accessible to all students, no matter their prior learning. Equally important, it makes the students who already are comfortable with a specialized disciplinary vocabulary think again about the meaning(s) embedded, assumed, or precluded by the abstract term itself.[19]

To return to Professor Chavez's antiracist writing workshop: aesthetic categories come with long histories. What does or does not constitute "high art" or "folk art" or "classical music" or "Great Books" or "non-Western art"? Professor Chavez challenges her students to think carefully about evaluative language and also about language that seems not to carry racialized judgments ("excellence") but that, in fact, embeds histories of approval or disapproval, acceptance or rejection.

Too often, she argues, the traditional "crit" session in art and design schools becomes a type of hazing, rejection, and even subjugation wherein the person in power (the professor) offers formal public criticism of student work. In this hierarchical situation, even approval comes at the cost of, at least implicitly, assuming or mirroring the value judgments of the professor.[20]

Chavez's alternative is "a more human, discovery-based model," where all students are offered an opportunity to find and *define* their own creativity, voice, and self-advocacy, regardless of race, gender, country of national origin, or other predefined factors.[21] Her principles of antiracism are not exactly the principles of active, participatory, engaged learning but, like the intersections of a Venn diagram, there is considerable overlap. Instead of accepting aesthetic categories of judgment that are the basis for the traditional crit session, she advocates discovery guided by four questions:

- "Who were you when you began this journey?"
- "What did you set out to do, and why?"
- "Where are you currently in your learning?"
- "What's next?"[22]

These questions require introspection, offer serious room for reflection, and give each and every student an equal opportunity to improve, learn, grow, and shine.

Critical Race Theory and Antiracist Futurism

Any instructor who has embarked on a discussion of race in a classroom—especially if you are not trained as a theorist or historian of race—knows the discussion is both crucial and laden with potential problems and pitfalls. This is especially true in this particular historical moment when conservative lawmakers in the United States (as well as in other countries including Australia and the United Kingdom) have proposed or even instituted laws banning "critical race theory" from public school textbooks. In fact, this is more political slogan than reality since current K–12 textbooks do not include "critical race theory," a body of legal scholarship developed in the 1980s and 1990s by Derrick Bell, Kimberlé Crenshaw, Patricia J. Williams, and others.[23] Critical race theory examines the disparate racial impacts and outcomes of certain laws due to changing and sometimes even subtle social or institutional processes.[24] In the United States, one result has been that, as of September 2021, ten US states have passed laws banning the teaching of history that includes mention of racism. Of the restrictive Tennessee version of the law, English teacher Mike Stein notes: "History teachers can not adequately teach about the Trail of Tears, the Civil War, and the civil rights movement. English teachers will have to avoid teaching almost any text by an African American author because many of them mention racism to various extents."[25]

Universities are not exempt, in the United States or in other countries where white supremacist movements are on the rise. Professors at public universities are being called to task for talking about race in classrooms, and some are being persecuted. In the midst of this politically controversial melee, the National Museum of African American History and Culture offers useful advice for "Talking about Race." This basic statement can be especially useful for instructors who are not scholars of race and racism and not trained to discuss this currently controversial subject that can come up in any classroom, in any discipline, at any institution:

> No one is born racist or antiracist; these result from the choices we make. Being antiracist results from a conscious decision to make frequent, consistent, equitable choices daily. These choices require ongoing self-awareness and self-reflection as we move through life. In the absence of making antiracist choices, we (un)consciously uphold aspects of white supremacy, white-dominant culture, and unequal institutions and society. Being racist or antiracist is not about who you *are;* it is about what you *do.*[26]

Understanding "what we do" is the primary focus of the Boston University Center for Antiracist Research founded by Professor Ibram X. Kendi, the author of two bestsellers, *How To Be an Antiracist* and *Stamped from the Beginning: The Definitive History of Racist Ideas in America.*[27] Kendi defines a racist policy as one that leads to a racially inequitable outcome. If your organization's outcomes are inequitable, no doubt its policies are what took you to that place. Kendi writes serious historical books intended for a general audience. He has also rewritten *Stamped from the Beginning* as a children's book and there is even a version for toddlers. He believes education never stops, cradle to grave.

Kendi defines an "antiracist idea" as "any idea that suggests the racial groups are equals in all their apparent differences—that there is nothing right or wrong about any racial group." In his scholarship, teaching, and workshops, he argues that being an antiracist requires "persistent self-awareness, constant self-criticism, and regular self-examination."[28] His approach relies on research and the deeply optimistic assumption that researching, making visible, defining, and calling out antiracism are the beginning, not the end, of an intellectual and social process.

Before offering readers his annotated syllabus of thirty-eight books "for those open to changing themselves and their world," Kendi notes:

> This antiracist syllabus is for people realizing they were never taught how to be antiracist. How to treat all the racial groups as equals. How to look at the racial inequity all around and look for the racist policies producing it, and the racist ideas veiling it. This list is for people beginning their antiracist journey after a lifetime of defensively saying, "I'm not a racist" or "I can't be a racist." Beginning after a lifetime of assuring themselves only bad people can be racist.[29]

The books on Kendi's antiracist syllabus, like his own research, examine the nature of human complexity and the idea that "people hold both racist and antiracist ideas and obviously support both racist and antiracist policies. . . . No one becomes an antiracist. It is only something we can strive to be . . . there is no destination, it's a journey of really consistently ensuring that we're supporting antiracist policies and policy-makers and that we're articulating antiracist ideas, and we're constantly unlearning this conditioning."[30]

By embracing rather than ignoring or denying difference, Kendi proposes a democratic pedagogy, one that identifies and uses any difference in a classroom for the benefit of everyone, not as the basis for bias, prejudice, discrimination, and racism. In the next chapter, we offer a method that prioritizes difference. "Collaboration by difference" specifically draws from the differences in our classrooms to ensure that every student knows that they belong in the university and that they have something invaluable to contribute and equally invaluable to learn.

CHAPTER 8

Group Work Without the Groans

There is perhaps no skill more crucial in the world beyond the classroom than being able to collaborate with others. Yet nothing elicits more groans from students than the phrase, "Let's work in groups." When that happens, we double down: most students do not yet realize that learning how to contribute successfully to group work is crucial to their success in the world. The *easiest* thing we can do is explain the importance of this essential skill and bolster explanation with inspiring examples. And the most *useful* thing we can do is structure carefully how the groups work together and not simply leave it to the students themselves to figure out how to accomplish successful collaboration. Group work is crucial. It's also a learned skill, one that takes practice and dedication.

In the everyday work world, just about everything requires collaboration: you may not like the cranky business manager but you cannot submit your contract or grant without them. When it works well, collaboration is magic—whether achieving excellent patient care, coordinating lights and sound in a theater production, or pulling off a potluck dinner with a little bit of something from and for everyone. Collaboration done right collates a wealth of ideas, often from different perspectives or different forms of expertise, and uses this variety of skills and knowledge to accomplish something bigger or better than any one team member could produce alone.

Some of the best science is generated by collaborations, including international seed banking, the International Space Station, the Human Genome Project, and the development of the COVID-19 vaccine. We all can think of myriad examples within and across every field. The climax of Ludwig van Beethoven's *Symphony No. 9* would not be the same without Friedrich Schiller's poem "Ode to Joy."

Yet collaboration is rarely easy, and far too often instructors act as if it comes naturally. Young adults need practice to become proficient in the social skills required for good teamwork, including self-awareness, self-regulation, empathy, and clear and effective communication. In fact, so few adults in the workforce possess these skills that *The New York Times* developed "An Adult's Guide to Social Skills, for Those Who Were Never Taught."[1] It doesn't take a lot of time to call attention to the skills students can practice in their collaborations. Collaboration becomes the most valuable learning experience when it is the *beginning* of a conversation. Participatory learning is especially effective in starting that conversation and guiding students successfully through group projects and their applicability beyond the classroom. The methods we advocate in this chapter are standard in the world of work: businesses spend millions of dollars every year training employees in how to collaborate across differences effectively. The participatory classroom is the exact right apprenticeship for a life of collaboration to follow.

In this chapter:

What Is Collaboration by Difference?

"Collaboration by difference" is a method developed by the online community HASTAC (Humanities, Arts, Science, and Technology Alliance and Collaboratory, pronounced "haystack"), a network founded by me (Cathy) and a colleague in 2002, and called, by peer reviewers at the National Science Foundation, the world's "first and oldest academic social network." Whether it is the oldest or not is hard to prove; suffice to say it's older than Facebook or even Facebook's predecessor MySpace. In 2002, there was not much educational theory around to address the optimal ways to conduct online interaction across radically different fields, linking young students, technology experts, or coders who might not have gone to college and distinguished professors and scientists. We never dreamed that this user-created social network would still be alive and well decades later. Now with over eighteen thousand members, HASTAC allows anyone who registers to the site to contribute any content that is relevant to its mission, "Changing the ways we teach and learn," and is respectful of its core value: "Difference is our operating system." HASTAC's first funding came from the National Science Foundation's Cyberinfrastructure Division. It was part of NSF's international "collaboratory" effort. Computer scientist William Wulf used this term to describe a "center without walls" in which researchers could perform their work "without regard to physical location."[2] Collaboratories and social networks were a shiny new idea when HASTAC was founded. Now they are, quite simply, how the world works.

To support collaboration online and across all of its constituent fields, HASTAC members advocated an inventory method specifically designed to solicit all of the diverse opinions in a group and, equally, to distribute responsibilities and work across all participants. "Collaboration by difference" requires participation from everyone, including the outliers, in order to ensure the best possible outcome. This means structuring the collaboration to encourage—not ignore—innovative, original, untrained, diverse, and even contrary opinions, so long as they are offered constructively and respectfully. Our method of collaboration by difference is essentially a prelude to successful group projects. It is an operating model made up of three basic rules:

1. Recognize and value differences
2. Let non-experts talk first
3. Always ask what we're missing

These three rules make room for everyone to contribute, setting the stage for more holistic approaches to problems and better outcomes.

Collaboration by difference can be really straightforward, especially *recognizing and valuing differences,* which can be taught even to toddlers. In fact, I (Christina) am currently working on a project designed to translate this method for preschoolers. Here's a short sketch of what it looks like in action: two preschoolers, Daryn and Adrian, want to pick apples from a tree but those red, juicy fruits are *just* out of reach of their tiny hands. Daryn is an adventurous, active child who likes to explore. Adrian is more cautious and careful. A parent suggests they work together and sets a small wooden crate under the tree. Daryn climbs on top of the crate to reach and pick the apples, then tosses them down onto the grass—such fun! Adrian carefully picks up the apples one at a time and places them into a small basket—"I did it!" Both children have used their different strengths to accomplish the same goal. That's the point.

It's not so different in the New College Classroom, albeit a little more sophisticated, when group members share the workload according to what each partner can best contribute to a project's overall success. Students make a preliminary effort to discover which member can contribute what, who has certain skills, passions, interests, or even character traits, who can climb high and who can carefully attend to what falls. Through collaboration, we familiarize ourselves with the discomfort we feel when we encounter differences. In healthy collaborations, we turn differences from deficits into resources that can be creative and generative for the group as a whole.

When we devote time to structuring activities to ensure the contribution of every member, we reassure our students that there is no room to hide and no room to take over. One reason students may dread group work is that, too often, one person ends up doing the brunt of the work. Others then either feel left out or feel like they are getting away with murder. There are many small ways to try to avoid unequal contributions. For example, if you've noticed a pattern or problem in discussion-focused work, you could put all the "talkers" in one group to help them learn how to listen and all the "introverts" in another to help them practice speaking up. This not only shakes things up but also makes room for every group member—now on more equal footing—to discover and value other, more unique and diverse skills they can contribute.

Rule 1: Recognize and Value Differences

The initial meeting of any group can be daunting. Whether in a classroom or in any gathering where participants are coming together for the first time, several preliminaries are important before the leader says, "Get into your groups!" If you were building a project team at a workplace, you would never just call for a random group of participants. You would assess what the task demanded and select the participants best suited to contribute to a successful result.

Asking, first, what each person contributes before establishing any groups helps students recognize and value the differences of all participants in a classroom. Most people are reluctant to simply state what they can and cannot do, so an inventory method puts all on an equal footing.

We recommend using one of the classic inventory methods described in Chapter 5 (for instance, entry tickets or interview) to give students a context for expressing what skills they possess. In a quick exercise (90 seconds always works—as do index cards), you might ask students to write out two or three talents they know they can contribute to the group. It's useful for the instructor to provide a sample list of skills for inspiration to remind students about their own. A skills list might include a range of academic skills (math major, library sciences); soft skills (public speaker, project manager); hard skills (speaking Mandarin or Spanish, coding ability, copyediting and proofreading, video editing); or even personality traits (an ability to work under pressure, deliver a product to specs and on deadline, or inject humor when the group is stuck).

After identifying their talents, students next list skills they lack or talents they hope someone else in their group will possess. They might say, "I don't know statistics and need to work with someone who understands regression and probability." This discursive method is particularly powerful in language classes. For example, at the University of Minnesota, Professor Lydia Belatèche has students in Advanced French Composition and Conversation meet in virtual cafés to have conversations about their roles and other topics. They submit the audio files from these peer-to-peer interactions for credit. Knowing that these conversations "count" underscores their value. She finds that her students form close bonds in group work, and these overflow into voluntary additional time spent working on creative final projects such as videos, paintings, drawings, and more, accompanied by artists' statements.[3]

Cristy Bruns, associate professor of English at LaGuardia Community College, begins each of her class meetings with icebreakers designed to support collaboration. She offers prompts to encourage students to discuss skills for success in school (such as "How are you at asking for help?"), to connect course content with their own experience ("What have you researched lately outside of school?"), or to check in with each other ("How are you holding up?" or "What's helping and what's not helping?"). The regular prompting to talk with classmates transforms the atmosphere of Bruns's classroom from one of anxiety and awkwardness to one where even shy students grow comfortable and feel like they belong. That feeling of belonging is especially significant where she teaches, with a majority of students who are low-income, immigrants, and people of color—students who may have grown accustomed to feeling unwelcome and unheard. This practice, and her overall effort to make the classroom a safe place for students to contribute and participate, led several students to remark that coming into their classroom felt like coming home.[4]

Rule 2: Let Non-Experts Talk First

The only way to ensure input from non-experts is by giving them the floor first or, even better, by using an inventory method that allows everyone to give an opinion in a low-stakes fashion at the same time so that the group can then see all the options at once (this might be polls, Think-Pair-Share, entry tickets, or another deep listening method). Unless the situation is structured for their contribution, it likely will be drowned out by the more "knowledgeable" voices.

The value in this rule goes beyond showing students that they matter: oftentimes, the non-expert is able to see glaring missteps, and they are more likely to critically question underlying assumptions behind common practices and traditions in a field. A sociology student might ask an English major why an eighteenth-century novel matters today, and that is a valid question. In some group activities, the non-expert may be someone from outside of class, such as a person the students are interviewing. Virginia Yonkers at the University at Albany organizes an activity with her Business Communications students in which she sends in-class groups outside to complete a task using leadership skills they are studying. The unpredictability of what happens "outside" the classroom challenges students with complex problems and situations beyond any artificial simulation in a classroom. An outsider's perspective—such as an interviewee—forces insiders to go beyond the assumptions of a field.[5]

In a project in Chicago involving low-income middle-school students that aimed to design ideal digital media for their after-school program, we (Cathy and her partners on the Digital Media and Learning Initiative sponsored by the John D. and Catherine T. MacArthur Foundation) made a rule that no one but a middle-school student had permission to speak during the first hour of our initial two-hour planning meeting. By having the students go first, the teachers, parents, and technology experts took a back seat. We were inspired by them and arrived at projects more imaginative than any of us had planned. We also had no problem getting the youths on board since they had originated the ideas and they were determined to show that they had made wise choices. Without this structure in place, this input would not have happened and we would have ended up with a duller project and less motivated participants.

In folk tales, it's the child or the naif who first points out that the emperor has no clothes. In groups, it is often the non-expert who sees something that those with more knowledge miss. The Vehbi Koç Foundation's Model School Project in Istanbul takes a similar approach when designing and building schools. A Third Teacher team, composed of an architect, a principal, and an anthropologist, meets with local community members, including parents and their kids, to assess their needs and dreams and to take them into consideration for the design of the school before breaking ground. Although the students may not be experts in architecture or administration, they give their input in the planning stages; students from each class level participate as representatives on the school board. Mesrure Tekay, who has decades of leadership experience in the Turkish school system, including serving as the head of Koç School from 1998 to 2013, emphasizes the "learner's agenda" instead of getting caught in the "teacher / student" binary. She says that "learner" is an important distinction: "nowadays a teacher cannot be described as a person who knows everything and distributes that knowledge to students. That was of the last century. It's better and more effective to encourage inquiry and exploration because we are all learners and things keep changing. If we stop learning, we will go backwards." The first model school has so far been a success: Tekay says that because the building is so special to the community, the students respect the school materials and take care of the building.[6]

Letting non-experts speak first is a simple reversal that accomplishes much of what we mean by collaboration by difference. It recognizes and values differences, and it helps the students with the most expertise to gain insights from those who may not know as much. In a certain way, it helps the group avoid yet another pitfall of teamwork that has not been structured equitably: it takes the pressure off the most prepared student by not allowing them to end up doing all the work. Successful collaboration means making differences useful for offering a perspective that can push the collective achievement even further.

Rule 3: Ask What You're Missing

Once a collaboration is underway, roles and workloads are assigned, and the first critical questions have been asked, it is important to end each meeting with the open-ended question, "What else?" or "What are we missing?" This is a good rule for any business meeting. First at the Futures Initiative and now at Transformative Learning in the Humanities, we (Christina, Cathy, and our colleagues) include "What else?" at the end of every agenda. Leaving room for questions at the end of a session is always a good idea. An even better idea is asking everyone in the room to suggest what might not have been covered yet. Using a collaborative document to gather these suggestions reframes the ending like the beginning: by making everyone in the room the expert on what needs attention.

To underline the importance of making "What's missing?" a routine question in the course of a project, consider an example of what happens when differences of opinion are *not* aired routinely in work culture. In the workplace, the consequences of collaborations that do not structure and support differences of perspective can be catastrophic. In *Disastrous Decisions: The Human and Organizational Causes of the Mexico Blowout,* industrial safety expert Andrew Hopkins analyzes the reasons for the Deepwater Horizon oil spill of 2010, which was responsible for the tragic loss of eleven lives and at the time was the largest environmental disaster in US history. Hopkins argues that the disaster came largely because of a "C-suite" (corporate) culture that rewarded confirmation and consensus, silenced divergence from the norm, and actively discouraged anyone who dared to deliver the "bad news."[7] Plenty of people, he argues, knew disaster loomed ahead but were afraid they would be punished for disagreeing with the majority opinion that everything was going smoothly.

While collaboration in a classroom is hardly a matter of such dire consequence, we all have witnessed failed group projects where everyone, like salmon, follows the majority upstream without asking critical questions or taking time to play devil's advocate. This is "groupthink," which discourages creative and original thinking. It becomes an overt or covert form of coercion.

In contrast, when those who see what is missing are given the power to act, the results can be positive far beyond what anyone could have anticipated. In 2010 and 2011, Christchurch, New Zealand, was hit by a crippling series of earthquakes that destroyed 80 percent of its downtown area, rendering approximately eleven thousand homes uninhabitable, and killing 185 people. Amidst the tragedy, over ten thousand University of Canterbury students knew exactly what was missing: they self-organized the Student Volunteer Army and provided essential assistance by helping clean up liquefaction, a quicksand-like substance, and distributing blankets, chemical toilets, and water. According to Billy O'Steen, associate professor of community engagement at the University of Canterbury, as important as students' labor was, it was their interactions with residents across the city that flipped the script: local community members went from perceiving college students as noisy and troublesome drunkards to seeing them as the helpful, thoughtful, and useful people that they are. Likewise, the students felt a sense of self-efficacy and relevance. While O'Steen witnessed this amazing display, he considered how to bring students' actions back to campus. He studied models of service learning, especially Tulane University's response to Hurricane Katrina. Finally, he proposed the course called Strengthening Communities through Social Innovation, to the president of the University of Canterbury, and, since then, the course has been offered every year to over a thousand students. Now community engagement is part of the four core campus-wide skills University of Canterbury students emerge with after graduation and a new degree program. This is a remarkable example of the power of asking, "What's missing?" both in a community and also in the core curriculum.[8]

Taking the Temperature of the Room

Before you dive headfirst into teamwork, take the temperature of the room—that is, make sure to measure the health and readiness of all members of a group for collaboration. This is good practice whether the potential collaborators are your students or colleagues in or outside of your department. Whereas K–12 educators attend workshops and receive feedback on their teaching all of the time, in higher education we rarely find ourselves on teams or in environments where exchanging feedback and encountering radical differences are the norm. Take it from us. Sometimes collaboration just doesn't work, no matter how hard one tries.

I (Christina) have worked on diverse and inclusive teams of all sizes, but I ran into a problem when organizing a panel for a major international conference. I had an idea for a special session on environmental literary studies, a field that analyzes literature from an ecological perspective. A friend suggested two scholars I might ask to collaborate on such a panel. They were both at the same or similar junior career stage as me. They knew one another, but I had not met either of them. In retrospect, it would have been a really good idea to set expectations for collaboration up front.

To make a long and painful story short, one participant never met deadlines and bristled at any hint of feedback or prompting. Eventually, he chose to drop off the panel. The other took the credit despite doing only limited work. To be fair, I had said this was okay when it wasn't. At the time, I feared that this colleague, too, would reject my leadership, so I stepped down. My stepping away had another consequence: it meant he didn't have a chance to step up. Based on subsequent interactions, I now know he's far more generous than that. The panel was successful by any *outside* measurement: it was accepted to the conference, it was well attended, and in the Q&A session, there was a very positive and fruitful conversation with the audience.

Yet here I am, several years later, still regretting that interaction. I felt like it was a failure then, and I still do. Contributions weren't equal, feelings were hurt, and relationships were damaged. A successful final product, in other words, is not all that matters in a collaboration. The process is also important. Whenever my students groan when I mention group work, I think back to this and understand their apprehension.

I learned three things from the experience. First, it is crucial to state expectations up front. For example, I could have been clearer about the purpose of the panel, the deadlines and requirements for each participant, and, in my initial invitation, I could have delineated what each member would need to contribute in order to be included on the panel. Second, before committing to a project together, we all needed to agree that we were comfortable with accepting and giving constructive feedback and that our aim was to be able to improve together. Third (and this one's not easy to determine), given that I was the only woman in this collaboration (is my frustration coming through here?), it would have been useful to acknowledge the power imbalance and gender dynamics at the outset. That did not happen either.

Years later, I had a chance to do things the right way from the start. The next time I was the only woman in a group collaboration, I was able to note the earlier bad experience and was relieved when my collaborators responded quickly and positively. They made it clear that they intended equal contribution, and they were as good as their word.

I've been able to apply this lesson in many situations, including in the classroom. When students break into groups and there are designated "roles" for group work, I remind them of the gender and other biases associated with roles like "secretary" or "notetaker." This can be a part of warming up the room, getting everyone ready to bring their best, most collaborative, and most team-oriented selves to the group work. I encourage students to break the mold by finding an arbitrary way to assign roles. For example, whoever has a birthday closest to (or farthest from) that day becomes the notetaker that day. This is a nonevaluative method for assigning tasks and, not incidentally, an excellent way for students to learn a little about one another without getting too personal. The painful lesson of that earlier panel has turned out to be crucial to ensuring more equal participation in subsequent collaborations and has become an important feature of the New College Classroom.

"Job Descriptions" and Work Assignments

Without explicit job descriptions or roles for each member of a group, time can be wasted at the beginning of an assignment waiting for participants to volunteer to complete tasks. Or, worse, one student might try taking on way too much while another doesn't seem willing to take on any work at all. Clearly defined roles help to focus the interactions of team members, reduce the chances of one person taking over, and they work to make sure everyone feels included and that they belong. Rather than leave it to chance, there are ways that you as the instructor can help teams distribute work clearly and fairly up front.

One way to do this is to provide students clearly outlined work assignments or roles. For example, in a dissection lab for a biology class, the instructor might group students into pairs and assign each student a clear role. In the first half of the lab, Student A reads the instructions for the dissection out loud while Student B handles the specimen. In the second half of the lab, students switch roles with their partners. Student B fills out answers to questions on a worksheet, recording what the pair has accomplished in the lab, while Student A handles the specimen. Both students must work together to follow the instructions, complete the dissection, and record what they did together, and each one gets a turn doing the "hands-on" work as well as the secretarial work.

Another way to do this is to ask students to divide group work among themselves and draft their own "job descriptions" for their roles in the group. Offering students a list of potential roles to choose from works to help them get started (for instance, "task manager," "timekeeper," "resource manager," "skeptic," "optimist"). In the world of online collaborative coders (and hackers too), the term *firestarter* is used to indicate someone with a knack for getting everyone thinking in a new direction, and *finisher* for the person who reins it in at the end to ensure deadlines are met. The list might include an option such as "Students' Choice" to show there is some flexibility as long as all group members agree that the chosen role is essential to the group's success. It is important in any collaboration to leave room for creativity because we hope the outcome will be something that will surprise and amaze us beyond our expectations of one individual working alone.

In one class, I (Christina) used group work to make a long and intimidating text, in this case, Herman Melville's *Moby-Dick,* more approachable. The assignment was to create a BuzzFeed quiz related to the text (for instance, "Which character from *Moby-Dick* are you?") and provide a rationale for every step of the quiz. In summary, the project asked students to translate their comprehension of the novel's meaning and the significance of the novel's characters to their own audiences (that is, BuzzFeed readers). In order to complete the work, students had to gain a basic understanding of the characters and of the plot of the novel. I played the role of "Peleg," a character in the book who assigns sailors to different ships: I assigned students to their "ships" (groups of 5–6 people) and chose the "captains," or group leaders, for these "crews" of "mates." I gave a printed worksheet (calling it a "scroll") to each ship captain on the first day, asking captains and their shipmates to decide on a basic plan and concept for their BuzzFeed quiz. They had to create a name for their ship and equally divide the work among themselves, letting me know on the scroll who would be

The Four-Quadrant Writing Prompt

David Syring, Professor of Anthropology, University of Minnesota-Duluth

One way that David Syring gets his students to think about their skills is to have them complete a four-quadrant graph. Students draw a line down the center of a piece of paper, then an intersecting line across the center, creating four quadrants. In the upper left quadrant, they write down, "Things I like to do and do well." In the upper right, they list "Things I like to do but don't do particularly well." In the bottom left: "Things I don't like to do but can still do well." In the bottom right: "Things I don't like to do and I don't do well." The four-quadrant writing prompt provides students ways to talk about skills, attitudes, and how their team can get things done.

doing what part of the work on the journey ahead. Then the "sailors" made their marks on the scroll as a kind of promise or contract to do their part of the work. This roleplay was as effective as it was fun in a class of 30–35 students.

Writing more formal job descriptions, role-playing positions for real-world jobs, would work for a class of any size. To emphasize the importance and relevance of writing job descriptions, we recommend giving students credit (if possible) and feedback on their descriptions.

Feedback That Keeps Group Members Accountable

Once students are clear about their work assignments, the next step is to ensure that everyone is clear about their own role, assignment, and expectation. In the workplace, a supervisor or a project manager is typically responsible for ensuring that the workload is distributed equitably across the group and that everyone delivers. The problem with this model is that the feedback only goes down. The stakes can be high. Failing to deliver what is required by the group can even cost you your job.

In a transformed classroom, the feedback goes both ways. Peers should not be put in the role of "supervisor." It is unfair to ask that of students, and it permits the most ambitious students to simply take over the tasks of those falling behind rather than confront them. Without a routine in place for evaluating progress, peer assessment can seem bossy, unfair and officious, and it can often be unproductive or even toxic.

A simple and effective way to coordinate routine evaluation is to begin with a checklist of all the tasks that need to be done, with students invited to identify and add to the checklist as new tasks emerge. At the beginning of each meeting, all collaborators in a group should take a few moments to review the checklist together. The list might even have names of collaborators assigned to each task (students can assign or volunteer for these themselves), which turns this list of tasks into an accountability check, too.

When a complex, long-term assignment or a multi-day lab is broken down into its component parts, the workload becomes easier to see and to distribute evenly. When someone falls behind and there are outstanding tasks that need to get done in order for the group to move forward, planned accountability checks at the start of each meeting help everyone see what is impeding the workflow. If it turns out that one or two people simply are not contributing, the checklist review also helps the instructor see the problem and offers evidence to justify intervention and perhaps having an individual discussion with the students who are falling behind. The checklist allows this discussion to be concrete, with a clear path forward. The outcome should not be shame but success.

We've all experienced failures in group work (and, if you haven't, watch any group project on reality television—*Survivor* and *Project Runway* are filled with eye-rolling, hair pulling, and other signs of frustration and strife). Checklists and job descriptions help to catch negative behaviors early and identify exactly what work is and is not being done as well as who is contributing too much, who is contributing too little. Ultimately, if the missing work cannot be resolved among student

The Role of Community Guidelines for Regulating Peer-to-Peer Feedback in Small Groups

CLEAR Lab, Memorial University, St. John's, Newfoundland, Canada

Founded and directed by associate professor of geography Max Liboiron, CLEAR Lab is a collective of researchers specializing in a variety of fields from ocean sciences to social work who study plastic pollution and who run equitable lab meetings informed by Indigenous, particularly Métis, principles. Their meeting guidelines include: "One Diva, One Mic," which means one person speaks at a time; if you've been speaking a long time, then you have to "step up into a listening role." Another rule is "Own Your Shit," which means taking responsibility for mistakes—mistakes happen, but no matter how good one's intentions, it's important to be accountable for them. Then there's "Don't Yuck My Yum," which means that you shouldn't disparage someone else's joy, ideas, or experiences.*

Establishing some basic coworking rules like these both calms students who are uneasy and provides each group with a foundation for troubleshooting problems. Depending on the length of the collaboration, student teams might spend 5 minutes or even 30 minutes (for a longer project) developing coworking guidelines before they get to the actual work on their projects. While community guidelines for a whole class might be more general, establishing ones specific to the students in each team can smooth the road ahead. For example, if one student shares that they do better with praise and incentive than criticism, whereas another student is driven by constructive criticism, then a team might make a rule like "everyone is entitled to the kind of feedback that drives them to become their best selves." Developing these rules helps students get to know one another and can help them self-regulate throughout the period of group work. Whether it takes 5 or 30 minutes, the time is well spent because students will learn best practices for future collaborations.

* "How We Run Equitable Lab Meetings," CLEAR, March 31, 2017, https://civiclaboratory.nl/2017/03/31/how-to-run-a-feminist-science-lab-meeting/. On the influence CLEAR Lab has had on place-based research, see Max Liboiron, *Pollution Is Colonialism* (Durham, NC: Duke University Press, 2021).

peers, the next step is to inform the professor—but we can significantly limit this negative escalation if we build early interventions into the project itself.

In Chapter 10, we look in detail at how to structure methods of peer evaluation in collaborative settings, whether that setting is an entire class, a lab, or a group project. By carefully including regular, even weekly, progress assessment, no one group member can fall too far behind, and the instructor can see where there are problems and, most importantly, contribute to ensuring that everyone gets on track again *before* the end of the project. When feedback is integral to the process, students learn how to deliver and receive feedback but, as we will see, are removed from having to nag, grade, or snitch on one of their classmates.

Online Collaboration That Actually Works

In a survey of more than three thousand undergraduates taking courses online during the COVID-19 pandemic, Vikki Katz, associate professor at the School of Communication and Information at Rutgers University in New Brunswick, New Jersey, along with her team of collaborators, found students to be so unhappy doing large-scale group projects that Katz and her colleagues summarized simply: "Group projects: just don't do it."[9] They emphasized that collaborative projects are important and advocated assigning *short-term* group projects, managing them with care and making them low in stakes. While many of those suggestions are helpful, we want to push back on the notion that managing group dynamics online doesn't serve students. To be fair, it is complicated—almost too complicated. However, guiding students in effective collaboration is one of the best ways to mentor them, both in a global crisis and beyond.[10] As difficult as it is, ditching online group projects now, as the world increasingly depends on them, does not prepare our students for life beyond college.

We suggest, instead, that we need to show students, again, *why* collaboration is important and *how* to be good collaborators. First, in most workplace settings, collaboration is necessary so that we can succeed at tasks that no one person could begin to manage alone. While writing this book in 2020 during the COVID-19 shutdown, we were, like everyone else, facing the fraught and stressful conditions our students faced—and so was everyone else outside academe who was lucky enough to still have the kind of job that could be done remotely. As we wrote "together" using collaborative writing tools (mostly email and Google Docs) and conferring by Zoom, one of us (Cathy) in Manhattan and the other (Christina) in Brooklyn, we could each hear the other's partner in adjacent rooms—also on group video calls. One partner works in finance, the other in publishing. Both were on Zoom constantly, doing exactly the kind of work the students in Katz's study objected to: group projects, under harrowing conditions, with stressed-out colleagues, 24–7. Collaboration online is difficult yet important to workforce readiness. That's a message we need to send students early and often, at the beginning of a semester, at the beginning of every class.

Second, we can show students how to be good collaborators by drawing from team-based and support-based learning models. In their survey analysis, Katz and her team missed the critical component of team work: community. They suggested that it is difficult online to manage students who fall away, "ghost" the class for a period of time or fail to contribute, leaving their peers to shoulder the responsibilities for the group. Katz wrote, "It serves neither you nor students to spend the semester managing group work dynamics that increase students' anxiety instead of building community." During the pandemic, some instructors used student teams to build critical networks of support, and a few professors had been using team-based and support-based models for years. Lea W. Fridman, professor of English at Kingsborough Community College, uses static (permanent) student teams with rotating team leaders in a specific form of teamwork that is framed and shaped as support.[11] She also uses a language of possibility to instill a growth mindset in her students. In this design, teams are permanent in order to build relationships of safety and trust over a semester, and they are connected via chats and their own Zoom accounts so that members can easily clarify assignments and check in on one another. Team leaders keep their members on track with academic work but also are required to encourage bonding within the team and to reach out to any team member who "ghosts" a class or is floundering. When a student doesn't pull their weight on their team, Fridman gives extra credit to the team members who pull up their sleeves to reach out and try to help their fellow teammates to come out of their shell or to catch up on work they missed. When using other forms of team and group work, Fridman found that there are always some groups that never gel. With the language of support and possibility, however, breakdowns become opportunities for breakthroughs. Students gain a sense of comfort in taking risks. Shy students overcome their shyness knowing they are safe from embarrassment or shame. Teachers in art, accounting, and English at Kingsborough who use what Fridman calls "Team as Support" find that the community created within teams helps their students flourish academically but also emotionally and socially—even in the midst of a pandemic. They also gain a readiness for the world of employment in which their collaborative and teamwork skills will be key.

Distance learning can alienate students by removing the human interactions we require to engage in deep and meaningful learning. An online course is an opportunity to double down by making group projects even more important and more valued. Instructors at the College of Arts and Sciences and the Sawyer Business School at Suffolk University in Boston, Massachusetts, offer examples of digital service learning that connect students to others through meaningful interactions such as developing a social media strategy for a community action group, designing marketing materials for a local nonprofit, and gathering data for a community grant application.[12] Because so many group activities can be accomplished asynchronously, collaboration also offers students a chance to work together instead of sitting alone for hours. Like all participatory learning, the goal of equitable group work is to give students agency—empowering them in a situation where their personal development and success are the goals.

According to an extensive study of over 180 working groups at Google, two important factors that make group work successful are the meaning and impact of the work: that the work is personally important to team members and that they believe their work creates change.[13] Ensuring that students are engaged in projects that matter, on topics where they can contribute their expertise in a meaningful way, is especially important for online projects. We admire the work by Michael Yarbrough, associate professor of political science at the John Jay College of Criminal Justice. He was teaching the senior capstone course in the school's Law and Society program to some twenty-five students when COVID-19 changed everyone's plans. Yarbrough pivoted this course in individual research into a group project on the pandemic. Notably, he did not dictate the terms of their collaboration or the topics. Instead, he offered students the chance to work collaboratively on an online group project under the most dire and complex of circumstances. The students write, on the homepage of the class website:

> This virus has left our city and society with immense heartache and grief. . . . Just like that, our senior year was cut short. To adapt to this sudden change, we decided to change our research project. Now it would be a group project about the impact of COVID-19, while experiencing it in real-time. We focused our research on the experiences of CUNY students and our communities. Our work helped us come together as a community and discuss the things that were most important to us during this time.

The students worked in subgroups on topics such as "Anxiety and Coping," "Work and Money," "Education and News," "Family and Relationships," and "Health and Healthcare." Four students took on the role of "editorial team" for the project. All kept diaries and timelines and shared those in group chats and published summaries of that personal work. They conducted interviews with two non-class members focusing on their topic and then worked together to publish their more polished findings on the websites.[14]

Not every online group project can have the urgency and importance of this one led by Yarbrough and his students at John Jay. Yet every topic should be meaningful—and should rely on the central element of collaboration: that the whole will be greater than the sum of its parts, that the whole could not exist without contribution by all of its members. This is equally true for collaborative projects that are not online.

Collaborative Studying for a Final

Collaboration works not only for research or course projects but also for an accomplishment such as studying for a final exam together. Dr. Richard Light, who is the Carl H. Pforzheimer Jr. Professor of Teaching and Learning at the Harvard Graduate School of Education, insists that every president of Harvard has asked him the number one key to success as a Harvard student—or a student anywhere—and he always gives the same answer: study groups. Nothing else comes close. Based on ten years of in-depth, personal interviews with hundreds of students from dozens of campuses, Light, an eminent statistician who spearheaded the Harvard Assessment Seminars program has found that students who study together thrive.[15]

One particularly effective method is studying collaboratively for a final exam. There are ways that we can help make that happen, assuring students that studying together isn't "cheating" but is instead one of the best methods for learning. In fact, collaboratively devising questions and answering them offers a tremendous benefit to students: they learn not just content but also from the testing process itself in a *formative* experience.

The most effective way to do this is by scheduling a collaborative review day onto the syllabus and having individual students prepare topics or questions for that class. Or you can have students work in small groups and come up with four or five final exam questions

Models from Inspiring Professors and Programs

Walter D. Greason, Professor and Chair of the Department of History at Macalester College in Saint Paul, Minnesota

Created in collaboration with digital designer Megan Allas and Professor Greason's Media Design students in Spring 2018, "Sojourner's Trail" is a virtual simulation of African-American neighborhoods in nineteenth-century Charleston, South Carolina, and twentieth-century Chicago. Greason teaches courses in Diversity and Equity in Digital Classrooms, Economic History, and History of Media Design. In "Sojourner's Trail," he not only uses the principles of diversity but also shows, using the mechanics of game play, how escape depends on networks, collaboration, and the sharing of different skills and positions of power and influence. Envisioned as an improvement on the classic "Flight to Freedom" online game at Bowdoin University in Brunswick, Maine, "Sojourner's Trail" allows students to explore an infinite variety of spaces and places across the African diaspora. More importantly, the content variations allow the platform to gamify almost any lesson plan. Professor Greason notes: "After a decade of work with innovative educators from a wide range of institutions, I committed to a collaborative philosophy of education that grew out of the civil rights training sites like the Highlander Folk Center and the American Friends Service Committee. By 2010, my students reported that their experiences during my courses changed the trajectories of their lives, especially those who felt marginalized by earlier educational settings."*

David Schultz, Professor of Mathematics, Mesa Community College; and **Hidetoshi Fukagawa**, retired high school math teacher, Fukuoka, Japan, author of *Sacred Mathematics: Japanese Temple Geometry*

A math teacher at Mesa Community College for over twenty years, David Schultz is renowned for working collaboratively on his research and in his teaching, across disciplines and cultures. If you are a student in one of Schultz's Calculus I or Trigonometry classes, you are learning not only the basics of these fields but also learning problem solving, data visualization, and animation plus a dose of Japanese culture and history. You will also be exposed to entirely new ways of thinking about math. Schultz gives students impossibly complex geometric problems and shows them how these problems can be solved by advanced trigonometry or calculus using the entirely different methods of *wasan*, a mathematical theory developed in Japan during the centuries when it was isolated from the West.[†] There is a classical mathematical problem known as Soddy's hexlet involving the proportional sizes of six tangent circles within a larger circle. It was thought to have been solved by an English radiochemist named Frederick Soddy in 1937, but the problem had already been solved in Japan in 1822, on a Shinto Sangaku tablet.

Schultz challenges students to work in collaborative groups of up to three but requires each student in the group to hand in their own signed, typed analysis of their solution and the process by which they solved it. They use a mathematical typeset (MathType or similar) in order to show all the algebraic steps they came up with together and utilize graphing software like Desmos, Maple, or MATLAB to illustrate the solutions they derive. He also has them write up their conclusions in a grammatical sentence (that is, with no equations). He encourages them to "pepper their write-ups with anything that seems to enhance the project." He sees math—and cross-cultural appreciation—as key to everything else his students do in the world.

The course websites for Schultz's math classes are full of beautiful animations that unfold like Japanese origami, posing problems and illustrating solutions to complex problems he sets for his students.

Harry Stecopoulos, Associate Professor of English, University of Iowa

In his honors English class, Harry Stecopoulos challenged his nineteen undergraduates at the University of Iowa to rewrite F. Scott Fitzgerald's *The Great Gatsby,* whose 1925 copyright had just expired.[†] They reimagined the main character as a Black, female art forger in their version, which they called *Gilded in Ash.* The university wrote up a short press release about their collaborative assignment on the school website where it was spotted by two producers who contacted Prof Stecopoulos with a series of thoughtful questions. Within two days, the nineteen students were approached by Independent Pictures and Fugitive

(continued)

Films about a film option. One student in the class talked with his parents, both of whom were lawyers, and they worked to create a limited liability company that they named Old Sport, after an expression Jay Gatsby often uses in the novel. A vice president at the university put the students in touch with an alum from the Iowa Writers' Workshop, now an agent with Creative Artists Agency in Los Angeles, who helped them understand the process and advised them on the terms of their contract. Not all group work has such a happy, real-world outcome, of course. Suffice to say, these students learned about adaptation, collaborative writing, project management, legal responsibilities and liabilities, and what it means to work with big-time Hollywood producers.

Reacting to the Past (RTTP), Barnard College

Barnard College has pioneered a series of student-led active learning role-playing games, "Reacting to the Past," that in effect deconstruct the generic textbook by having students take on assigned character roles. Entire courses, or portions of them in shorter games, become collaborative—and even the games themselves are the product of faculty collaborations across institutions and disciplines. In any one of the games, students' roles depend on the actions of other classmates. They research their roles and literally enact them through communication and collaboration throughout the term. Some textbooks and games are about political science, such as "Threshold to Democracy: Athens in 403 B.C." or "The Needs of Others: Human Rights, International Organizations, and Intervention in Rwanda, 1994." Other courses, such as "Puzzling the Carbon Question, 1976" or "Food Fight: Challenging the FDA," are designed for both majors and non-majors in traditional science, technology, engineering, and math.

* Cathy N. Davidson, "Learning from Prof Walter Greason's Real-Time Video and Social Media Classroom Innovations," HASTAC, November 17, 2019, www.hastac.org/blogs/cathy-davidson/2019/11/17/learning-prof-walter-greasons-real-time-video-and-social-media.

† Fukagawa Hidetoshi and Tony Rothman, *Sacred Mathematics: Japanese Temple Geometry* (Princeton, NJ: Princeton University Press, 2008).

‡ Emily Nelson, "Iowa Students Sign Film Option for their Reimagined 'Gatsby,'" University of Iowa, https://stories.uiowa.edu/university-iowa-students-film-option-gatsby-retelling.

together. In the next part of the exercise, one half of the room asks one of their questions with students in the other half of the room answering, and then the process flips. This, of course, is another, active version of "metacognition" or reflection, an opportunity for students to think together about what has been important in the course.

In no way is collaborative preparation for a final exam "dumbing down" or "catering" to the least prepared students. Studies of collaborative test taking and test preparation tend to find exceptional improvement for "low performers" and continued high achievement for those who typically perform well. Going back to the 1950s educational research of Benjamin Bloom, we have ample evidence that socialization, interaction, and motivation are all enhanced when students study with one another for a final exam. According to Bloom, as we reach toward more complex goals and need to solve more intricate problems, we benefit more and more from socializing ideas with others.[16] In contrast, one wrong impression or idea can easily lead to failure when left unchecked in isolation. We achieve better outcomes when comparing notes, testing ideas, developing understanding through conversation, and sharing strategies and tactics for arriving at the best answers. Just one day devoted to collaborative study can boost student performance and students' confidence in their own answers as well as *how* they arrived at those solutions.

CHAPTER 9

Research That Inspires Creativity

During a public interview at an academic conference on popular music, the Canadian singer-songwriter Alanis Morissette confided to music critic Ann Powers that whenever she's hitting a blank wall or feels like she's grinding out another song without a real sense of purpose, she asks herself one question: "Who are you?"[1] That question is not one we usually associate with the academic research project, yet it is a great place to start, since it reminds us that, etymologically, "research" is, literally, a search, a question, an exploration. "Who are you?" is the very question—and it's not an easy one—many people go to college to answer. In the best circumstances, the research project gives students the opportunity to get closer to answering that question. It can be the culmination of a student's hard work, a chance to think independently and to take what they've learned and translate it into a project that is uniquely their own.

In this chapter, we extend the methods of the New College Classroom to the way students conduct their own research for course assignments. The research project is, intrinsically, active learning: students learn by defining a topic for themselves and finding the best way to research and present their findings. At the same time, there are many equitable principles that we, as instructors, can build into these assignments to ensure that they inspire curiosity and are not simply busywork, another assignment on a syllabus.

We insist that any research project has the best chance of success when we follow three guiding principles: (1) engage students with the project and the critical thinking process early on; (2) sustain students' curiosity and motivation to search and learn throughout the project; and (3) break the assignment up into smaller, more manageable milestones with multiple touchpoints or "check-ins" along the way. By breaking up the research process into a number of smaller components we teach students the best practices in project management and give them the support they need to produce something polished and of consequence. We say "polished" instead of "final" because we want students to engage in an inquisitive, creative, and critical learning process that will continue after the last day of class.[2]

By helping students accomplish research that matters, we offer them an unforgettable experience. In the best instances, the research project helps students move closer to shaping themselves as credible, responsible individuals in response to the never-ending, always evolving life question: "Who are you?"

In this chapter:

Research That Matters
Helping Students Choose (and Narrow) a Topic
Keeping Students Motivated
Students Will Get Stuck (We All Do): Scheduling Check-Ins
Sticking to Schedules
A Public Contribution to Knowledge

Research That Matters

Nothing about our systems of education nor our ideas of research exists in a vacuum. Whether students are doing a chemistry capstone experiment or a research paper in history, they will be more engaged and less likely to procrastinate if we make clear that the stakes are not simply "fulfilling a requirement" but an opportunity to find out "what *really* happened." The best research makes knowledge-seeking a pursuit. The researcher is a detective putting together clues and evidence to solve a mystery.

In a final project, even in the most conventional of educational settings, students are required to pursue a significant undertaking on their own. The method of "collaboration by difference" becomes "research by difference," where students are invited to negotiate among competing methods and approaches and a range of empirical evidence in order to conduct their own experiments, test their own hypotheses, make their own judgments, and arrive at their own conclusions.

The research project can offer us a singular opportunity to interpret and analyze with fresh eyes. Students can—and should—ask "why?" This fundamental question seems simple, but it's necessary to understand traditions of research that obscure certain topics and make others "fixed," and it helps students connect what they are doing in school to real-world issues relevant to their lives. The goal of participatory learning is to unfix ourselves and try something original and meaningful to students.

In *Decolonizing Methodologies,* Linda Tuhiwai Te Rina Smith, professor of Indigenous education at the University of Waikato in Hamilton, New Zealand, challenges readers to push further, ask deeper questions, whenever a method or project is defined as a "journey of exploration" or a "discovery." Whose journey? Whose discovery? Some ideas are not *new,* but they may be new to the particular researcher. Ethical, responsible research honors that individual's discovery as personally meaningful without appropriating someone else's ideas or traditions. Research that matters teaches students that difference.[3]

Smith uses the classic example of the British explorer James Cook, who returned to England with knowledge and goods from his exploration of the South Pacific. He left behind diseases that wiped out countless Indigenous people, all while using their knowledge to map the South Pacific for further exploitation. No student venturing into a research or capstone project is going to be able to correct hundreds of years of colonial practice. That's not the point. Grasping a colonial legacy helps students become more aware, responsible, and honorable as they conduct inquiries and choose journeys that matter. In any discipline, students can become familiar with the conventions and methods of research in their field and then use them to ask what questions are still unasked or to learn the basic tenets of a discipline to break its outdated assumptions, to critically analyze its methods and suggest a better way.

In *Floating Coast: An Environmental History of the Bering Strait,* Professor Bathsheba Demuth of the Institute for Environment and Society at Brown University asks, "What is missing?" before she begins her exploration. Writing from the position of the "foreigner," the term used by Indigenous people in the Arctic for those who are not from their three main Indigenous nations, she is keen not to replicate the appropriations of past foreign explorers. She begins with the year 1848, when the first commercial whalers from New England crossed through the Bering Strait "to kill bowheads for the energy in their blubber." She writes, "The process they began is the focus of this book: the reduction of ecological space, in all its complexity, to a source of commodities."[4] Think about all that is left out of a history of this region (or any research project) if we only regard it as a "source of commodities": all the aspects of nature, all of the nonhuman animals, all of the different and complex cultures of the Indigenous peoples who long inhabited this seemingly "uninhabitable" land.

Thousands of scholars and students around the world are contributing to an ongoing project at Michigan State University seeking to trace and record the history of every family separated in the African diaspora. "Enslaved: The People of the Historic Slave Trade" is a research hub designed to aggregate existing databases of economic transaction records and ship registries in Britain and West Africa; language dictionaries compiled throughout Latin America and the Caribbean; and diaries, personal letters, photographs, and quilting catalogs collected from individuals, communities, art museums, and historical societies in the United States.[5] One purpose is to break through the "Brick Wall of 1870," the first US Census to officially record and track the families of former slaves.[6] "Enslaved" is not only a research project that matters to the historical record, but it may well provide the basis for future claims for reparations for the descendants of former enslaved people throughout the New World.

A parallel approach to asking "What is missing?" can be found in cross-disciplinary multinational science projects. A 2017 breakthrough in the science of pathogenic fungus resulted from a novel methodological approach called "convergent bioscience." An international team of scientists, engineers, and students worked together to address the real-world problem of antibiotic-resistant *Candida albicans,* the most prevalent cause of fungal infections in humans. This fungus is responsible for sickening two million people annually and resulting in some eight hundred thousand deaths each year. By deliberately putting aside the traditional pharmacologic solution of searching for yet another antibiotic fix, teams led by Professors Jérôme Govin and Carlo Petosa from the Université Grenoble Alpes and Professor Charles McKenna from the Michelson Center for Convergent Bioscience at the University of Southern California had a major breakthrough involving the BDF1 gene-regulating protein that blocks the growth of *Candida albicans.* Student researchers, both undergraduate and graduate, were encouraged to think about treatments in a world where antibiotics were off the table. Successful discovery relied on pushing aside traditional approaches and working within new paradigms for combatting deadly fungal infections.[7]

These three projects offer students inspiring examples of research that carves out new pathways partly by acknowledging the legacies and the omissions of previous research. By encouraging our students to question both themselves ("Who am I?") and their disciplines ("What is missing?"), we help them overcome the feeling that there is nothing that hasn't already been covered or been done better by someone else.

Students can join existing projects already underway or invent their own, and they are capable of astounding inventiveness when given the freedom to solve some of the world's most puzzling problems. A design-based approach practiced in over four hundred Dutch primary schools affords students some flexibility by focusing on—and devising potential solutions to—new challenges as they arise, challenges that students themselves decide are worthy of taking on. In Amsterdam, two Montessori school boys built a battery-powered river-clean-up device. Once a class narrows down students' ideas—say, some are interested in solar power and others are interested in reducing air pollution—they might use math skills to determine if a plane can operate on solar energy.[8] The point is that the projects are not predetermined by instructors but generated by the students. The possibilities are endless: interviewing members of one's community to learn from one's elders to producing a documentary or a podcast; designing a solution for a drought; or imagining what might have happened if a famous historical figure, such as Mahatma Gandhi or Ruth Bader Ginsburg, had studied accounting or engineering instead of law.

The guiding principles in all of these examples are the same: students learn the methods of a discipline to meet the requirements of a course while making the journey meaningful to them and, if possible, producing something that contributes to the public good. Ample research shows that students demonstrate more positive learning outcomes when they grapple with real-world problems.[9] When basic statistics students in the Open Space Lab at Ca' Foscari University of Venice model the probability of Venice being underwater by 2050, they have not just the tools but the motivation for research across many disciplines that might help their beloved city stay above water—a metaphor and model for research that matters.

Experiential Research

Ronald N. Miller, former Biology teacher at Manchester High School West, Manchester, New Hampshire

Ronald Miller, while teaching at Manchester High School West, had his biology students select their own invertebrates that they would raise (read: keep alive). The lab was filled with tanks of scorpions, crawfish, leeches, and even a pair of lobsters. Students showed tremendous care for these creatures, and their interest and sense of personal responsibility spurred rigorous research to understand their invertebrates. They willingly took on extra work to keep these invertebrates happy, visiting the lab before and after school to check water temperatures and measure salinity. One pair of leeches had babies, much to everyone's excitement. The group of students with lobsters later released them, wading into New Hampshire's ocean shore, and shared pictures with their classmates. Their research was intense and thorough, and the lessons were unforgettable.

Miller also encouraged students to bring in samples of anything they would like to see under the microscope. Some brought in plants they found while exploring their backyards. A couple students brought in moldy Tupperware from lunches forgotten in their lockers. In the winter, Miller placed an open petri dish on the lip of a fish tank, and the class identified streptococci and other bacteria growing in the dish, which meant it had been in the air they were breathing. These exercises encouraged students to treat their local and familiar environments as new fields of inquiry and study.

Helping Students Choose (and Narrow) a Topic

The "research" in a research project begins with choosing a topic or question. Even with flexibility and choice, it is the instructor's job to be clear about the parameters and requirements of the research project and to be supportive during students' data collection. Giving students the freedom to work on "anything you want" doesn't serve every stu-

Online Adaptations

Laken Brooks, Doctoral Student and Adjunct in Digital Humanities, University of Florida

During the COVID-19 pandemic, digital humanities scholar Laken Brooks used community-based service learning in her online classes to make remote learning more relatable to students. Students could volunteer their research service to their local libraries, including by interviewing local authors or reading stories online to children at daycare centers. While doing good for others, they also wrote up their work as research, new experiences that made "valuable human connections during their physical isolation." Brooks's students used digital outreach projects as opportunities to express optimism in a future even amid college shutdowns, public health crises, and inequality. Her students ended up with a wide variety of relevant, practical research projects including a technical writing project that developed online instructions for 3D printing face shields and a literary project in which students suggested books by Black authors to be narrated by open-access audiobook libraries like LibriVox.*

Nerve V. Macaspac, Assistant Professor of Geography at the College of Staten Island

Nerve Macaspac challenged his students in Urban Geography to do field research on the environmental, political, and demographic impacts of the COVID-19 pandemic on Staten Island. They carried out their research by producing a "day in the life" autoethnographic film, which was then published as a short documentary called "My Pandemic." The film premiered on December 18, 2020, on YouTube. The road from an idea to a premiere required all of the different talents, skills, and experience various students brought to the course. The field research and co-production of the film served as the course's main assessment.†

* Laken Brooks, "Reimagining Service Learning in the Digital Age," *Inside Higher Ed,* September 23, 2020, www.insidehighered.com/advice/2020/09/23/how-adapt-service-learning-hybrid-or-online-classes-opinion.

† "My Pandemic," *Geospatial CSI,* December 18, 2020, www.youtube.com/watch?v=VFPzTMQ91uE.

dent well, despite our best intentions. After many years of teaching literature, we (Cathy and Christina) know that clearer, more specific writing prompts lead to better essays. Vagueness at the level of topic selection turns original research into a dispiriting guessing game, where the student's goal isn't to answer an urgent question but to try to figure out what the professor thinks is important.

With thoughtful framing, any of the world's complex problems is big enough for every student to develop an original research project, whether they work independently or with peers. In *Design Unbound: Designing for Emergence in a White Water World,* architect Ann M. Pendleton-Jullian and computer scientist and entrepreneur John Seely Brown raise the stakes, arguing that we need new ways of teaching if we are going to prepare students for what they call a "white water world" that is in constant rapid change and complexly connected. They write: "We all recognize that we are becoming much more global and urban, meaning there is greater diversity in closer proximity. And we are increasingly vying for resources that are more limited every day. . . . The result is we are engaged in a whole new set of issues and conflicts that are without a clear resolution or end state."[10] They argue that we need new ways of learning to imbue students with the confidence to tackle increasingly complex and fraught conditions.

Pendleton-Jullian, a former dean and professor of architecture at Ohio State University, offers one model for a new way of teaching and learning. She describes a game design studio she led in 2006 in Shanghai, China, in which she challenged students to tackle the complexity of improving the quality of life in a megablock housing site along the northern bank of the Suzhou River by addressing the problem of a vast informal recycling (garbage) facility that had become a "black-market marketplace that thrived when legal authorities were looking the other way." Rather than simply dive into the often-disastrous process of urban renewal and reform, she led students in a game theory approach to help them see connections between such things as the historic opium trade that formerly inhabited the site, the surrounding middle- and working-class housing developments, and contemporary street life. Before even beginning to tackle the problem of the site, Pendleton-Jullian had students spend a full, intensive week playing and analyzing strategic games all day, every day, including "chess, Go, Mahjong, Quoridor, Quarto, and the video game Starcraft." They studied games, mapping gameplay over time, creating information visualizations to chart flows, decisions, connections, and rules made and broken.

The exercise not only built a strong collaborative team that allowed each member to recognize and appreciate the other's different skills and strengths (collaboration by difference) but helped students to look anew at this megablock housing site along the Suzhou as a similarly complex system with interconnected rules, where one change would result in other changes and causal connections. The game play and analysis was foundational, fundamental research that kept students alert to complex interconnection. It challenged them to think not just about "fixing things" but also about ways to connect and dissent, adapt and question, and look for large solutions while addressing the local contingencies and contexts. The final result was a suite of "highly sensitive and pragmatic proposals for . . . development of the site, and even the surrounding neighborhood."[11]

Some advocates of "research-led teaching" in the social sciences across Australia and the UK suggest recycling pre-collected or archived data from the instructor's own research that has already passed an ethical review board's approval (a time-consuming process) and giving students a free hand to use the data to address new topics and issues or to offer additional perspectives.[12] Other instructors prefer to offer students a broad list of predetermined prompts to choose from to give students the opportunity to design the research question themselves, with feedback from the instructor. If the project is collaborative, you might allow students to form their own teams based on practical

The STAR Method

Borrowing a method from the business and finance world, I (Christina) use the STAR method to help students narrow their topics while also establishing stakes for their projects. STAR stands for "Situation, Task, Action, Result." In a research abstract, proposal, or even thesis paragraph for a paper, the STAR method can help budding writers see what they need to do to either accomplish the project they envision or dial it back.* I've used the method when applying for grants and fellowships. Here's an example adapted from one of my first successful grant applications:

> The work of my dissertation addresses ["Situation"]. Within the grant period, the project would benefit from ["Task"]. My audiences at conferences and my students would also greatly benefit from ["Action"]. When this project becomes my first book, it would contribute ["Results"].

Identifying a situation, the tasks involved, appropriate actions, and probable results has the additional benefit of clarifying the "So what?" question of a research proposal and, implicitly, addressing the equally persistent question: "Who are the stakeholders?" The STAR method makes overt what is at stake in all projects that students undertake in any course.

S is for Situation

The situation is whatever event or context will offer a clear idea and example of "the stakes" of a project. Where, *specifically,* is the need for this research and work? First, a researcher must establish that need. For example, a student might introduce a problem or a gap in knowledge that the project will work to address in its Task or Action list. Essentially, the situation is the "Chekhov's gun" of the proposal. Chekhov insisted one must never place a loaded rifle onstage unless it's going to go off. Everything has a purpose. The situation needs to be addressed by the end of the abstract or proposal.

T is for Task

Task is a fancy way of saying "goal." A researcher needs to outline the goals of the project, and note that here it is most helpful to keep students' lists to *attainable* goals in relation to a specific part of a situation they hope to address. This task list offers you, as an advisor on the project, an opportunity to point out what is and is not within the scope of the class, the budget (if applicable), and the timeframe for the project. The list also should build toward achievable action items: it may sound like a great idea to achieve world peace, but we can't do everything. When it comes to writing project abstracts, I ask students to set up parameters for the project that help them paint its *successful* future.

A is for Action

In addition to listing future things students *will* do, here writers also list action items that are already complete. For example, a completed task might be that students have contacted a librarian or selected and narrowed a topic. It's always good practice, in any project pitch, to show its successes. Action items are simple, clear, and detailed. Finally, if this is a team effort, researchers should outline individual roles and contributions.

R is for Result

My advice to students: be confident, be bold. This is the place to really "sell" a project, but it will only be successful if it seems reasonable. There is no room for overselling—it should feel real and optimistic, not implausible and over the top. If students successfully introduce a situation that needs addressing as well as detail task and action lists that are feasible within the timeline of the project, then it's time to show some pride in what they have accomplished and will accomplish.

There are many reasons not to skip this step. It may seem strange to ask undergraduates, particularly nonmajors in a general curriculum required course, to produce "results." We are not asking for groundbreaking science or a major philosophical intervention. What we are asking for is the *transformation of the student.* If students become more advanced critical and creative thinkers than they were before they signed up for the class, that's a win. That is within their power, and it ought to be included in the "results" the same way we include learning outcomes on our syllabi. It is a step toward the interventions they *will* make if and when they exercise their skills and talents in their future careers.

* Sarah Cook, Coaching for High Performance: How to Develop Exceptional Results Through Coaching (Cambridgeshire, UK: IT Governance Publishing, 2009).

alignments such as compatible calendars or on similar interests and aspirations.

Some preliminary peer-to-peer work to hash out ideas can afford students a much-needed sounding board as they develop various research plans. An interview at this stage serves the purpose of helping students brainstorm ideas that are personally meaningful and that give them something concrete to start with, think about, and respond to. We like to follow this interview activity with an assignment to write very short, ungraded, rough abstracts of one or even two or three proposed research topics for the next class.

The next part of the process is winnowing. Here, students pair up with a different student than the one with whom they completed the first exercise. In the entertainment or business worlds, this might be the "pitch," where the student proposes each of the two or three possible topics to another student, the "interlocutor," who asks questions—no more than 5 minutes per topic. Then the interlocutor writes a few sentences about which topic they prefer and why.

The next phase is usually the office hour. Students either come with both "pitched" ideas or only the preferred one and present their topics one on one. I (Cathy) know from experience that this works especially well online, with the mirage of intimacy and distance being useful (rather than an obstacle) to the one-on-one discussion. The goal is to support a student working toward defining, narrowing, and building a research proposal or prospectus.

Before a pitch meeting, I sometimes offer students the traditional journalistic template to flesh out their topic: "5Ws+H," or "Who, What, Where, Why, When, and How." These questions or identifiers help students define their argument and specify what aspects they are most interested in. It also serves to narrow the field of inquiry and identify particular areas that will be easier or harder to tackle responsibly. Ultimately, the whole pitch meeting forces students to confront the problem they wish to solve or the argument they want to make in the clearest terms possible.

Keeping Students Motivated

Based on what we know from neuroscience, students retain what they learn when they feel motivated.[13] Ideally, a research project is an opportunity for students to synthesize all the content and methods learned in the course and practice applying them. This requires a great deal of students: they must successfully retrieve information and methods learned in the course and know when and how to use their newly acquired knowledge. This task should be fairly straightforward for your students as long as your expectations for the project are clearly outlined, you space out content and techniques of your discipline, and students regularly recall and reflect on them as well as *how they were learned* throughout the semester (metacognition again).

It can be difficult to keep students motivated as they work through the nuts and bolts mechanics of an assignment. One simple way to do it is to acknowledge the accomplishment of every step taken (even some backward steps can lead to leaps forward). A list of requirements for a large project is a perfect place to explain how certain skills or content areas will be applied and refined at each stage. This concise written explanation is doubly powerful when supported by a verbal conversation in a class meeting, in a lab, or during office hours. Under each required step or deadline, have each student add one sentence explaining the purpose of that component for their project. Alternatively, you might design a callout box or another creative way to remind students that they already have the skills and knowledge base necessary to be successful. For example, one step of writing a research paper might look like this. We'll use Sociology 101 as our model here:

> Incorporate feedback on your draft.
>
> *Purpose:* Identify what needs development; seek out resources to build your skills (ask for help if you don't know where to begin); and apply new skills to strengthen your draft.
>
> *Sample student contribution:* In my project "How Italians in Chicago Became White," I will use standard bibliography on ethnicity and urban

> history, supplemented by interviews with elderly Italians (i.e., my grandparents and their friends). I've never done ethnographic interviews before and would like to talk to graduate students in our department before I begin these interviews.

Essentially, this is an opportunity to tie specific learning goals for the course to each component of the project. This exercise is most effective when students have multiple opportunities to make these connections throughout the semester. It reminds students of what, why, and how they are learning from the research and helps to keep them on track.

There are a variety of ways to do this but the key element is retrieval: having students make the connection between something already known (such as learning outcomes for the course) and something new (their own research). In their book *Powerful Teaching: Unleash the Science of Learning,* cognitive scientist Pooja K. Agarwal and middle school teacher Patrice M. Bain call this retrieval method the "power tool" of teaching. In their decades of experience teaching in higher education and K–12, Agarwal and Bain have witnessed the benefits of retrieval for retention and information comprehension for diverse learners, from the most academically prepared to those who come to college without adequate prior training.[14]

Students Will Get Stuck (We *All* Do): Scheduling Check-Ins

Scheduling check-ins affords *every* student—not just those brave enough to ask for help—opportunities for care, mutual support from peers facing similar challenges, and mentoring from instructors. The research project is a time when care is especially important. It is all too easy for students to become overwhelmed, lost, or paralyzed by the thought of an original research project. This all-important final capstone project (whether research paper, thesis, or dissertation) often comes at a monumental time of personal transition, right as students are thinking ahead to moving from the ordered world of college, graduate school, or professional school to the open-ended and anxiety-producing challenges of finding a first (or next) job or taking a step toward promotion in their chosen career.

The research project is about encouraging student independence while also giving students mentorship and support. Checking in, making sure there are landmarks and milestones along the way, and offering formative feedback will help the student feel confident in finishing.

Organizing students into teams or groups and coordinating weekly peer-to-peer check-ins can become a lifeline during long-form projects. Peer support might be something some students know to seek out on their own, but not everyone has that essential skill or that level of confidence. To guide students to turn to one another to troubleshoot challenges along the way, you might group them into support teams and assign rotating team or group leaders who are responsible for reaching out or following up with a peer who seems stuck or behind on their research. This extra work could be rewarded with extra credit. Another way to foster networks of support is to hold group office hours in which you meet with small groups of students and troubleshoot problems together. I (Christina) have done this in my online composition course, and at the end of group office hours, I recommend that students exchange contact information or create a WhatsApp group—if they feel comfortable doing so—so that they can continue to support one another outside of our class.

I (Cathy) once did a variation of this in a doctoral seminar called "This Is Your Brain on the Internet" (neuroscience and computer science) by having each student claim an area of expertise for a "research hackathon." Every student visited every other student with a specific question or area they wanted feedback or help on. Given that several students were computer programmers, I was not surprised to learn that, although my evening class officially ended at 9 P.M., some students worked together literally all night.

For instructors, mentoring students throughout long-term projects means guiding them to focus on the *process* and not just the final *product* and also emphasizing how a research project isn't "busywork" but a way of gaining tools that will help throughout one's career. Navigating and working through stressful projects and challenges to specifications and on a deadline are invaluable higher-order skills. Our mentorship at this juncture can have lasting impact. Breaking down milestones at the start helps make a looming project feel more manageable and models for students how to set reasonable expectations about the workload ahead—for this research project and also for the first time they have a major project due at a new job.

Check-ins might include a meeting during office hours; a poll to see how students are feeling about their projects; a homework assignment demonstrating progress (for instance, students submit a component of the project); and progress reports in which students update the class, a small breakout group (for more intimate peer-to-peer support), or the instructor on what tasks have been completed and identify next steps. This last idea—requiring progress reports or updates—is from *The Online Teaching Survival Guide: Simple and Practical Pedagogical Tips* by online distance learning experts Judith V. Boettcher and Rita-Marie Conrad. They recommend using progress reports as opportunities to celebrate success, teaching students that sharing success builds community: "As they share their completed steps and identify their next steps, other students often praise, encourage, and suggest, building a stronger network of learners."[15] We like this activity because it keeps students motivated while offering practical, focused support.

Boettcher also shares a useful tip for students and colleagues alike. Along the same lines as asking students to list their next steps, Boettcher leaves herself a note about the next task that needs to be done when she stops work on a project—*any* project, even quilting—and then when she returns to it after some time away, her next step is right there waiting for her. This is effective, even when we're not actively working on a project, because it gives us some ideas to think through while we're away.

We hasten to add that we practice what we preach. In writing this book together, largely online and often editing asynchronously, we constantly left notes for ourselves about our progress and also for one another, including marking difficult areas that we wanted to return to later, after we had a better handle on the research, or that needed careful rethinking in the final round of edits.

Sticking to Schedules

All instructors wear multiple hats, especially adjuncts who sometimes teach at more than one institution, with different term schedules and deadlines. It's a true talent to keep all the balls in the air because when one falls, the whole stunt is over. As Professor Emerita Raewyn Connell of the University of Sydney puts it in *The Good University,* "Like research, a great deal of teaching is collective labour. The public image may be a solo lecture by a star performer. The everyday reality is a team of technicians, administrative staff, tutors and lecturers moving in a ballet in which that lecture is only a passing moment."[16] Given our experiences managing our multiple roles as teachers, researchers, and university citizens, we can be excellent models for our students when we show them the tools we use to stay organized (and sane).

A Gantt chart, named after the mechanical engineer Henry Gantt, is a bar chart that maps a project's schedule across time, essentially illustrating time to make it easy to comprehend the schedule at a glance. The tasks that need to be completed are listed on the vertical axis on the left (and can be broken down into micro-tasks), and the estimated time it will take to complete those tasks is broken up into intervals along the horizontal axis. Then the project manager fills in the amount of time they have allotted for each task to be completed, creating a bar chart for a project schedule. This works especially well when certain timelines for tasks overlap (for instance, running tests or scraping data in the background while reviewing the code for the next set of tests).

Lest this sound too much from the realm of engineering, I (Christina) found Gantt charts extremely helpful in mapping out my dissertation and showing my dissertation committee my "progress to degree." Gantt charts are effective tools to map out *any* project with multiple moving parts so that all members of a team (or review committee) can see a coherent timeline, locate where they are in that timeline, and determine what needs to be done next. Most importantly, building a Gantt chart helps us foresee potential delays (holidays, other due dates, vacation time, etc.) and find a way to work around those delays.

Gantt charts not only help us anticipate some bottlenecks in advance but also offer a look backwards at how past projects played out. When Gantt charts become a frequent practice, they help us see how much time we have spent on a task in the past and predict how long it will take to complete a similar task in the future. This can be extremely helpful when plotting out a timeline for a grant proposal, for example. However, we know all too well how a timeline can go down the drain in an instant when something unpredictable happens. When *doesn't* something come up? Always add at least a little cushion to each phase of a project. That is what we did when we planned this book. Cushion time may seem "lazy" or a waste but, having now witnessed a global pandemic, we can personally attest that some cushion is critical to the success of a project. Even our editor expressed surprise when we managed to deliver our manuscript on time.

A Public Contribution to Knowledge

There are few sadder sights in academe than an ancient box of research papers moldering outside an instructor's door, all carefully annotated with professorial feedback that will never be read by students (or anyone else). In some ways, that mournful spectacle is the ultimate expression of pedagogical failure: a student spends weeks or even months conducting research and distills it into a report or paper read by one person whose job is to grade it. We can't presume to know why students don't read or pick up comments on their papers, but we suspect that, the more a research project is seen as a required assignment designed to be read by the professor so they can give students a final grade, the less likely students are to see it as having anything real to contribute to their life and future. In this case, the student can feel "done" the moment they've turned it in. The feedback is irrelevant to completing the assignment.

We believe the purpose of higher education goes beyond students earning grades that add up to a diploma. Their hard work on research that matters deserves a better audience, as does our constructive feedback. We strongly advocate for research that has an audience beyond the instructor, research that makes a contribution to the public in some way.

The extensive research conducted by Professor Emerita Andrea A. Lunsford of Stanford University and her collaborators reveals that students write more clearly, persuasively, and with fewer errors (grammatical or syntactical) when they write for a larger audience, including (counterintuitively, perhaps) on social media. She has studied samples of student writing from all over the United States and finds that quality and motivation both increase when students see their writing as having a purpose beyond one instructor grading them in a course.[17] Student engagement increases when they write for publication and real-world conventions and rules must be adhered to and deadlines must be met. Students might contribute to a public class blog or a professional peer-reviewed journal. They could deliver a paper at a student or professional conference, make a presentation at a local club or community group, or create a poster for a university symposium.[18]

The possibilities for presenting research to a public audience works in every discipline. Computer science students can form teams to enter a regional competition in the International Collegiate Programming Contest (ICPC), which presents teams with real-life problems that they must solve together within five or six hours under the scrutiny of a panel of judges. To start, a computer science instructor could present a class with one of the ICPC's problems from years past, choosing from over forty world competitions, such as calculating the best location from which to take a picture of Saint Basil's Cathedral in Moscow in 2020's "Domes" problem, or establishing interstellar communications between bases in 2012's "Asteroid Rangers" problem.[19] In a photography studio class, students can submit their work to photo contests such as the ongoing *New York Times* "Show Us Your Generation" feature.[20] While preparing to submit their own final portfolios, students can evaluate the winning photos from previous years. Or the authentic audience could be more personal: if a senior student wants to apply for graduate school, they might present their research project following whatever format the graduate school application process requires, assuming the audience of an admissions committee.

We can model innovation by using multimodal public tools as well. K–12 and higher ed teachers from all over the world use the technology provided by the Finnish education and media company ThingLink to create an unlimited number of interactive lesson plans for free. Instructional technology coach Ornella Cappuccini created a virtual house tour at the Istituto Comprensivo Rovereto Est in Italy to teach her students German. Professor Barbara Antoniel at the Andrea Scotton Technical Institute in Bassano designed a virtual tour based on the novel *Siddhartha* by Hermann Hesse to immerse her literature students in a flipped classroom experience. Proving that online learning materials do not need to be dull, difficult, or expensive, these educators break the mold when it comes to presenting their lessons online, providing a perfect model for students to do the same. Students can design StoryMaps using Esri's ArcGIS or create other interactive presentations using Neatline. Ideally, they will have an example to follow from their professor's multimodal presentations.[21]

Despite the extensive research on the benefits of having students address real people who are interested in the topic—not instructors reading for a grade—it's important to include some cautions. Some institutions interpret Family Educational Rights and Privacy Act

(FERPA) rules to mean that faculty are not allowed to require their students to publish work publicly. Before building a course website or CMS page where your students will post their work, it is essential to know if publication is allowable and, if allowable, if it can be required or only suggested. We recommend making publication voluntary or for extra credit, even at institutions without such restrictions. For students who do publish their work, we recommend that faculty help them write out a citation that students can list on their résumés.

Erin Rose Glass, senior developer educator at Digital Ocean, a commercial cloud services provider, designs class activities that give students the tools to protect themselves online. In one exercise, Glass assigns students a close reading activity in which they locate the "Terms of Service" that they agreed to when they downloaded an app or tool for a course. After completing their close reading, students collaborate to develop a public resource or analysis of the "Terms of Service" and post their assessment using a freely available tool such as MLA Humanities Commons, Neatline, HASTAC.org, or Hypothes.is.[22]

In order to help students develop a sense of what counts as worthwhile research, we ask them to search for research published by students at other colleges and universities. Seeing what peers in their field have done helps them gain a sense of how to frame a topic, how to limit it, and how to present it. For example, the search term "undergraduate research topics" at Virginia Commonwealth University leads to a page rich with advice, lists of student topics, and even four student posters from a university-wide annual research symposium in 2020: "RNA Purification Through Fluorous Activity," "Significance of Nucleus Accumbens Core Astrocytes in Alcohol-Seeking Behavior," "Neorealism, Violence, and the Spaghetti Western," and "Head of Bed Elevation and Prevention of Ventilator Associated Pneumonia." It's hard to imagine a wider range of topics or a more exciting and relevant way for students to showcase their research than in a university-wide symposium.[23] If your institution doesn't currently offer one, suggest it to your dean of

Four Ways to Model How to Do Serious Research

Susan Smith-Peter, Professor of History, and **Joseph Frusci**, Adjunct Assistant Professor of History, College of Staten Island

Shortly after the COVID-19 pandemic sent New York City into quarantine in 2020, Professors Susan Smith-Peter and Joseph Frusci created a Facebook community page so that the Staten Island community could share their stories, digital photos, and videos to show how the pandemic was impacting their lives. Frusci had students conduct oral histories, while Smith-Peter's archival studies class cataloged the digital collections of the Facebook page. The oral histories and the material collected through the Facebook page were integrated into coursework, allowing students to become the historians of their communities. The Museum of the City of New York chose seven items from the Facebook page out of more than twenty thousand submissions for their exhibit *New York Responds: The First Six Months,* which dealt with COVID-19 in New York City. These seven items made up most of the representation from Staten Island in the exhibit. The exhibit demonstrated how meaningful students' hard work was outside the classroom, showcasing the value of students' public contributions to the whole city.

Denise Cruz, Professor of English and Asian American Literature and Culture, Columbia University

In Fall 2020, Professor Denise Cruz was faced with teaching a lecture class of over one hundred students remotely when New York City was in the throes of the COVID-19 pandemic. With over 20 percent of the class made up of international students prohibited from returning to the United States, Cruz (who had never taught online before) decided to use her own progress learning a new skill to exemplify for her students the process of researching, learning, and doing at the same time—an essential life skill. Cruz worked with her teaching assistants and Columbia's Teaching and Learning Center to develop an engaging, participatory online version of her popular Introduction to Asian American Literature and Culture course. She began by sending the students a video designed to inspire them and whet their appetites: "This will be a fall like no other. We're ready. We can't wait to meet you."*

Importantly, she told her students why she was doing certain kinds of restructuring, such as redesigning the course with short modules that students would unlock sequentially throughout the term. She used digital whiteboards and synchronous chat functions to engage students, continually inviting them to position their contribution and that of their communities, literally in cities across Asia, as parallel to themes in the Asian and Asian American writers they had read. She underscored the importance of imagination, creativity, reflection, and community to resilience.

She introduced their final research project on "PJ day," during which she, like the students, Zoomed into class wearing flannel pajamas. Having told them she was using her "stay at home" time to learn to play the guitar, she also played a song for them, Mitski's ballad of youthful anxiety, "Class of 2013." She used her own performance as an improving amateur to challenge them to be bold and to take risks. Instead of a conventional term paper, she invited them to use the technology affordances she'd absorbed and introduced throughout the term to think of creative, multimedia ways of presenting their own research. Nearly 70 percent took up the challenge. For example, a student in Singapore created a lyrical stop-motion animation of her own calligraphy, translating the Asian American literature they had been reading in class into a new form of multilingual, artistic, multimedia art, accompanied by a professional-level taxonomical "storyboard" with a spreadsheet of plots, characters, and actions charting these multimedia translations. "Scientists have long traditions and methods for rewarding experimentation and risk," Cruz notes. "In the humanities, we focus more on the final product. We need to find ways to remind students of the joy of discovery and process."

Arini, Dean of Education and Social Work, Thompson Rivers University, Canada, and **Sereana Naepi**, Associate Director of All My Relations: An Indigenous Wellness Research Network, Thompson Rivers University, Canada, and Lecturer at Auckland University of Technology, Aotearoa, New Zealand

In their essay "Knowledge Makers: Indigenous Undergraduate Researchers and Research," Naepi and Airini discuss the mission and the remarkable success of the award-winning Indigenous undergraduate research program at the University of British Columbia, Canada.[†] The

(continued)

goal of the Knowledge Makers program is to support cross-disciplinary Indigenous researchers by drawing from the knowledge of Indigenous ancestors, methodologies, and legacies. Seeing higher education's "historical and continuing research practices as a core threat to indigenization," the Knowledge Makers program reframes research as a legacy of and contribution to multiple Indigenous worldviews. Students design research that draws from many fields, qualitative and quantitative, critical and creative, that merge disciplines kept separate in Western Enlightenment divisions of the academy. One project addresses environmental law and mining operations, another mixed-race legal and political identity issues as they have an impact on governance and leadership models in health services and social welfare programs. Still another reimagines photography and indigeneity. Graduate and professorial researchers work side by side with vocational students learning trades including horticulture, culinary arts, diesel engine repair, and nursing, bringing experiences and insights across these networks.

Within the first three years of its creation, the Knowledge Makers program included forty-two participants and the publication of research papers by each of the students. The program also resulted in numerous graduate scholarships, advanced degrees, and international scholarships and internships. Core principles include honoring one's ancestors, expanding the research canon, undertaking research as a form of service to the community, and conducting research as a commitment to one's legacy. From one-on-one meetings with advisors to e-portfolios, from intensive research workshops to conversations with Elders, the program is designed to encourage students to reflect on "values they admire" as exemplified by "someone who inspires them." Collaboratively, workshop members discuss one another's proposals and research topics and offer feedback toward eventual publication across a diverse array of topics. In "The Importance of Research and the Value of Knowledge Makers," student Marcus Wally Scherer, whose ancestors come from both the Ojibway and the Secwepemc Nation, describes a two-day Knowledge Makers workshop: "I learned how to use my personal and community values to guide my curiosity and questions, physically formulate my goals based on my current skills and achievements . . . and formulate achievable goals based on the STAR acronym. I now look at research from a new perspective—one that is closer to who I am, and not based solely on what a specific institution's ideals and expectations are."[†]

Myron Campbell and **Junjie Zhu**, Professors of High Energy Particle Physics, University of Michigan, Directors, Summer Undergraduate Research Experience

Every year, dozens of undergraduate science students from around the world come to Switzerland to hear lectures by the renowned high-energy particle physicists and to conduct their own research at this famous science research center that operates the world's largest particle physics laboratory. CERN has a network of six accelerators, a decelerator, and the enormous Large Hadron Collider, the largest high-energy particle collider—and the largest single machine—in the world. Besides producing numerous Nobel Prize winners, CERN is the official birthplace of the World Wide Web, begun as the ENQUIRE project initiated by Tim Berners-Lee in 1989. Since 1998, the University of Michigan's Summer Undergraduate Research Experience has selected approximately fifteen students to join students from across Europe as well as from two national programs in Japan and Canada for nine weeks at CERN. Myron Campbell and Junjie Zhu, both professors of high energy particle physics at the University of Michigan, currently direct this program mainly for physics, math, and engineering students. Student research projects run the gamut of topics: biomedical imaging, volcanic island seismology, neural engineering, robotics, and climate change. Professor Thierry Gys, who specializes in hybrid photon detectors, teaches one of the introductory lectures and stresses the importance of risk and creativity to true research. The epigraph on his website is a quote from the great Spanish philosopher and writer Miguel de Unamuno (1864–1936): "True Science teaches, above all, to doubt, and to be ignorant."

* Cathy N. Davidson and Dianne Harris, "Making Remote Learning Relevant," *Inside Higher Ed,* August 5, 2020, www.insidehighered.com/views/2020/08/05/colleges-should-throw-out-conventional-pedagogical-and-curricular-playbook-fall.

† Airini and Sereana Naepi, "Knowledge Makers: Indigenous Undergraduate Researchers and Research," *Scholarship and Practice of Undergraduate Research* 2, no. 3 (Spring 2013): 53.

‡ Marcus Wally Scherer, "The Importance of Research and the Value of Knowledge Makers," *Knowledge Makers* 1 (2016): 11, www.tru.ca/__shared/assets/journal-201645318.pdf.

students or teaching and learning center. Or offer students extra credit for planning and mounting such a symposium. More than once I (Cathy) have offered students the chance to put on a public panel showcasing their work as an alternative to a final exam. After the event, I helped them describe their complex effort—including project management, teamwork, communications, and the research itself—as essential skills on their résumés.

All of the methods for guiding research projects suggested in this chapter are based on the idea that intellectual curiosity is a quality to be nourished and respected. Students matter, and their research matters. We also know that when students present their original research to their peers, they learn even more. Learning-by-teaching is a well-researched subject and has long been used in medical training as an exceptionally effective and efficient method for learning.[24]

If students know their hard work will make a difference in the world and will be read by someone and taken seriously, it inspires them, even at the end of a course, a semester, or a frazzled senior year of college or the final year in a graduate or professional program.

CHAPTER 10

Feedback That Really Works

Transformative feedback is based on a central tenet: revision is a continual process, and its purpose is to end up with the best result possible. Learning how to give good feedback, how to accept feedback, and how to use it to improve our work are all crucial life skills. In the classroom, good feedback should be supportive. Even when critical, the ultimate goal of feedback should be helping students to see their own work more clearly and to help them improve it. Sadly, many of the foundational premises of most of higher education contribute to feedback that can be harsh, negative, and far more about saying what's wrong than offering guidance on the way to improvement. Or it's feedback by the numbers, which does not serve the purpose of fostering growth: ranking, rating, selecting, certifying, credentialing, and grading. These are almost antithetical to the goals of helping each and every student become their best selves. In transformative learning, the instructor's role is to support students in their journey, not to judge or shame them when they fall behind.

Many years ago, when I (Cathy) was fresh out of graduate school and taking various adjunct and other part-time positions around the

Chicago area, I worked for a year at the Fermi National Accelerator Laboratory planning arts and humanities events for the Russian and American higher energy physicists who felt that humanists would have a calming influence on their stressful work lives. Since the scientists found the Fermilab's modern open floor plan too public for something as personal as a book discussion, our first task was to set up a committee of arts and humanities professors to work with the Fermilab's architect to design a more congenial and private meeting space. When he showed our humanities team his drawings and his architectural maquette, we attacked. We laid on critique after critique of what he had designed for our new room.

He was shocked. Little did he know of the sharp elbows of critical theorists. We were there, as far as the scientists thought, to "humanize," but here we were, serving up criticism without offering any constructive alternatives to build upon. His solution was to hand us each a blank sheet of drawing paper and ask us to take two or three minutes to sketch our own ideas for an ideal meeting space. Once we could see all the alternatives (however crudely drawn), we were able to focus on what was positive, not all the nitpicking negatives, and build—together—on those.

Ever since then, I've adopted what I call "the architect's method" whenever I am responding to writing by colleagues or students. Instead of writing, "This is confusing," and stopping there, I will write: "I'm not sure I'm reading your intentions correctly here. Let me try to paraphrase what I think I'm reading." And then I jot out a very quick, sketchy rewrite—not for the writer to copy but to offer an alternative vision to build off of.

Victoria Pitts-Taylor, professor of neuroscience and gender studies at Wesleyan University, starts her Introduction to Women's and Gender Studies class with one basic challenge: "It's easy to be critical and far more difficult to be generous. Let's be generous this semester and see what we can find of value in these texts, some of which are very old."[1]

This is what Eve Kosofsky Sedgwick, one of the founders of Queer Theory, called "reparative criticism."[2]

We take a similar approach to feedback. Research shows that students who learn how to give generous and thoughtful peer review also come to see themselves as independent thinkers, more responsible for their own learning.[3] We look at different models of formative, generous feedback designed to help students succeed, including peer review and self-evaluation. We also discuss offering students the opportunity to give constructive feedback to their instructors for improving their courses or assignments. Care must also be taken to ensure when students offer feedback that they do not replicate the forms of dominance we sometimes see in traditional higher education—there's no room for acting high and mighty when we share the goal of mutual improvement.

As Felicia Rose Chavez shows in *The Anti-Racist Writing Workshop,* too often feedback—such as in the art, design, or architecture "crit"—becomes a thinly disguised public hazing that can contribute to the replication of systemic bias (race, gender, class, neuronormative, or other forms of bias). Transformative peer-to-peer feedback makes three major research-based interventions: it gives the students being reviewed opportunities to ask for the feedback they want and need, emphasizes growth and self-directed learning, and fosters a generous, mutual sharing of strengths and strategies.[4]

In this chapter:

Giving Feedback That Counts
How Students Can Give Themselves the Feedback They Need
Student-Centered Coaching
"My Students Don't Read My Feedback"
Roleplay: Modeling Constructive Feedback
Peer Evaluation: 360 Feedback
Asking Students for Feedback

Giving Feedback That Counts

"Feedback has no effect in a vacuum," conclude John Hattie and Helen Timperley, professors of education at the University of Auckland in New Zealand, in their exhaustive study "The Power of Feedback." They show that feedback is tremendously useful for learning outcomes only when its purpose is to help one grow and improve ("formative feedback," in the terminology of learning science), not to sum up the worth of a finished product ("summative feedback"). If we want our feedback to help students become proficient, we need to communicate with students as soon as possible after they hand in the work; provide them with constructive suggestions for how they might improve; and, most importantly, model how to develop one's own criteria for self-evaluation. By contrast, comments appended to a grade on an assignment where there is no opportunity or guidance for improvement have no impact on students' learning. We might as well not waste our time. The impact is "effectively nil."[5]

Hattie and Timperley have been studying the effects of formative versus summative feedback since the 1990s. Their conclusions are derived from a synthesis of "over 500 meta-analyses, involving 450,000 effect sizes from 180,000 studies, representing approximately 20 to 30 million students, on various influences on student achievement."[6] Evaluating these studies against numerous measures of student success, Hattie and Timperley have devised a simple, effective template for formative feedback, distilled into three questions posed by the instructor and, ideally, by students themselves:

- "Where am I going?" (What are the goals?)
- "How am I going?" (What progress is being made toward the goal?)
- "Where to next?" (What activities need to be undertaken to make better progress?)[7]

These questions (sometimes known as "discovery" or "inquiry" learning) help students to evaluate how far they've come on their chosen journey and how far they still have to go.[8]

Hattie and Timperley argue that formative evaluation works best coupled with "instruction": feedback that offers students specific ways to improve, to find better ways to learn, and to demonstrate what they have learned. We would add a fourth element, which is to model how to overcome difficulties, setbacks, and struggles so that all students, including those who struggle most, can believe in their own ability to better themselves. Creating an environment where student development is prioritized over "getting the grade" means that, in addition to offering progress-oriented feedback, instructors have to rethink their role as the final arbiters of success. We need to create "360 degrees" of feedback where student self-evaluation, peer-to-peer evaluation, and teacher evaluations are utilized all together and become the norm.

In the words of Harvard University law professors Sheila Heen and Douglas Stone, truly successful, formative feedback requires "coaching the coach."[9] Instructors, as well as students, must learn how to give constructive feedback—and how to listen to it. We must invite students to become self-reflective, collaborative partners *with us* in order to determine what works best for their learning. The best feedback is not about telling students what they're doing wrong but about helping them figure out the best ways to get things right. As David Gooblar notes in *The Missing Course,* "much of learning is failing."[10] Feedback recognizes that setbacks and missteps are part of a process on the way to learning more and better.

Too often, most of us instructors have imbibed the assumption that our primary job is to inform students when they've made a mistake. That assumption itself is a mistake. It turns out most of us—and most students—know when we're doing a poor job. What we need is help figuring out how to repair, straighten up, resume work, and do a better job. In a global survey of four thousand people conducted by *Harvard*

Business Review, 74 percent of respondents indicated that they already knew about a problem in their work before it was pointed out to them. They were not surprised when they received "negative or redirecting feedback," and most would have fixed it themselves had they known how.[11] According to this study, three out of four people said knowing something was wrong wasn't the issue. What they needed was positive guidance to help them figure out a way to fix the problem.

In a classroom, that pattern is tragic. College should be the place where you come to learn, not where you are reflexively told of your mistakes. Carol Dweck's idea of the "fixed" and "growth" mindsets illuminates the internalized modes by which students judge themselves to be capable or incapable of progress. Feedback that doesn't encourage students to see themselves as able to advance can inadvertently fuel negative feelings and destroy the motivation to learn. In a study of a hundred students, Dweck and her research team gave all the students the same ten questions from a basic IQ test. After they graded the results, they presented students with their scores and told half of them: "Wow, you got [X many] right. That's a really good score. You must be *smart* at this." They told the other half of students: "Wow, you got [X many] right. That's a really good score. You must have *worked really hard.*" Significantly, although both sets of students were praised enthusiastically, the ones who were told they were "smart" were more likely to reject a chance to take on a challenging new task. They did not want to jeopardize their fixed position as "smart." Stunningly, over 90 percent of the students praised for having "worked really hard" were willing to take on the more difficult task.[12]

All forms of evaluation should help students see how they can use good, constructive feedback—in class or anywhere else—to succeed. (And how to recognize bad or unhelpful feedback when it happens and how to find ways to ask for the real feedback that they need.) Every time we are about to make a comment, whether oral or verbal, on a student's work, we might ask ourselves: does what I am saying, in the position of instructor, help my students toward their goals? The next step should be observing any progress and commending it, not simply omitting it as a given. Constructive feedback is difficult, and it is equally difficult to process and evaluate feedback and figure out how to incorporate it into your work.

Whether you teach in STEM fields and are working to support more women majors, or if you're seeking more ways to support nonwhite students, considering a students' self-evaluation is crucial. Pausing briefly to ensure that our feedback is focused on the development of the student can positively influence the lives of our future graduates and even the future of our profession. We will never reach anything like true diversity or inclusion if we continue to assume that every student needs "tough love." Minority students, female students, first-generation college students, immigrants, and those from the lowest income groups have been stigmatized throughout their educational careers as deficient, or, worse, as failures. While ample resources may be available to them, such as a tutoring or learning center or a professor's office hours, we can't assume that they automatically feel welcome in those spaces, especially when traditional education has fed a "fixed" mindset instead of fostering a belief in each student's potential.[13] If feedback is to be constructive, these social factors need to be considered thoughtfully.

Even when a student is excelling in a course, rather than giving them an A as if that were the end of the matter, we can make it clear that feedback is part of a lifelong process. It is not an end in itself. We can share with students what their next learning goals might be, say, if they wanted to major in the discipline or apply to graduate school to pursue further study in the field. The goal is to recast feedback as developmental: to frame it as an opportunity to grow, an opportunity that every student is fully capable of realizing.[14] In her history class at Knox College, Professor Catherine Denial holds one-on-one conferences with students where she learns and listens when they share their concerns and the significant life issues that impinge on their ability to write. She holds these conversations as a follow-up *after* students have turned in assignments and completed self-evaluations, a way of affirming that the assignments are a beginning, not an end, to a process of lifelong learning. The conferences prove to be meaningful to both the students and their professor. Denial writes that evaluation became "an actual delight. It wasn't about words on a page, but about meeting someone in their humanity and sharing my own."[15]

How Students Can Give Themselves the Feedback They Need

Perhaps the single most valuable feedback any student can ever receive is the feedback they give themselves. The technical term for this is "self-regulated learning." It's a habitual process where students learn how to work toward goals they set themselves, are able to evaluate how close they are coming to those goals, can give themselves feedback on better ways to achieve their goals, and then try again, repeating the process. Self-regulated learning has been shown to contribute to traditional measures of academic success, and it proves to be equally effective in the workplace.[16]

There are excellent ways of helping students regulate their own learning, and the good news is that these methods don't have to take an unreasonable amount of an instructor's time. In fact, if these methods take too much of your time, *you* are regulating the students, and that undermines the whole process.

Sarah J. Schendel, assistant professor at Suffolk Law School in Boston, Massachusetts, has devised an especially effective method for helping her students evaluate what they are learning, and it doesn't require her to spend extensive one-on-one time with them. She overtly builds a process of self-reflection into her exams to help students become what she terms "self-regulated learners," learners who have skills for more accurately assessing what they know and do not know. She then gives them advice, as a group, on how they can use that basic self-knowledge to determine where they need to pay more or less attention, in her course and in all future situations.

Schendel argues that, for a lawyer, excessive self-evaluation can be as disastrous as a lack of confidence.[17] Once the law degree and bar exams are over, lawyers must continue to learn in order to keep up with their constantly changing profession. We would argue that that is true for any and every profession.

For her law students, Schendel adapts a technique called "cognitive wrapping," a method also used in physics, chemistry, and second language acquisition courses. Cognitive wrappers are special questions inserted into the beginning or end of any exam or assignment that are designed to have students reflect on the exam or assignment itself, on their study skills, or their time management, such as: "What grade do you expect to earn on this exam / assignment?" or "How many hours did you spend studying for this exam or assignment?" Students are informed that they are required to answer these questions and they should try to answer accurately even though their answers won't "count" for their exam grade.

When the exam or other assignment is returned with a grade and comments, Schendel takes a few moments to walk the class through an exercise where they compare their expectations and preparation with the grade earned and the evaluative comments they received from the instructor. If there is perfect alignment, that is one kind of information (for instance, "I know if I study for fifteen hours and feel confident that I'm earning an A, I'm likely to earn an A; therefore I know I thrive when I have enough preparation to enter a situation confident"). If there is a disparity, the instructor can invite students to think about why. She asks the class what they can learn about themselves from the difference between the preparation and self-assessment they reported on the exam and the external result they achieved. Of course, an instructor can invite any student to come talk about the disparity during office hours if they wish. Whether or not they do, the exercise in itself provides information that can be invaluable in school and beyond.

Versions of the cognitive wrapper help students think about themselves as learners, think about their process, and think about how those things can be improved. Educational consultant Starr Sackstein suggests an easy and effective method of self-evaluation. After returning a graded exam or assignment, she asks students what the exam or assignment was missing. What did students learn that wasn't covered (or accounted for) in the exam? This is, Sackstein notes, "an opportunity to give students more of a voice in the process. If we take the time to let students reflect, to share with us what the assessment may have missed, then we get a fuller picture of the students in a way that might make more sense for them."[18] This is a quick, simple way to create a bidirectional assessment process, one that works in every classroom no matter how rigid the institutional rules may be.

At Stanford, Nobel-winning physicist professor Carl Wieman offers his physics students a variation on this exercise. He builds into his curriculum opportunities for students to reflect on their homework after it has been completed. Each new homework set begins with a question about the last one, such as, "Select a problem from the last homework set that you did incorrectly and explain what you did wrong and what should be done differently to obtain the correct answer." This prompt puts the spotlight on students' solutioning process, demanding time to reflect on feedback—even if delivered indirectly during class or in an answer key—to improve and practice.

We like to invite our students to come up with their own questions for self-evaluation and offer them a few ideas to get them started. When we do this frequently, over time we gather a list of questions from former students to share. Whether remotely or face to face, students can work in groups or in breakout rooms to come up with three or four different self-evaluation corrections per group. When the class reassembles, each group reads out their evaluation questions and then enters them in an online collaborative tool. In just a short period of time (15–20 minutes), students in a class of thirty or fifty or even a hundred can come up with a strong set of questions that can guide their self-assessment throughout the course.

Student-Centered Coaching

Coaching is a specific form of evaluation that isn't limited to the playing field: it can be usefully employed in every classroom and in every job. In their bestseller *Thanks for the Feedback: The Science and Art of Receiving Feedback Well,* Douglas Stone and Sheila Heen define coaching as "frequent, close-to-real-time suggestions, and the chance to practice small corrections or improvements along the way."[19] Feedback is most useful when the work is still fresh in students' minds and it affords them more time for application. The trick is to find quick ways to turn feedback around.

In *Teaching Naked Techniques,* Goucher College president José Antonio Bowen and C. Edward Watson, director for the Center of Teaching and Learning at the University of Georgia, recommend "advance organizers" as a way to help students become "self-directed learners." Advance organizers are preparatory surveys, checklists, rubrics, or open-ended questions that help students before they actually begin to approach a task, whether completing an assignment or preparing for an exam.[20] Having students participate in preliminary discussions about how and why certain lessons, assignments, and activities work helps them to understand and achieve their learning goals and to be realistic about other goals. These are ways to check for student understanding of the tasks ahead and to provide clear parameters for each assignment. Although this may seem too intuitive to be called "coaching" from a college professor's standpoint, it *is* coaching.

In *Improving How Universities Teach Science,* Wieman advocates yet another form of coaching. He recommends brief, frequent "tasks" as opposed to high-stakes, end-of-term summative varieties. Coordinating these as in-class and class-wide tasks affords him the ability to coach all his students at once. He supports students in "productive practice" by offering positive and negative examples of what performance looks like and the type of work that would and wouldn't meet the course goals. Having asked former students how long they took to complete a task or assignment, he is able to give current students "realistic expectations about the amount of practice required by giving guidelines for the amount and type of practice that will be needed." As students become more proficient throughout a course, he modifies criteria to maintain an appropriate level of challenge. After a task is complete, Wieman shares common errors with the whole class, focusing on key elements to avoid overwhelming students with negative examples. He communicates strengths and weaknesses, pointing out if students made progress. He does this in class in real time by collecting group responses on colorful note cards or electronic clickers. With frequent practice and real-time coaching, students "can determine where their strengths and weaknesses lie—in time to make corrections" before an important, high-stakes exam.[21] He recommends students self-assess these assignments, thus freeing instructors to direct more attention to mentoring students at more critical stages in a semester.

Although Wieman's students are studying physics, his advice applies to teaching in any field. Wieman shares coaching responsibilities with his students, involving them in the planning of assignments and projects. He then asks them to submit drafts of their plans, and both he and their peers respond to those plans. The exercise helps students externalize their strategies while affording the instructor an opportunity to offer guidance.

Entrepreneur and educational evangelist Ted Dintersmith calls this kind of academic coaching "preparing students for life, not standardized tests."[22] Together, a whole class might compare and contrast study strategies, or they might compare different ways they each plan to tackle a problem or construct an experiment. The instructor's role, in this coaching situation, might be to walk students through the planning process to show how they would troubleshoot problems and then ask the class to offer other methods. Students might ask themselves, "What assumptions am I making?" or "Is this task taking me too long? Why?"

Collaboratively developing rubrics with students is another useful coaching technique to develop self-evaluation skills and practice constructive peer-to-peer evaluation. It is also another activity, like cognitive wrapping, that can help a professor who is teaching a large class or many sections of a class to save some time grading. Rubrics become formative when they are not accompanied by a grade; they become transformative when students create them.

For example, one can begin simply by asking students to make a chart or checklist of the basic requirements of an assignment. They can refer back to the syllabus for information or come up with a checklist themselves of such seemingly obvious (to the instructor!) items as a cover page, a project title, research notes, site descriptors, a methodology, documentation and citations, and so forth. Students might develop other rubrics for what constitutes an excellent assignment: accuracy, clarity, and establishing urgency, for example. Or, in a literature class, comprehension of a text, a convincing interpretation, or a sophisticated theoretical framework. In other kinds of courses, rubrics might emphasize analytical skills, statistical methods, case reviews, and more. In all cases, students are already "doing" the assignment in their advance planning and engaging in a deep and meaningful learning process by working on specific aspects of the rubric in a short timeframe. An instructor or teaching assistant could comment on these and offer suggestions for how to approach meeting these goals. Then, when assignments come in, refer to these rubrics in your own feedback. Rather than writing feedback from scratch each time, rubric users (instructors or students) can circle the evaluative content that applies.

Inspired by LaGuardia Community College professor Bethany Holmstrom, I (Christina) have used the categories "Passing," "Almost There," and "Not Yet" as evaluative rubrics in my classes. By lining these categories up together under each skill set on the rubric, students can always see what the next steps are, what they need to do to strengthen that skill and get from "almost there" to "passing." Brief, targeted comments can be added to adapt it to every student.

Finally, when it comes to coaching, less is more: one or two areas that could be strengthened, focused on, and improved before the next assignment. More than that may be unreasonable and even discouraging. Mentoring in comments might include identifying one pattern you observe (at most two) and sharing a tip or strategy you might use to develop that skill. For those teaching very large classes or several classes at a time, a glossary of tips and strategies with links to further reading can supplement a rubric. Again, this can go from efficient to transformative by having students contribute here, too.

"My Students Don't Read My Feedback"

If you've been teaching for a while, we know you've witnessed this: students flip their exams or essays to the last page to look at the grade and then put them away. This is one of the most frequent complaints we hear among colleagues: "My students don't read my feedback."

Understandably, it is very disappointing for educators who spend hours tailoring their feedback to each student to have those comments disregarded. However, if students aren't paying attention to comments and feedback, that could mean they are proficient in being schooled but have missed the importance of learning. As we will see in the next chapter, students have been enculturated by many years of formal education to equate "grades" with "accomplishment." If their grade is satisfactory, the feedback that would foster their betterment and overall improvement may seem redundant or, worse, get completely ignored.

If students don't understand the value of feedback, if they don't understand that the most important part of learning happens when *applying* the lessons learned, then it may be because this is a lesson they've quite literally never had before. Think of ignoring the comments as a symptom, not the problem itself.

One way to slow students down to focus on feedback is to give them *only* comments designed to inspire them to think about strategies for improving their work. One business tool that resonates with students, sparks a desire for improvement, and effectively delivers constructive feedback is the classic "SWOT" analysis (strengths, weaknesses, opportunities, and threats). The goal of any project is to make it as good as it can be. Some people who dislike the idea of "threats" modify this business prototype to something like "contradictions" or another term signaling an opposing point of view.

In a research project or paper, an "opportunity" might be a new direction in which students can elaborate or extend their work. This positive framing matters: it shows students a way to improve and gives them a vote of confidence that we believe they can and will. A "threat" might be some counterargument. For example, in a biology class, a threat could include research that points toward an opposite conclusion. Threats give students exciting new challenges to take on. Through SWOT, students learn to take advantage of opportunities, to examine and take measures to strengthen their work when confronted with a contradictory argument or conclusion.

With only feedback, students focus on their personal development, especially in critical thinking, testing out hypotheses, and clarity in presenting their work. There are no grades for these assignments—only "complete" and "incomplete." To self-regulate, students *have* to read the comments to gauge how their work is going and to find out what to look out for when it comes time to prepare for final research papers or projects. To make this work, the comments and feedback need to be formative—whatever method you choose, growth mindset, SWOT, or something else, to do this well requires coaching students to build up the work to the next level. Ultimately, grades are calculated by completion of work, allowing students more latitude to test, try, fail, regroup, and try again.

There are other ways to ensure that students read feedback. Students can submit revised work with a cover letter or cover sheet explaining how the current submission incorporates feedback from the previous one. A variation on this method is to require students to complete a brief survey when they submit an assignment or exam. This might be as simple as a checklist where students check boxes next to all the requirements of an assignment (or all the practice steps they took before an exam), such as "Carefully read instructor's comments on previous work to understand each suggestion" and "Revised my approach based on comments." Or the survey could ask, in a multiple-choice question, "How much time did you spend reading comments on previous work?" If a student doesn't check all the boxes or indicates a lack of time spent processing feedback and then repeats similar mistakes, the reasoning behind the results should be obvious. Student responses provide a starting place for coaching when students follow up in our office hours.

Finally, when students excel, when they consistently ace the skills an introductory course requires, we spend our time in office hours talking about next steps in their development or what our expectations would be if the class were an advanced course for majors or a graduate seminar. Simply saying, "You're doing great," isn't helpful feedback, and it doesn't incentivize students to value our comments in future.

Whatever alternative feedback method you choose, devote time and thought to showing students why *applying* feedback is crucial to their learning. You'll likely stop saying, "My students don't read my comments."

Roleplay: Modeling Constructive Feedback

I (Cathy) go back and forth on how much or how little to model feedback for students. Sometimes it can seem like a little guidance sets them free; other times I feel like I'm micromanaging and limiting their creativity. There's no one right way, for sure. Often, in preparing students for the vagaries of evaluation of all kinds, I tell them a story from a memorable week in my own life as an undergraduate. During this week I had a philosophy paper on the visionary geodesic theories of semiotician Charles S. Peirce returned with negative, even sarcastic, comments from my professor scrawled over every page. I could make no sense of all the criticism on a paper that earned an A+. That same week I had a quantitative political science assignment returned with a B grade and the sole comment "Good work!" For several weeks I kept the two papers pinned to a bulletin board above my desk, proof (as far as I was concerned) that higher education was a mess.

With hindsight, I realize that it's not just higher ed that has a hard time figuring out how to give the right amount and type of feedback. In the workplace, this is another area that managers struggle with (and hire coaches at top dollar to consult on).

Roleplay activities solve the problem of micromanaging. By design, they let students explore how good feedback works and how to identify, respond to, and clarify feedback they find unhelpful. Roleplay affords everyone an opportunity to practice with fictitious low-stakes scenarios. In a partially scripted roleplay, students take turns giving and receiving feedback on an imaginary project. Students might break into pairs or small groups or, for an in-person lecture even of four hundred students, each student can turn to the student next to them and take turns, beginning with an initial script about an imaginary project where the goal is to help the project improve, not simply critique all its flaws.

We give students a template script about a fantastical made-up project to start with. The script might look like this: "What you do well in your research on flying water buffaloes is [name strength]. One thing you might focus on before delivering your oral presentation on [deadline] is [name a skill—organization, introduction, presenting evidence], which I think could be developed more by [suggestion for a way to strengthen this weaker area]." This is only meant to spark a conversation, break the ice, and then students can use a similar script for their real projects down the road.

When teaching remotely, we organize the same activity by assigning students to breakout rooms of 2–3 people. If you would prefer to have more oversight, or if you would like the whole class to observe the roleplay and talk through how it went in a debrief session, you can ask for two volunteers to role-play what they accomplished in their breakout session and then peers might comment on what they observed.

To make the roleplay more effective and fun, after the first scripted exercise you could ask for new volunteers (or have students find new in-person partners or assign them new virtual breakout rooms) and ask that students deliberately give extremely vague or unhelpful feedback. Remind them it is meant to be fun, maybe even a little dramatic. As a facilitator, keep this very short and light. You might even organize this as a class-wide Mad Lib. Then, in the debrief, talk about how to respond to unclear criticism and some ways to ask for more directed, helpful feedback. Again, in a virtual classroom, the chat function allows students to correct the vague or harsh feedback in real time.

Role-playing puts students in the driver's seat and shows them that they have agency and the ability to insist on thoughtful responses to their work. What's more, this helps students gain a greater awareness and understanding of the process of giving and receiving feedback. No feedback is final—even if it seems so. Perfecting the art of receiving useful feedback is as important as delivering it. It is yet another invaluable skill that contributes to students' professional growth and will serve them throughout their careers.

Peer Evaluation: 360 Feedback

There are many ways to conduct peer evaluations, including using a simple form or survey that students fill out at the middle or end of a project, ideally one that also serves as a teaching tool for giving good feedback in the future. A more complex form of feedback often used in the workplace is the 360-degree performance review. It is one of the most holistic and democratic professional feedback methods that we can adapt to a college class. It works.

In the workforce, a 360 review is meant to capture all 360 degrees of an employee's performance. It includes self-evaluation, peer evaluation, and evaluation by those who supervise them. It's a tool for helping managers understand better where they are performing well and where they have room to grow into the next role. The format of a 360 review is easily applicable in the classroom. Students complete self-evaluations, reflecting on their performance and what they have contributed to the class as well as the direct results of their contributions. Students then seek out reviews from their peers, say, four to six classmates with whom they have worked in pairs, in small groups, or on long-term projects. In addition, students receive discursive feedback from their instructor that synthesizes the self-evaluations with the peer evaluations and provides any additional insights the instructor may have.

This is precisely what I (Christina) did in my in-person American Literature: Origins to the Civil War course at Hunter College in New York City. At the end of the semester, I asked students to complete self-evaluation and peer evaluation forms. I had announced in my syllabus that peer evaluations for group work would be coming: these forms were published at the end of the syllabus, so students knew, from the first day of class, the criteria by which they would be evaluating themselves and their peers. Throughout this course, students frequently worked in groups (the same people in the same groups for the whole semester). At the end of the term, I handed out printed self-evaluation slips, which students filled out first (to practice on themselves before judging their peers), then the peer evaluation slips, which students filled out for every member of their group. The peer evaluations guided students through thinking about assessment in sophisticated ways that allowed them to understand what it means to judge and to be judged and how evaluation can lead to excellence and confidence, not mortification and humiliation.[23]

The preface to the form itself read: "Take a moment to think about how you worked with your peers and how they worked with you this semester. Working in groups helps us practice listening and leadership skills as we organize different points of view through effective communication to achieve common goals." The preface was written such that students viewed the evaluations with a growth mindset: instead of being "good" or "bad" at something, students were encouraged to consider this to be a *practice* of certain skill sets they have used and will use beyond the class. Then, the form offered students a list of thought topics for their consideration, such as preparedness for group work (for instance, did they complete the homework all, most, or only some of the time?) and listening skills (did they take peers' opinions into account all, most, or only some of the time?). The topics also included group leadership, volunteerism, and other service qualities students could apply and improve upon in the future.

Finally, to complete the 360 review, I synthesized students' self-evaluations with those of their peers to offer each student a summary of their progress and contributions to the class as well as some gentle suggestions for improvement in future courses. What surprised me was that almost all students voluntarily added discursive feedback for their peers (this part of the form was optional). It turned out that the short-answer format of the self-evaluation forms encouraged students to use the same thoughtful evaluative practices for their peers as well. In my synthesized reviews, which I sent to students via email after the last day of class, I anonymized any direct quotations from peers and included some of these positive comments. Because the forms were framed with a growth mindset, students' comments about their peers were generous, encouraging, and uplifting in addition to being constructive.

In response to receiving 360 feedback, one student wrote: "I've never seen that sort of feedback before and think that every class should include introspection and positive critique of a student's ability to work together with others." This is the opposite of grade-grubbing, of cringing and becoming defensive about feedback. The student had clearly come to understand feedback through a growth mindset, not as "criticism" but as something powerful, helpful, and, sadly, unique. Everyone in the course became a colearner, and, in the words of one student, "a real educator, not just a teacher."

For an example of "a real educator, not just a teacher," look no further than progressive educator, MFA student, and TikTok sensation Phoebe Eligon-Jones (@blupoetres), who generously shares her most effective teaching methods for participatory learning online. Her participation grading model encourages students to think of participation grades as a 360-degree evaluation *and* a 360-degree reward for being actively engaged in the class. Most importantly, her model works: her remote class in 2020 had almost 100 percent visual participation (for instance, actively raising a hand). In Eligon-Jones's class, over a six-week marking period (approximately thirty days of class), students need to earn 20 participation points. Each time they raise a hand, they get a point, as she explains in a November 2020 TikTok video (with over sixty-nine thousand views in one day). She incentivizes students to do more than the bare minimum: the first student to get to 20 points wins an extra 5 points. Students can bank the extra points and use them on a quiz, homework, test, essay, "or they can be decent human beings and donate their points to someone in the class who might be shy or quiet." This method is effective: her remote class—when most dropout rates were only going up—boasted almost 100 percent visual participation, *and* the students loved it.

Asking Students for Feedback on Our Course Design and Teaching

As engaged teachers, we tell our students that everything is a "process" that can be improved, that we learn from mistakes or weaknesses, that that's what learning is. Asking our students for their feedback is an important step in becoming colearners and an opportunity to practice what we preach, applying the lesson of "process" over "product" to ourselves as well. However, asking students to give *us* feedback on our teaching or on a course, especially in the middle of a term, can quickly raise our hackles. Why wouldn't it be difficult? Giving students this much say can be intimidating, even to those who have done it before.

It's worth the anxiety. Inviting students to evaluate and offer feedback on a course is beneficial for them and for us. As bell hooks notes, "When students see themselves as mutually responsible for the development of a learning community, they offer constructive input."[24] To us, "constructive input" means, in application, two things: first, guiding students to use a "growth mindset," and, second, directing their attention to the entire learning community, not just one individual instructor.

The ideal way to solicit student feedback is, first, to frame it as productive, formative, and welcome. It has to be cast as a net good for everyone and a process to which everyone contributes. Feedback might be solicited as often as regular exit tickets at the end of class meetings, asking students, "Was there anything we missed today that we should have covered?" You could coordinate a one-time check-in at the beginning of the semester in which you ask students what assignments are most interesting to them and then drop the one with the least votes, or you could conduct a midterm survey asking students how the course is going and whether anything needs tweaking (do they want more or less lecturing, more or less time for group work?). Soliciting feedback on a course could, in and of itself, be built as a project for group work. Either way, the instructor should be very much included in the discussion. Instructors can show students different paths toward the same learning goals, such as sharing previous syllabi from the same course or syllabi on the same topic from different instructors. Taking it one step further, of course, is asking students what they might do, and an extended version of this would be to ask them to design a future class or assignment transformed by their insights. When students offer an alteration, they imagine what might be done *differently* rather than saying what has been done "wrong," which isn't constructive. The common denominator across these various ways to organize student input is to structure the conversation to meet the needs of the learning community in a low-stakes (ungraded) conversation that is formative *for you* as an instructor and also for students. The best way to grasp how to read and follow a syllabus is to play a part in shaping one.

The key factor here is supporting students in learning to give practical, real, constructive feedback to someone who has the power to judge them or even fail them. It won't be the last time they have to give advice, a suggestion, a complaint, or a refusal to a supervisor who may well have the authority to fire them. Learning how to deliver constructive feedback in a delicate situation is a life lesson they will never forget.

Mid-course correction, given and taken, is far more beneficial, for students and instructors alike, than end-of-term teacher evaluations. The typical teacher evaluation is multiple-choice, generic, often jargon-filled and bureaucratic. These summative evaluations do not foster a sense of "mutual responsibility" due to their timing and anonymity. Moreover, they are handled by a third party—an "impartial" person or digital system—to protect students and guard against any potential retaliation in final grades. This process normalizes and even fosters hostility instead of encouraging personalized, home-grown feedback by and for the learning community. Multiple studies have shown this form of student evaluation to be unproductive (they don't inspire professors to change). Even worse, they replicate gender and racial disparities in the academy and society at large. One white, male professor who taught two identical online courses did an experiment: he went by a gendered male name for one section and a gendered female name for another section. The course evaluations were skewed more positively toward the "male" iteration of the course—he was called more authoritative, knowledgeable, persuasive, effective.[25] The results skewed more negatively for the section taught under the "female" name. Evaluations tend to skew even more negatively when the instructor is a woman of color. Importantly, the results are more helpful, detailed, concrete, and less biased when evaluations occur in real time, not after the course is over, and when we take a moment to discuss gender bias in evaluations—throughout the term—with our students.[26]

Before leaving this topic, we want to address vulnerable professors (those who are part-time, adjunct professors or even full-time professors without tenure) to take special care with student evaluation.

Models from Inspiring Professors

Jessica Spencer-Keyse, Pavel Luksha, and **Joshua Cubista,** *Learning Ecosystems: An Emerging Praxis for the Future of Education,* **SKOLKOVO & Global Education Futures, Moscow School of Management**

In order to manage their ongoing and ever-changing collaboration across more than forty different educational, civic, and corporate institutions, the Global Education Futures group has designed an interactive peer feedback system that is based on an ecological model of thriving. Each project communicates findings and plans with the other. Their learning "ecosystem" affords a better way of thinking: it serves as the environmental model of the resilient, mutually-sustaining interdependence they aspire to.*

A motto of this consortium is "Unlearn-Reimagine-Relearn." They argue: "Evaluation and assessment systems of the past may not be best suited for guiding people toward desired combinations of skills for the 21st century. We need to acknowledge the limitations of assessment and redirect the impact on people's life, especially for young people so that evaluation and assessment can be experienced as valuable and encouraging feedback" (23–24). The collective focuses on "Univercities," meaning partnerships between universities and communities, in a range of projects involving tens or even hundreds of thousands of participants. These include: "CityMart," an integrated community care system in Dallas, Texas, that coordinates environmental, health care, nutrition, literacy, and other neighborhood-based activities; "Change the Script," a storytelling system based in Denmark designed to train environmental activists; and "Nature Farming," a Japanese consortium that ties balanced biodynamic farming and spiritual practices. Another ambitious project is the indigenous Yakuts climate change program in Yakutia, Russia. Yakutia is the largest single jurisdiction in the world—larger than Argentina—and has the coldest temperatures on inhabitable Earth. Students there are prototyping a future "way of being" using solar energy and hydroponic architecture.

The project directors give as much attention to "Guiding Questions for Execution," an attentive and serious collaborative feedback method, as they do to their environmental goals: "To what extent do you cultivate the conversation between leaders in your area, or your sector, on how to become more eco-systemically oriented? . . . To what extent do you ensure there are feedback loops on research and processes, ensure that all feel heard and have the space to safely share their concerns? To what extent do you increase visibility and promote the journey of your ecosystem so others can learn from you, support you and celebrate your successes?" (157). To solve the catastrophe of our natural ecosystems, they argue, you first need sustainable, respectful, "thrivalist" educational ecosystems.

Luis Bonilla, Professor of Practice and Director of the Digital Audiences Lab at Arizona State University's Walter Cronkite School of Journalism and Mass Communication

Professor Luis Bonilla directs a professional immersion program in which journalism and communication students work with real clients to meaningfully grow, engage, and measure their audiences. Students work in teams in an agency-like environment and put their strategies to work with real social campaigns and more, all happening in real time as they learn. Bonilla even runs his office hours to bridge the classroom to the workplace. He conducts one-on-one meetings with every student on a biweekly basis. He reflects, "I have found it to be a crucial opportunity to build trust, provide and take transparent feedback, and to genuinely understand how each student would prefer to learn." These meetings aid both student and instructor alike, allowing the student to share concerns about lab work and providing Professor Bonilla some insights that inform adjustments to the curriculum. Bonilla explains:

> Setting the tone for the one-on-one meetings starts before the semester begins during student orientation, where I set the expectations of what we will discuss, how long we will hold the meeting, and the casual nature of the dialogue. Then at the beginning of the first one-on-one, I reiterate what we'll use this time for (such as reviewing any concepts that they don't want to bring up in front of the group or even events or challenges outside of our classroom) and begin asking a few questions. Some are relevant to the coursework, while others are more customized to the student. . . . I want the tone of the meeting to be open and eventually a safe space for students to express their thoughts, but that only happens over time and after showing that I care not just about their success, but for them as an individual.[†]

Every student and every meeting is different and unique, but there is one trend: conversations at the beginning of the semester typically focus on coursework and then evolve, later in the semester, into broader

(continued)

concerns about managing course workload and finding employment after graduation. Bonilla offers himself as a resource to students to help them succeed both in his course and in their careers.

* Jessica Spencer-Keyse, Pavel Luksha, and Joshua Cubista, *Learning Ecosystems: An Emerging Praxis for the Future of Education, Educational Ecosystems for Societal Transformation* (Moscow: Moscow School of Management SKOLKOVO & Global Education, 2020), http://learningecosystems2020.globaledufutures.org/wp-content/uploads/2020/11/LA_eng_1.pdf.

† Tatiana Ades, "Bridges into the Workplace: One-on-One Student Meetings with Professor Luis Bonilla," HASTAC, February 16, 2020, www.hastac.org/blogs/tianaades/2020/02/16/bridges-workplace-one-one-student-meetings-professor-luis-bonilla.

Faculty from marginalized groups (that is, women, professors with accents or from minority religious groups or lower social classes, etc.) face the same discrimination in a college environment that they do off campus.[27] When the feedback goes in every direction (self, peer, and course evaluation), it keeps students' attention on productive, collaborative engagement in course content and the learning process, counteracting such bias. Sharing research on social bias sometime before student-to-student evaluation establishes the foundation for addressing bias in student-teacher evaluation. This helps instill in students a sense of responsibility for their learning experience rather than a leap to judgment.

Chavella Pittman, associate professor of sociology at Dominican University in River Forest, Illinois, argues that an integrated, thoughtful process might help to mitigate some of the student incivilities that disproportionately marginalized faculty experience in conventional teaching evaluations. Pittman proposes that a shift to student-centered peer review methods "might result in increased focus on the actual course work and less student resistance and reaction to marginalized faculty's grading." At first, "Faculty may feel these strategies may further make them invisible or disempower them in their classrooms." While she acknowledges and understands that perspective, Pittman notes that student-centered learning practices still give faculty "a lot of classroom power as they are the ones choosing the course material, planning the active-learning activities, giving short lectures, facilitating classroom discussions, evaluating student work, and so on."[28]

The through line of these different methods of giving and receiving feedback is that we often waste a lot of time—hours or even days—worrying about problems alone. The best solution is almost always to simply *ask* those around us for new ideas and approaches. We solve problems better together than we do in isolation. We grow and develop faster when nourished from multiple sources of experience and perspective. And we are smarter when we collect insights and wisdom from different knowledge sources. A wealth of ideas is often readily available to us—at our fingertips ("Hey, Google, how do I boil an egg?" or "Alexa, what does a panda sound like?") and in those we sit next to (or Zoom next to) in a class. In a great classroom, each interaction helps students be confident enough to trust their peers (and themselves) to offer the feedback that all of us, including instructors, need to thrive.

CHAPTER 11

Grades—*Ugh!*

A new group of students sits in your classroom on the first day of the semester, quietly reading over your syllabus while you talk them through all the requirements and deadlines.[1] They are wondering, "How do I get an A in this class?" You may wish they were thinking about the exciting learning ahead but, really, it's all about the grades. This is the first-day-of-school ritual that we've all experienced, year after year. It's exactly what we did when we were students sitting in those desks. Now we are instructors, and the piles of grading accumulate so fast we can hardly keep up, and with those comes the all-too-familiar last-day-of-school ritual: students knocking on our door (or our inbox) pleading for a higher grade. It's a vicious and unhappy cycle that brings out the worst in everyone.

Almost all of us—instructors and students—have gone through systems of formal education that place a high premium on testing and grading. From preschool on, we have learned that grades have consequences. We have been screened, ranked, and rated by our test scores practically from birth. Our grades have determined what schools we go to (magnet schools for exceptional students or competitive private schools), whether we're selected for "gifted" or "special ed" programs, and if we're considered "college material." By the time students enroll in college, they equate "school" with "grades." Implicitly and structurally, traditional higher education is about grades, thinly veiled by terms like "outcomes," "learning goals" (not the learning *process* itself), and "assessment."

Grades cause problems. They are not a substitute for evaluation, and they give the appearance of objectivity and certainty even where there isn't consensus about what they might mean. We have abundant research on this, going back many decades. As we will see, grades raise student anxiety and decrease motivation, detract from actual learning, and reduce the different ways a student learns and the uneven ways they might absorb material to one letter, score, or number—a blunt instrument, to be sure.

Grades themselves are a problem for instructors, too. Practically every instructor has struggled with every aspect of grading, from cheating to claims of grade inflation. While many of us would relish an opportunity not to grade, it's hard to know where to begin when a system is so firmly in place and has gone largely unexamined.

We are not advocating doing away with final grades. That's an institutional decision. In the United States, less than a dozen institutions eschew grades (including Brown University, Evergreen State College, Hampshire College, and Sarah Lawrence College, among others). We are advocating approaching the methods we use to evaluate student work with thoughtfulness and care. Even at this time when institutions around the world are increasingly opting for grade norming, standardized metrics, and predetermined rubrics and outcomes, there are also instructors everywhere working to develop responsible tactics to supplement the final grade required by their institution with other forms of assessment that are more useful to students.

In this chapter, we offer research, suggestions, tips, and advice to help instructors design purposeful, constructive methods of evaluation. We discuss "ungrading," a range of alternatives to traditional grading, including contract grading, peer assessment, and peer badging.

Through alternative assessment systems and creative ways of adapting final exams (even multiple-choice exams in classes with hundreds of students), professors have found ways to evaluate students that emphasize student autonomy and judgment and help prepare them for all the complex ways they will be judged (without a report card) once they graduate from college.[2]

Advocates of participatory learning like Jesse Stommel, Alfie Kohn, and Susan D. Blum use the bold term "ungrading" (others call it "going gradeless" or "de-grading") as a deliberate provocation and deconstruction of traditional grading.[3] Rather than a summary of achievement, ungrading redesigns assessment as a formative process, offering feedback with the goal of improvement. It helps students to ask profound questions: *Where am I going? How am I going? Where to next?*[4] In the words of Knox College professor Catherine Denial, ungrading is "a spectrum of collaborative feedback strategies that can, at some institutions, replace grading altogether, and at others, make for a better partnership between student and faculty member as they determine what letter grade a student's work should get."[5]

In some of the models of alternative assessment that we explore in this chapter, students themselves determine what constitutes success for themselves and others. When we ask students to evaluate their own progress and define their own ideas of success in a course, we shatter old habits and expectations, including our own. Everything about a course changes when we deemphasize grading and front-load our commitment to student success and ask students to define success for themselves.

Imagine a transformation of the first day of class: you begin by looking students in the eyes, and you ask them, "What is 'success' in this class for you? And how can I help you achieve it?" Students may not know how to answer these questions at first, because in all likelihood they have never been asked such questions *before* a class begins—if ever.

In this chapter:

A Brief History of Grading

Educational ranking systems are not new. They go back at least thirteen hundred years in China, and to medieval and early modern Europe, when public, debate-like oral examinations were "marked" with letters and even pluses and minuses.[6] There's some debate about whether it was Yale president Ezra Stiles in 1785 or Cambridge tutor William Farish in 1792 who first decided that some students should be marked higher than others ("optimi" or "inferiores"), but throughout the industrializing nineteenth century, grading was in the air. Uniformity, productivity, standardization, and automation were all signs of modernity in the new world of factories. Educators began to propose ways of adapting the new ways of measuring worker productivity to education.[7]

With the rise of Taylorism at the end of the nineteenth century, it was perhaps inevitable that institutions would decide that it was important to rank and rate student work. In the United States, the first institution to move from discursive, oral, or written-out comments to letter grades (awarded as a summation of all of a students' work on a project, a paper, or an entire course) was Mt. Holyoke, the elite women's college in Massachusetts. Aspiring to train the "modern woman," Mt. Holyoke adapted what seemed like a more "objective" system. Instead of student conferences and long, written-out comments evaluating a student's work throughout the term, Mt. Holyoke opted to award single A, B, C, and D grades at the end that would stand in for or "summarize" the overall quality of all the work in an entire course. The problem came with the lowest grade, which should have been, for consistency's sake, the *E*. Fearing the letter *E* would be confused with "Excellence," Mt. Holyoke invented the *F* grade for "failure"—the only referential grade in the system. Not insignificantly, other early trailblazers in this arena were in the meatpacking industry. Ironically, they were less concerned about the ambiguous *E* grade than they were about reducing something as complex as sirloin or chuck to a simplistic overall letter grade.[8]

These Industrial Age histories live on in our everyday practices. We like to pretend that affixing a letter grade or a number to a students' accumulated course work is somehow more "objective" than a written evaluation of their intellectual labors. It's not. Arthur Chiaravalli, a high school math teacher who also advocates alternative assessment methods, calls grades a "false currency."[9] A grade seems to stand for something—but it's not clear what, how accurately or objectively, or for what purpose.

As we shall see, every component that goes into the affixing of a final letter or number is filled with areas of discrimination and judgment, typically determined by someone (presumably an instructor or, in some cases, a department or institution) who has achieved expertise in that field. Reducing all those processes to one grade or number doesn't change all the specific, individual, and varying factors contributing to that assessment. As retired University of Oklahoma professor Laura Gibbs (who tweets as "OnlineCrsLady") notes, if one is teaching typing, measuring improvement in speed and accuracy *is* a valid way of assessing learning, but grades are not "real measures" or comparable "stand-ins for real assessments."[10] Doctoral committees make determinations all the time if a student has done enough to earn the highest degree conferred in their profession. Typically, the committee appends comments, much like their nineteenth-century predecessors at Mt.

Holyoke and elsewhere used to do. Affixing a letter or a number grade at the end adds no evaluative content, nor does it offer the student feedback to help them learn better in the future. It is not a useful proxy.

Ironically, we now live in the great age of formative feedback. Grades, scores, marks, IQ tests, and multiple-choice tests are products of the Industrial Age. More than that, they are an anachronism. The Internet Age offers a vast and ubiquitous array of opportunities for all of us to share our feedback on just about everything we do. In the modern workplace, for example, employees typically participate in annual or semiannual performance reviews evaluated by supervisors; in many traditional companies, employees are asked to write a self-evaluation. Whether they are promoted, given a merit raise, or, in the worst cases, fired will partly be determined by how well they negotiate that evaluation process. Everywhere else, too, in daily life we are constantly providing specific feedback, often in a highly individualized manner—on the books we buy on Amazon, the recipes we try, Uber rides, and everything from restaurants to dentists on Yelp. These reviews, often coupled with a five-star rating scale, accumulate into an average, so there are hundreds of evaluations made by many people engaging with a service or product in various unique ways, all averaged together. In short, in car rides or restaurant reviews, the person receiving the evaluation typically receives more evaluative information, from a wide variety of perspectives, than a student might receive in a course. Formative feedback is happening everywhere now. It's an ideal time to think about better ways to evaluate student work.

So What's Wrong with Grading?

It's the middle of term, and instructors at my (Christina's) institution are required to submit "progress reports," by which the university means midterm grades. These grades are purely speculative at this point, because students have only completed half the work. This process was put in place by the university, ostensibly to address low performers early and trigger a support system to follow up and offer students help. Later, when submitting my final grade roster, I notice that, despite setting off the alarm bells at the midpoint, students marked as failing then still failed the course in the end. Where did the *system* fail students? What's wrong with *my* students? Or did *I* do something wrong?

It turns out they responded quite predictably to being alerted to their potential failure. In 2015, Astrid Poorthuis, assistant professor in developmental psychology at Utrecht University in the Netherlands, demonstrated that students who are issued low grades in progress or midway reports rarely improve. In fact, the majority do worse in the latter half of the grading period.[11] Instead of inspiring development, issuing low preliminary grades undercuts it.

We now have decades of research confirming that "grading orientation," as learning science experts call it, actually hinders learning. In 1991, Drs. Hall P. Beck, Sherry Rorrer-Woody, and Linda G. Pierce demonstrated that students who cared primarily about their grades struggled academically, socially, and emotionally compared to peers who had somehow (through their past educational or family experiences) been rewarded for and absorbed a "learning orientation." Those students who wanted to learn, explore, and discover are the ones who excelled in the end.[12]

Professors Matt Townsley and Tom Buckmiller throw down the gauntlet: "Traditional grading practices have been used for over one hundred years, and to date, there have been no meaningful research reports to support it."[13] They argue that, although most educators think grades are "objective" and therefore "meaningful," the evidence runs in the opposite direction. We may think grades are "motivational," or that students work harder for a grade, but Townsley and Buckmiller insist the building evidence suggests it is long past time to rethink grading.[14]

Alfie Kohn, author of over a dozen influential books on schooling and parenting and one of the most outspoken critics of grading, notes that we educators often confuse "excellence" with "rankings." It's not enough to do well; we assume that some have to do better than others. Kohn argues that the apparatus of standardized tests, rankings, and grades demands a hierarchy. It *requires* some failures. If some students don't fail, then others can't be excellent.

Kohn has designed an intriguing thought experiment to prove his stark hypothesis that failure is built into our idea of excellence: "Suppose that next year virtually every student in your state met the standards and passed the tests. What would the likely reaction be from politicians, businesspeople, and the media? Would these folks shake their heads in frank admiration and say, '*Damn,* those teachers must be good!'?"[15] We all know that if everyone met the standards and passed the tests with perfect scores, the response would be consternation, not elation. As Kohn notes, immediately there would be commissions bringing together educators to diagnose what had gone wrong. He observes that when New York state's math scores rose unexpectedly in 2009, the chancellor of the state's Board of Regents insisted: "What today's scores tell me is not that we should be celebrating but that New York State needs to raise its standards."[16] By contrast, if we were assessing the success of a space shuttle launch and everything went off seamlessly, no one would say the bar was set too low.

Kohn's thought experiment reveals an assumption at the base of traditional education: no one is ever good enough. What's wrong with celebrating those math teachers who went above and beyond? Kohn would argue that failure is foundational to modern formal education, which implicitly assumes the "bell curve" argument that some must fail in order for others to succeed. We argue that we could think more carefully about how and why we evaluate student work, identify our priorities (for instance, student learning) and focus on how best to achieve our goals. The Dickensian pedagog Thomas Gradgrind, the notorious educator in *Hard Times* who wields his pointer like a saber, does not inspire student trust, and neither do summative evaluations like grades.

Thoughtful, formative feedback brings student learning back into the central focus of our evaluation.

There are other problems with grading. In Kohn's fictitious example, everyone would get upset if all students achieved perfect scores on a statewide exam. However, it turns out that, especially in elite higher education, most students actually are getting A's. As geologist Stuart Rojstaczer and computer scientist Christopher Helms have documented in their studies of grade inflation, the single most common grade given in higher education today is the A.[17] In reality, grade inflation correlates with the cost of tuition. A's are given more commonly at expensive private universities, where students pay large tuition bills, than at public ones. And to return to Kohn's thought experiment, there is little public outcry when students at elite, private prep schools all get A's.[18]

When we talk about K–12 public education, failure is our metric. When we talk about college, A is the most common grade. Although grades and test scores seemingly mean everything about getting into medical school, eighteen of the top twenty medical schools themselves give only pass-fail grades.[19] It's a flawed, archaic, and confusing system. No academic that we have ever met enjoys grading. To the instructors out there: do you?

Since late 2020, "ungrading" has become something akin to a movement. Over a thousand people have participated in reading groups, webinars, Twitter threads, podcasts, workshops, talks, conferences, and other forums to discuss Susan D. Blum's edited collection of essays, *Ungrading: Why Rating Students Undermines Learning (and What to Do Instead)*.[20] Many of these events are organized by volunteers, sometimes spontaneously. Clearly, we are on the verge of a change.

"You do what you can within the confines of a current structure, trying to minimize its harm. You also work with others to try to change that structure, conscious that nothing dramatic may happen for a very long time," writes Kohn in his book *Punished by Rewards: The Trouble with Gold Stars, Incentive Plans, A's, Praise, and Other Bribes*.[21] Maybe it's time to ask, in a serious and responsible way, if grades have outlived their usefulness and to explore what we can do instead.

I Can't Just Give Up Grades—I'd Get Fired

Grading is one of the most regulated aspects of all higher education. Before you embark on alternative approaches to grading, including grading contracts and peer evaluation, we have one important recommendation: talk to your department chair, dean, or registrar's office first. The answer may be as simple as: if you offer the same contract to every student, then what you do in class is fine as long as the final grade calculations conform to department and university rules. But it may not be that simple, and it's good to check.

Alternatives need to be presented to administrators (and students) with care and reinforced as meaningful, documentable, responsible, credentialed forms of for-credit learning attainments. Most institutions of higher learning have elaborate rules specifically designed to oversee and standardize grading: how, when, where, whether you can change a grade; when and what to do when students dispute it; and so forth. Pay attention to those rules! There are ways to be responsive to the research on the benefits of alternative assessment systems without—let's be blunt—getting fired. (Losing your job does no one any good.)

This caution applies to your students as well. While the research on alternative assessment methods supports the efficacy and benefits of various ungrading methods, in the real world in which most students live, if they are paying tuition, they also want something more concrete than a sense of their own personal advancement. Students expect a grade, a degree, a diploma, and other forms of formal, institutional recognition of the effort they have invested in their learning. (Otherwise, why not just learn from a friend, a book, or a YouTube video?) We have found that students respond to the challenge of taking their own level of learning seriously if they believe that the instructor takes that challenge seriously, consistently, and for a reason. Explaining "why" is vital when you are changing the status quo.

Extensive research, going back to Ruth Butler's studies of the 1980s, shows that providing comments on students' work without any grade at all is the *most* effective form of feedback we can offer students.[22] Replicated many times, Butler's studies showed that grades not only distract students from learning but they also *detract* from learning even when accompanied by careful feedback. Grading has had such a powerful influence throughout a student's life that, when they see a grade, it negates the impact of the feedback. They find it hard to see past the grade to the comments designed to strengthen their learning. The reverse also has been replicated numerous times in different contexts and with consistent results: when given feedback without grades, students show more motivation toward learning.[23]

If an administrator protests about institutional rules, you can abide by the requirements *and* find other ways to supplement grading with formative feedback. At the University of Missouri College of Education, Rosalie Metro, an assistant teaching professor, has come up with a responsible, professional, and inspiring alternative form of grading. Teaching nearly a hundred students a year who will go on to become teachers themselves, Metro has to ensure that her students meet state certification standards. Instead of allowing those standards to work against her students, she has designed a humane standards-based assessment, which she uses for both her online and on-site courses. In certifying teachers of English as a second language, she incorporates the competencies required by the Missouri Department of Elementary and Secondary Education in her "standards-based" form of grading.

In her "assessments *for* learning" approach, students' comprehension and understanding of the skills needed to fulfill the state's teacher competencies are assessed during the learning and teaching process, not after it. Instead of a summative grade on assignments, she gives students feedback on whether they are "developing toward, meeting or exceeding learning targets (e.g., adapting a lesson plan to meet the needs of emergent bilinguals / English learners)." Those who meet or exceed the learning targets are finished. Their work is complete. No additional work is required. For those still developing, Metro offers support and opportunity for revision to improve their work. She also uses a range of other activities, including discussion boards, quizzes, and lesson plans to help them acquire the skills necessary for certification. She assesses those separately, giving feedback not only on outcomes but on process and work habits such as meeting deadlines, professionalism in communicating with fellow students, and so forth.[24]

Metro's logic is clear: if her students—future teachers themselves—achieve proficiency in all that the state certification board says they should, then a separate, high-stakes, one-off graded exam adds only anxiety.

Grades Encourage Cheating

Another institutional byproduct of traditional grading warrants our attention here: cheating. When all that counts for a student is a grade, that both cheats the student and, inevitably, encourages cheating and cutting corners. Paper mills, where customers (students) pay for someone else to write a paper for them, know this. Indeed, the same companies that employ freelance writers to write papers for students also contract with companies that sell automated plagiarism-detection systems such as Turnitin to make sure their products pass another customer's (an institution's) cheat test. In the words of John Warner, author of *Why They Can't Write,* this broken model has reached "peak absurdity." Not incidentally, paper mills also pay their writers better than most universities compensate the average adjunct professor. One week of paper writing, in some cases, amounts to half a semester's salary for an adjunct.[25] Where is the incentive to grow as students and to grow as educators?

Nik Valdez, an adjunct instructor in the Writing Across the Curriculum program at the City College of New York, has designed an intriguing response to dishonesty: they use formative feedback and a form of "light" contract grading in a course that emphasizes decolonial and nonbinary gender principles. Valdez does not grade the three writing assignments for the semester except for Pass / No Credit. They allow every student to revise, talk with them about feedback, and revise and resubmit a paper as many times as they wish. Additionally, Valdez invites students to recommend a different assignment and a different structure if the timeframe, type of writing, or anything else does not work for them. They insist that "finding a voice" is the objective in the course, and so they make every part of the learning process negotiable—except plagiarism. Using someone else's "voice" violates the overt "compact" or community-based "social contract" of the course. Since everything else is in process and since students are given a free hand in that process, Valdez finds that students have no reason to cheat, and they do not.

Contract Grading

When contract grading is fully built into the foundations of a class, the instructor presents a student with an actual contract that lists all the different requirements in a course and posits final grades a student can achieve by successfully completing part or all of the required work. Students sign up for the grade they aspire to achieve. If they satisfactorily complete that work, then they have fulfilled the contract and earn the grade.

In the world beyond school, this is how contracts work. One party commits to do certain work and the other pays if the work is completed to satisfactory standards. If you contract with a plasterer and they do a shoddy job, with poor workmanship, failure to meet the deadline, and gypsum chalk tracked across the carpet, they aren't paid the full amount. If they do fine work, on time, and under ideal conditions, they are paid in full. If the work is extraordinary, they might even receive a tip or bonus.[26] It's not much different in a course, with requirements spelled out and agreed to, with a result (a grade) guaranteed if the work is satisfactory.[27]

Why a contract? Contract grading alleviates some of students' grade anxieties and allows them to focus on the content and methods of a course rather than worrying over why they earned a 93 percent A instead of a 98 percent A. Instructors who have never tried contract grading often assume no one will ever aspire to less than an A. That's not true. I (Cathy) once had a student contract for a C because they were an athlete and it was the season of their sport; they were also the lead in a play at the university. As a graduating senior with a job already lined up, they did not need an A, so they contracted to do enough of the assignments to earn a C, which also allowed them to choose assignments that did not conflict with a big game or opening night. This student did such superb work on the assignments that I tried to give a higher grade. They refused it. They believed in the integrity of our contract and did not want a grade higher than they felt they had earned. Instead, I gave them—this "C student"—one of the best reference letters I've ever given a student.

Professor Deborah Jenson, a French and global health professor at Duke University who has led several Health Humanities Lab ventures, tried contract grading for the first time in a Romance Studies course (taught in English with a French preceptorial section) cross-listed in Global Health, mostly taken by premed STEM majors. Most contracted for A's because that's what worked for their chosen career demands for entry into medical school. What she found remarkable, though, was, once they knew what was contractually required for their A, the classroom dynamic changed. They spoke up more, were more confident talking about critical theory and philosophy, and delved into difficult philosophers such as Michel Foucault and Robert Esposito they might otherwise have shunned. Rather than being competitive, students repeatedly spoke of their respect for and excitement over the work of students doing presentations, peer leadership, and peer assessment of the satisfactoriness of others' work. They were less defensive, were less inclined to put down what they were learning as "gibberish," and took the work seriously. They were engaged.

Without anxiety, they had no need to be dismissive. They could, simply, learn.

Giving students more autonomy is *not* about cutting corners—not for us, not for them.

Contract grading, combined with peer review, works well at any kind of institution and with any level of course. Between the two of us, we've used contract grading in a highly diverse middle school after-school program class with students who have learning and attention issues; at an Ivy League and other elite universities; at a liberal arts college; at public universities in the South, Northeast, and Midwest; at a community college; and in a doctoral course. We offer one other institutional caveat. Size *may* matter. Neither of us has used contract grading in a course with more than forty-five students. We have, however, interviewed or observed instructors who have done it with far more students. Professor Courtney J. Sobers Swindell, assistant teaching professor of chemistry at Rutgers University in Newark, New Jersey, teaches first-and second-year chemistry courses, General Chemistry Lab, and Organic Chemistry Lecture, with between one hundred and five hundred students enrolled at one time. These often are considered the "flunk-out" courses for premed or prenursing students. Sobers Swindell offers her students a form of contract grading, including a combination of peer teaching units and "concept quizzes" that students are allowed to retake an unlimited number of times. Her students hope to have perfect grades on the way to applying for health professional school. Sobers Swindell acknowledges that while some value these alternative methods, others fear them and worry that their grades will suffer. They'd rather cram for the traditional midterm and final exams, as they've done successfully throughout their career.

Sobers Swindell helps students understand that the grade is never all that matters for medical school. "I tell students that if they don't do well, it gives them a story to discuss [at their medical school interviews]. Why didn't you do well? What about the teaching methods forced you to grow as a learner? Did your academic performance in the subject improve? Did your academic performance in other subjects improve because of general skills learned in the course?" As she notes, if she did her job in the way she intended, her students "learned chemistry on the way to learning how to be a lifelong learner when you're not in a classroom."[28]

Peer Badging—Online and Off

Contract grading takes the guesswork out of what students are required to do for a grade. In the terminology of Asao Inoue, professor of rhetoric and composition at Arizona State University, it is "labor-based grading." Students complete the work in a satisfactory fashion, fulfill the terms of the contract, and then receive the grade for which they contracted. Simple. But how do you, as their instructor, decide what counts as satisfactory work?

Let's circle back to the plasterer analogy. If there are cracks and bare spots, missed deadlines, and chalk dust ground into the carpet, it is obvious to everyone that the contract was not satisfactorily fulfilled. But what about a mediocre job, with no real flaws but also nothing exceptional? Who determines if that is "satisfactory"? If we simply assume that judgment is an instructor's prerogative, we end up back in the top-down, teacher-to-student mode of transmitting information in one direction. Ambiguity is mitigated by the contract but not solved by it.[29]

Peer badging is one way of inviting students to decide quality without being in the untenable (and potentially unethical) position of grading and judging their peers. This method has both egalitarianism and excellence at its core. Students collectively create a list of all the characteristics of exemplary work, either as individuals or in collaborative projects. Students reward exemplary work. They don't say what is "bad," and they certainly don't fail one another.[30] In groups, if they note a partner is doing something exceptional, they give it a badge. Each person then can see all those areas where their peers think their work is admirable. If there's a long list of characteristics that no one has chosen to badge, that's the best feedback they need to consider where they might improve or where they might follow up with questions to aid that process.

Peer badging can easily be adapted to the in-person or online classroom. The method was originally developed, decades ago, by open-source computer programmers to counter the problem of anonymity in freelance, online collaborative projects. When coders sought global partners (sometimes even partners who did not speak the same language), they needed a way to verify that the person they would be working with could deliver what they promised. Résumés and letters of recommendation are notoriously inadequate and cumbersome. So developers began awarding badges to collaborators on sites like Stack Overflow (https://stackoverflow.com/). In addition to badges in specific technical areas, other developers could see a number of badges awarded for character traits invaluable in collaborations. Some of the terms used: "altruist," "benefactor," "curious," "tenacious," "organizer," and "Socratic."[31]

Peer badging has been used extensively by gamers as well as for commercial purposes. In 2005, the video game industry, led by Microsoft's Xbox 360 Gamerscore badging system, adapted video game achievement systems to those playing video games so participants could easily initiate gameplay with other gamers who shared their interests and skill levels. Around the same time, a parallel method was developed into an algorithm by Amazon researchers in the now familiar "readers who like X, might also like Y" format.[32]

In 2007, Dr. Eva L. Baker, president of the American Educational Research Association, encouraged educators to think about these evaluation methods. She advocated adaptations of the peer-badging achievement system as a way to recognize and credential skills that students and lifelong learners had gained in their extracurricular activities, a way of augmenting schoolwork with a variety of life experiences.[33] Soon after, online tutoring programs, including Khan Academy and P2PU, two nonprofit online educational organizations, adopted digital badge systems to give credit to those completing their free, online courses.[34]

When I (Cathy) introduce peer badging to my students, they typically take to it with alacrity. I ask students to develop their own categories for evaluating what we do together in class, especially in collaborative projects. What matters in your work? What matters in successful collaboration? These categories might include: "originality of topic," "depth of research," "insight of thesis or argument," "persuasiveness," "clarity of the writing," "examples," "application," and the "significance of the project." For group work, they might include "timeliness," "ability to synthesize different points of view," "project management," or even "congeniality." By laying out all the qualities important to successful completion of the contracted work in a class (individual or group work), students think in advance about what is expected of them and of others.

The biggest dividend: students learn how to recognize and reward with clarity, developing standards as they go. They do not need to depend on the relative "failure" of anyone for the system to be useful. Instead, they can decide that their goals are achievement, accomplishment, and success—or perhaps a specific skill or badge they wish to develop most—and decide if and how each member of a team contributes to that collective mission.

How to Ungrade a Midterm or Final Exam

Although we prefer using alternatives to quizzes and tests to determine students' proficiency, we have each given our share of exams. In some ways, an entry or exit ticket might be considered a type of quiz depending on the prompt and if it counts toward students' final assessment. Likewise, discussion boards where students must demonstrate that they thought critically about the homework are another form of quizzing. However, in many situations, a midterm and a final are required by the instructor. Fortunately, many instructors have come up with ways to turn even traditional, timed, high-stakes, midterm or end-of-term exams into valuable learning experiences.

Dr. Siqi Tu, a postdoctoral fellow at the Max Planck Institute for the Study of Religious and Ethnic Diversity in Göttingen, Germany, has made it a practice in her sociology classroom to incorporate her students into the process of writing the final exam. By including them in the process, she creates an alternative assessment structure. Students become cocreators of the evaluation, determining what deserves their application and practice to demonstrate proficiency and what the markers for quality and success will be. This formative cograding structure allows students to decide, in advance, what does or does not get evaluated and how to measure the quality of what *is* evaluated.

For her collaborative examination project, each student prepares one short-answer question for each of the assigned readings prior to the exam. Students construct their own questions, provide their own correct answers, and identify what pages in the readings prompted them to ask their questions. Tu collects these and distributes them during an in-class review session, typically in the class meeting prior to the exam. Working in small groups, her class discusses each question and selects those they believe should be used to construct the examination. The professor chooses questions from these proposals, and the students take the exam in the next class meeting. In the process, students "put themselves in a professor's shoes," familiarize themselves with the course materials, report feeling "less stressed about the uncertainties of the exam," and acquire the skills they need to craft both good questions *and* good answers.[35]

The standard dictionary definition of a grade is "a mark indicating the quality of a student's work." In a typical "closed book" midterm or final, the grade is actually a mark indicating a student's ability to answer a question they haven't seen before without any assistance from outside sources. By having her students write the exam questions and argue about the best answers to those questions, she provides a deeper, more complex, and more transparent form of evaluation of how much students have learned.

Professor Jonathan Sterne, James McGill Chair in Culture and Technology at McGill University in Montreal, Canada, has devised an equally effective way to turn a traditional exam into a valuable learning process. He is the rare professor who reads books on pedagogy, cognitive neuroscience, and other fields that address learning and then incorporates the best ideas as practical solutions in his courses. He might have as many as six hundred students in a lecture course in acoustics or contemporary media. Some kind of "objective" final exam is required in a course of that size. He notes: "On the syllabus, I am completely clear about which evaluation methods are coercive (those I use to make them keep up with the reading and material) and which are creative (where they must analyze, synthesize and make ideas their own)." He wants students to reflect on those differences (itself an important pedagogical lesson), and then he works to make even the "coercive" exams pedagogically valuable. He insists that his "credo" is: "Multiple choice exams are an imperfect solution in an imperfect world. They can still have pedagogical value."[36]

He has come up with a number of brilliant workarounds that tick all the boxes of formative learning. One such workaround is inviting students to create a "crib" or study sheet for the course and bring it to the exam. They hand it in, signed, along with their final. Online, they upload it to the course tool as part of the exam. He likes to give each class specific instructions for their study sheets. In one, he might say all their information needs to fit on a large index card; in another, an 8½ × 11-inch sheet of paper, one side only.

What Sterne knows from the research is that the real learning happens in figuring out how to organize all of the term's content on that crib sheet. That's a very different cognitive exercise than cramming for a final. Since the 1880s experiments of the "forgetting curve" conducted by Hermann Ebbinghaus and replicated numerous times in the last

150 years, we know that when we memorize something for a high-stakes event (like a final exam), we forget as much as 75 percent of the content within days after the test is over.[37] By contrast, the more often we retrieve information, the more likely we are to learn it, remember it, and have it available in the future, to be adapted to different situations.[38] In both Tu's and Stern's alternative assessments, students are *required*—by design—to retrieve and even assess information multiple times, guiding them toward better, more effective study habits. From making the study sheet, Stern's students review what they've learned, synthesize it on a page, and even go through the metacognitive thinking about how best to represent it so that it is useful during the exam. All of those mental functions aid retention and help students to learn more about how they learn best—an invaluable life skill.

Sterne learns from those study sheets, too. He observes several hundred different ways that people organize knowledge, anticipating what he will ask on the final, and the areas they might have the most difficult time remembering. For some, it might be a list of dates or proper names; for others, complex theoretical concepts; for still others, statistics. The recurring patterns he sees in the crib sheets help him be a better teacher, too. If nearly every student is writing out quotes and concepts from Gilles Deleuze, he might, the next time he teaches the course, spend more time on Deleuze. Or, if there is a common mismatch between what students put on their study sheets and the questions he asks, he might do a better job explaining the exam the next time he teaches the course. The study sheets also help him to see how hard individual students have prepared for an exam and how much they have studied. He never lowers a grade because of a sketchy crib sheet (some students don't learn that way and don't need them, so theirs tend to be rather minimalist). He does learn, though, whether a student who fails is doing so because of lack of preparation (that is, a sketchy study sheet) or is a differently abled learner who might be brilliant and understands and knows the material but is not able to translate that competence into a bubble test. He often reaches out to those students and offers the study sheet and possibly an extra essay question as an alternative method.

Lately, Sterne has gone even further in his experimentation. In some recent online courses during the COVID-19 crisis, he has adopted a system he calls "open everything": students can consult any book they want, ask friends, get help, and even do online searches for answers. However, he advises them to still make a condensed study sheet for the exam since there won't be time for an extended search for every answer. Interestingly, he has found that the test scores have improved less than 0.5 percent in his "open everything" exams—but anxiety is minimized.[39]

Other instructors have come up with ways of assessing and enhancing student learning. Professor Virginia Yonkers, who teaches technology and organizational psychology and communications at the University at Albany, replicates a final exam form that she picked up from her own economics professor when she was a student.[40] She uses this method both on-site and online. She gives students a multiple-choice exam and offers them the option of writing an explanation of why they chose the answer they did. She tells students before the exam that she will offer full credit for either circling the right answer or giving a great, thoughtful explanation for an answer even if they circled a wrong one.

In the methods of these professors, thinking about thinking—metacognition—is an implicit part of the students' exam preparation. "What—from all we studied this term—do I need to write down before taking Professor Sterne's multiple-choice exam?" "Why did I choose this answer to Professor Yonkers's question?" "What's going on in your life on the other side of the computer screen?" Formative feedback is not about "making the grade." Rather, it's about students learning. It's about helping our students to thrive, in the classroom and beyond.

Retrieval in Practice

Catherine Denial, Bright Distinguished Professor of American History, Chair of the History Department, and Director of the Bright Institute at Knox College in Galesburg, Illinois

Catherine Denial has designed ways to structure multiple occasions in which students are required to recall or retrieve information and apply what they remember (see https://catherinedenial.org/blog/uncategorized/ungrading-in-a-pandemic/). She instituted two sets of short-answer questions to which her students responded each week. The first, due every Monday, asked students to engage in retrieval practice by sharing three things they remembered as important from the week before. The second, due the morning of their weekly Zoom session, asked students to reflect on the week's readings by articulating what new things they learned, what the class should talk about that week, whether they were confused by anything, and whether they had anything else they wanted to share. Denial's question sets included extra room for students to free-write on anything else they wanted her to know and prompted students to share how much of the reading they had done—not to penalize or to judge them but to help Denial plan for class. Both sets of questions were ungraded, and yet everyone consistently, diligently filled them in. This allowed Denial to identify and email students who were having difficulty getting work done, who didn't understand some of the concepts in the reading, or who were struggling for any number of reasons. She also shared in students' delight as they discovered new information about the past and used their answers to shape discussions to make them cocreators of each class session. These weekly question sets initiated and maintained a constant flow of information back and forth between Denial and her students and established a relationship in which graded assignments were not the primary method of communication.

CHAPTER 12

What Could Possibly Go Wrong?

The young think that failure is the Siberian end of the line, banishment from all the living, and tend to do what I then did—which was to hide.

—JAMES BALDWIN

At a conference in Vancouver, Canada, we (Cathy and Christina) presented participatory learning methods to an engaged workshop of innovative educators. Our ideal audience. We felt pretty happy about our presentation, challenging hierarchies of knowledge and traditional methods of teaching and learning. When we were done, we asked for questions, and one person in the audience immediately shot up his hand: "I did the same thing you did, and it didn't work. I invited the students to come up with a syllabus, left the room, and when I came back, they'd done nothing. The experiment failed."

That's not what we expected—but "what we expected" is, itself, a formulation that needs to be tested. Others in the room were nodding their heads knowingly, as if they too had tried active learning once, discovered it didn't work, and returned to the safer shoals of the traditional lecture. We took a breath and then asked follow-up questions. That, again, is the method of participatory learning: to ask the "why" and "how" questions; to learn from mistakes and failure. Learning is a process, not an outcome—especially when there's resistance and especially when you think you're the "expert."

In the conversation that followed, we learned that this instructor had done *literally* what he said: with the best intentions to give his students the opportunity to transform the curriculum and make it theirs, he left the room. However, he left them without giving his students a solid foundation and sense of community, without offering them the insights and reflections about active learning that we have been stressing in this book. We suggested that his ambitions were great but, without a foundation and even a little scaffolding, it was not surprising that they would clam up, balk, or shut down.

Some students love the freedom of being given a choice, and others panic without detailed instruction. When things go wrong, we rebalance the scale between our oversight and student autonomy to offer students something closer to the middle. Some learners need help focusing, while others cannot wait to cut the reins. It's not easy to keep in mind every learner, especially when each is uniquely different. Encountering turbulence is normal, and all we need to do is readjust course.

Professorial resistance is another factor. The instructor in our audience communicated, through his facial expression and body language, that he himself was not convinced by active learning. Yet he was there at this conference and attended a panel on "The Classroom as Training Ground for Digital Democracy." We had to wonder if, despite all the negativity, he might be leaving himself (and us) a second chance. We've all been there when a class suddenly takes a tailspin.

We asked other participants if they had also experienced failures and what they had done in those moments. We invited them to share failures and recovery methods. We also asked why they were still interested in a panel on active learning even after they had experienced problems in their own classrooms. The session became exceptionally lively and candid, with all of us sharing experiences, do-overs, and ideas about what corrections might work at different types of institutions and in different class sizes and levels. We may not have changed the grousing professor's mind that day, but the entire session felt more productive, interactive, and lively *because* of what had seemed like a roadblock.

Something similar happened a year later. At the height of the first wave in the COVID-19 pandemic, we were invited to give a presentation at an online learning conference to an audience of over two thousand international participants. Once again, we introduced a history of the traditional academy, talked about the importance of inventory methods, reflected on the value of reflection, and offered examples of successful, effective, interactive online learning methods, from Think-Pair-Share to ungrading. As we spoke, the chat window on our video conferencing tool filled up with report after report of failed attempts at active learning via Zoom or other digital platforms. From this back-channel conversation, one would have thought it was impossible to engage students actively online.

So we turned the Zoom camera around, so to speak, from us to the audience. Instead of telling them what to do, we wanted to show them how online participation can flourish. We finished our presentation with a slide that read "Your turn" and invited all 2,000-plus participants to take 90 seconds (no more) to jot out their single best tip for engaging students online in the same chat box where negativity had prevailed. Suddenly the chat space shifted from grumbling and critique to energy and excitement. It seemed everyone had at least one tip to contribute to the group. The success stories on the screen sped by so quickly it was literally impossible to read them all in time. We pledged to save the chat and make it available to the attendees.

We learned many things from these two encounters. First, if the idea of failure makes our students want "to hide," in James Baldwin's words, it also makes us, as instructors, fearful and hesitant too. It's intimidating to give up the traditional learning methods by which we succeeded when we were students, that we're accustomed to using in our classrooms, and that are rewarded by our institutions. The yardsticks by which we measure an instructor's success—student evaluations, colleague observation—are too often harsh, summative, and surveillant.

To make a change to radical pedagogy in the face of rigid judgment can be terrifying.

From these two conferences, we also learned just how much success depends on more than explaining *why* participatory learning works. We also needed to invite participation in order to demo participatory learning's merits as a method and show how the fellow educators we were addressing had already succeeded. By doing what we were advocating—soliciting 100 percent participation—we were able to create a more egalitarian space even in the singularly top-down hierarchical atmosphere of an academic conference. In this chapter, we focus on a few examples of what we can do when things go wrong. For nearly every participatory class we teach or hear about from colleagues, there is originally some minority of students who resent being unsettled. When we listen to those students, it becomes clear how important trust and community are to guiding students into something new and challenging that might even contradict the modes in which they've been taught most of their lives. We are asking students to take a leap of faith and have to earn their trust to take it together.

Sometimes, those students—and colleagues, too—can't make the change. In fact, there are better and worse times for change: when our environment is in flux, keeping some things the same can provide a degree of relief, comfort, and security. We witnessed this during the COVID-19 pandemic when we would ask students to work through a problem together in breakout rooms and some would suddenly report a bevy of tech problems that precluded their joining the group. Even for the greatest teachers in the world, sometimes the mysterious chemistry that makes a class great just doesn't happen. Sometimes even Think-Pair-Share, the wonder drug of participatory learning, fails to spark inspiration. It's hard at those moments to remember that from failure comes learning. To get ourselves unstuck when that happens, we try to take a three-pronged approach, though sometimes only one or two of the three is needed: reflection on what's not working; specific attention to the problem; and a platform for all present to contribute to a solution. Like an athlete trying to correct a weakness or achieve the next level of success in the field, in the pool, or on the court, growing as a great, engaged teacher requires practice, practice, practice.

We can all learn from "teaching fails."[1] A growth mindset applies to everyone, including educators.

In this chapter:

What to Do When Nobody Does the Homework
Learning from Failure and Regaining Student Trust
Getting It Right 85 Percent of the Time

What to Do When Nobody Does the Homework

There appears to be an invisible fork in the road when we encounter a silent classroom and it seems like no one did the homework. We often assume it is up to us, as instructors, to decide which pedagogical path to take, whether to respond with anger or kindness. Depending on the circumstances, we might decide it is the students who have done wrong—after all, the required homework was on the syllabus—or we might blame ourselves, figuring that we misjudged the workload or over-assigned during midterms or holidays. There is, however, a third option: bringing students into the solution rather than shouldering this burden ourselves.

Our surefire go-to process whenever students sit in stony silence: we ask students what they need. We next ask them what's the best way to address that need.

We like to use an anonymous inventory method—entry / exit tickets with index cards when face to face or a poll if online. We ask low-stakes but real questions such as: "What did you think about this week's assignment? Too long? Too hard? Too boring?" Ninety seconds. Anonymous. No grades. Low stakes. Follow-up question: "What do you think would make a better assignment for next class?"

We can't know what's misfiring unless we ask. The more we ask, the more students know their input makes the class a success and is not meant to be a confession of their inadequacy or failure. The lower the stakes of an inventory method, the better the solutions. "It sounds like no one's doing the reading because I'm assigning way too much reading," I (Cathy) said, reading yet another index card with that message out loud to one class. Everyone laughed, and the relief was palpable—including my own.

This was many years ago, in the introductory, general education "digital literacy" course I taught in a brand-new program at Duke University that I had helped to design called "Information Studies and Science." I could not have been more excited. The class was a mix of computer science and engineering students as well as digital arts, humanities, media studies, and social science students. Most of the articles we were reading were pre-prints, exciting new work with new ideas written by and for computational scientists trying to think about the social and human aspects of such things as social networks (new at the time) and artificial intelligence or algorithmic bias. It was cutting-edge work, a new field, and we were reading the smartest new thinkers in the world. I had steeped myself in this work. I was so thrilled by this course and new program that I couldn't wait to share my enthusiasm with these adventurous students willing to take a class in an entirely new cross-disciplinary program.

But I had a head start on this new way of thinking. The students didn't. Excited, I had assigned the same amount of reading I would have in a more typical course. I hadn't adjusted for the newness of the field with all of its geeky insider terminologies. "Algorithmic bias"? Students barely knew what an "algorithm" was. Affordances, RAM, ROM, plug and play, DIY, hypertext, collaboratory, mock-up, dyadic ties, hacker? All these terms seem more common now than they did in 2001. Even "social network" was a new term—MySpace, the predecessor to Facebook, hadn't been invented yet. The students couldn't even look up the terms in Wikipedia—it hadn't launched.

"For next week, what if we read one paper, not three? Even better, let's vote on which of last week's readings we want to reread for next week's class," I suggested. "And let's discuss some of the terminology first." The students applauded. *Literally.*

The magic of the index cards is that everyone counts—yet no one student is accountable. These were smart, adventurous students in a brand-new program. They didn't want to seem like failures. They didn't want me to feel like one either! No one wanted to say that they were having a hard time understanding the readings. Those index cards allowed them to save me.

Learning from Failure and Regaining Student Trust

If something goes wrong, inclusive, low-stakes inventory methods can turn a class around. Exit tickets are especially effective in most participatory emergencies. A prompt might be: "Today's experiment would have gone better if . . ." or, with a light touch: "Everyone acted like a zombie in class today because . . ." Or, our go-to favorite, "If *I* had designed today's class, I would have . . ." It's almost impossible for students to pass up the opportunity to outshine their professor. All these on-the-spot solutions can save a class that's turned into a flop, but if we're being honest, we don't always think that fast on our feet. Sometimes a flop happens with only a few minutes left on the clock and there's no time to repair the damage. On those days, we often think of a solution only after class has ended. Any of the above methods can be adapted to a quick homework assignment emailed to students after the fact.

Alternatively, at the beginning of the next class, you might try a new 90-second entry ticket: "What would help you most at this juncture in the course? More time? Less homework? Office hours? Something else?" Students write more freely if the entry tickets are anonymous, although it can also work to invite students to sign their card (on a purely voluntary basis) if they want to use the opportunity to communicate their struggles with you directly and privately. Whether the class is small or large, you can speak to students' responses to address the most common pitfalls and difficulties. When students see us trying to help in whatever ways we can, it builds (or regains) their trust, even when we fumble.

One college biology professor—we won't say who—teaching a large introductory Biology I lecture class for nonmajors made the mistake of writing the first exam as if the room were full of premed students and biology majors. The class average was way below par. Both the students and the professor were shocked by the results. The big question was whether or not the students themselves (and, importantly to them, their grades) could recover. No retakes were allowed—retakes were not a standard practice in the department or at this particular private institution. Fortunately, the professor recognized there was a problem with the exam (and the textbook) and said so to the students. After handing back graded exams, the professor offered additional office hours and revised lecture presentations going forward to better prepare students for the next time around. When proctoring the next exam, the professor handed out chocolate, a nice gesture to lower stress levels. What's more, the students enjoyed activities during office hours, which took place in the lab and provided more time for hands-on, participatory learning. (We know this because one of us was a student in this class.) Many in the class decided to sign up for Biology II with the same professor.

Getting It Right 85 Percent of the Time

No one gets it right all of the time. No one.

Recently, I (Cathy) co-taught a pedagogy graduate course on transformative learning with Eduardo Vianna, a Brazilian expert on the esteemed Russian psychologist Lev Vygotsky. Vianna, a psychiatrist, had returned to graduate school after attaining an MD to earn a PhD in psychology.[2] We structured the course along participatory learning principles, laying them out in the first part of the first class. We used Vygotskian scaffolding and discussed the debates on the term and its practice. We challenged students to self-organize into groups and design four topical units for the last half of the class. And, good Vygotskians, we left the room so that the students could self-organize.

We did everything right, if I do say so myself. We had big sheets of poster paper mounted around the classroom with the dates for each of the group presentations in order to help students with scheduling. We had passed out sheets with potential individual assignments or "job descriptions" the different members of the group could choose, and we had suggested that they come up with mini-deadlines and check-ins before the actual date of their presentations to ensure that everyone was contributing to their project. All of the group and project management methods were carefully explained.

When we returned at the end of the hour, three of the four groups had their topics defined and group members were assigned to roles. They even had started on timelines with deliverables. However, the fourth group—including members of the class who had already shown themselves to be knowledgeable about the topic—had spent their time simply talking, without deciding on seemingly anything at all. Their giant white wall poster was blank. They said, "We decided we'll all contribute to everything and we'll all figure out our topic together as we go along." I asked about their roles. "We don't approve of fixed 'roles,'" they insisted. "We're more *collaborative* and collective than that."

My heart sank. Having seen many amorphous groups fail, I worried that this project would never come together. Vygotsky's "zone of proximal development" ran through my mind. Maybe the members of this group really didn't need a formal structure to reach their full potential? Or maybe they were naive about the difficulties of collaborating on the fly.

To make a long story short, the three groups that had perfectly planned their group projects did wonderful work—as did the fourth group. The students had accurately assessed their compatible personalities, experience, knowledge, commitments, and temperaments. They didn't need the scaffolding or the hints and lessons and exercises we have described throughout Part II of this book. On the contrary, what they needed was an absence of constraint and the faith that they would make it right and succeed. They did.[3]

The important point here is that what works for some, doesn't work for others. What works beautifully in one course might not work at all in another.

Some students of Vygotsky have worked to quantify the insight that some small amount of failure is key to learning. We are more likely to learn when we have faltered than when we have eased to the finish line without a pause or a hitch. Some insist that 15 percent failure is ideal for maximum successful learning.[4] Whatever the percentage, some imperfection goes a long way. The students in the Vygotsky class showed us that, sometimes, scaffolding can limit and constrain rather than support learning. Sometimes, the best thing an instructor can do in participatory learning is *not* participate—back off and hand over the reins.

~

ONE KEY TAKEAWAY from these examples of teaching fails is that we, as instructors, have a lot more power in a classroom than we realize. When we give students autonomy, we have to trust them to be independent, even if it means failing a little some of the time. Recognizing that not everything is a win is especially hard for new teachers and those new to participatory learning.

Stumbling, even a little bit, is also difficult for students. When we instructors cede any degree of control, our students can hardly believe it. Some are suspicious when we change the norms. In their minds, we are the default authority, the default expert, and the best equipped in the room to lead. All it takes is one comment, one mark or erasure on a blackboard, a hint of skepticism, and, typically, students will look to the teacher in the room instead of searching, among themselves, for effective solutions. For truly transformative participatory learning to work, we have to prepare our students with clear expectations from the outset and then step away, while also giving them a platform (such as low-stakes inventory methods) for asking or showing us when they need our assistance.

Sometimes, magic happens in a classroom. Sometimes, no matter what we try, no matter how hard we work, a class never gels. I (Christina) taught two identical courses back-to-back and the one that met right after lunch was quiet as could be. When I asked my next class identical questions about identical homework assignments, it took work to get the groups to *stop* talking. My rowdy class met in a windowless basement room under clinically bright fluorescent lights, yet because I was their last class of the day, they were ready to engage with their peers. I called them my "happy hour" class. Learning flourishes even in imperfect settings and in unexpected ways, sometimes when the odds are most against it. The earlier class, which met in a sunny room with floor-to-ceiling windows, became my toughest challenge: my best, most fiery questions fell flat, which forced me to become an expert in planning and coordinating group work. *Fifteen percent.* Accepting some amount of imperfection is not only good learning theory for our students but is healthy as we evaluate ourselves as instructors too.

Active, participatory, radical learning is some combination of solidity and creativity, institutional constraint and rebelliousness, trial and error. The process of learning does not stop with a class that takes a wrong turn, nor does a temporary derailment mean we need to return to a hierarchical, traditional model of higher education. In fact, participatory methods, designed with students' learning at the core, are the most reliable and effective tools for pivoting and getting back on course. "Caring educators," bell hooks writes in *Teaching Community: A Pedagogy of Hope,* "open the mind, allowing students to embrace a world of knowing that is always subject to change and challenge."[5] Many of those challenges happen in the classroom itself. We can model for our students how to overcome fear of shame or fear of failure by addressing our own fears.

Push yourself a little further than you dare. The purpose and ultimate goal of changing our classrooms and inviting students to become co-creators with us is to provide them with a sense of self, agency, and empowerment. Our teaching does not have to be perfect all the time. The best gifts we can offer our students are a set of tools to support their courage and a vote of confidence to try. We can model that boldness too, by giving ourselves, as instructors, the freedom to change and try something new even if it means getting it right only 85 percent of the time.

Conclusion

Changing the World

It always seems impossible until it's done.

—NELSON MANDELA

"What if we are the people we are waiting for?"

We end this book with this crucial question and challenge posed by Radical Hope, an initiative by a network of educators dedicated to finding beneficial environmental policies and solutions. They come from universities around the world—Athens, Austin, Belfast, Cape Town, Caquetá, Dublin, London, Munich, Taichung—and are convinced that, by working together, by pooling the abundant resources of our universities, labs, archives, think tanks, and observatories, we have the ability not just to change the world but maybe even to save it.

They call their effort "Radical Hope" because they want to affirm the potential of change, not perpetuate the language of crisis. They invite all of us anywhere—scientists working with humanists, policymakers alongside technology designers—to join this effort. Their starting point is an open-access, free, crowdsourced global syllabus created by educators, students, and dedicated citizens and designed to make available great ideas, resources, and successful practices that can be replicated and furthered the world over. As it says in their "Full Syllabus," "We have all the technology, policies, and resources we need to create a more hopeful, sustainable future."[1]

Impressive. Yet can academics really move from theory to actual practice, from the classroom to the world? The answer is yes, and yes again.

What if we are the people we are waiting for?

Taking charge, making a change, using all of our years of specialized education, all of our well-honed research skills, we are capable of changing ourselves, our classrooms, and, yes, even the world.

In 2018, a coalition of US and Latin American academics responded to raids on undocumented peoples living in the United States. Calling their project "Torn Apart / Separados," this loose, transnational network of academics organized via the phone app Telegram in a mere six days to respond to the "Zero Tolerance Policy" suddenly instituted by US Immigration and Customs Enforcement (ICE).[2] The ICE policy was meant to block asylum seekers at the various ports of entry in the United States. In reality, children were being separated from parents, disappeared seemingly without a trace. An instant coalition of concerned academics rapidly combined information available in public archives to locate and amass information and find ways to alert local activists to what they could do to find, track, and, ideally, reunite these families. Publicity was one goal of this project, as was disseminating accurate data to dozens of ally and aid organizations in the United States, Mexico, El Salvador, and elsewhere that would help them reunite children and parents and focus media attention on some of the worst abuses of this international humanitarian crisis.

What if we are the people we are waiting for?

A simple list of transformative projects academics are undertaking around the world would be longer than this book. We need look no further than the COVID-19 pandemic to see the greater public good of higher education.

No vaccination has ever before been created in such a short timeframe. It took wide-scale collaboration to make it happen—scientists, policymakers, health care providers, doctors and nurses, supply chain experts, many different kinds of manufacturers and experts in cold-storage shipping. In the United States, the National Institutes of Health (NIH) launched a public-private collaborative endeavor called the Accelerating COVID-19 Therapeutic Interventions and Vaccines (ACTIV) partnership to speed the development and clinical trials for viable vaccinations against the virus. Both the pooling of resources from public and private investors as well as the call for clinical researchers to swiftly share results were unprecedented. The effectiveness of the global, interconnected response may have established a collaborative framework that would quicken our responses to future pandemics.[3]

Usually in academia it's a crisis when you find someone else is working on the same research you are. In this case, a willingness to share results from labs working independently on the same problem may be saving the world. We are stronger, more efficient, and more successful when we work together.

What if we are the people we are waiting for?

Instead of hand-wringing over the various crises of education, in this book we have offered many small and large ideas for transforming your classroom with the goal of helping your students to transform their lives—and with, ultimately, the greatest goal of contributing to a more just society. Social innovation. What universities, at their best, are designed for.

Our current moment is ripe for bringing new and original ideas into our teaching practices and using them both in and outside the classroom to transform higher education. As we emerge from a global pandemic and yet totter on the edge of climate, political, and economic pandemonium, universities offer the next generation forms of training, knowledge, skills, confidence, and connection to address problems, and even solve them, no matter how daunting.

What if we are the people we are waiting for?

The human story behind the developers of the first COVID-19 vaccine is one parable of higher education's promise and an example of how excellence, efficiency, and equity go hand in hand when the goal is knowledge for the public good. Uğur Şahin, the lead in developing one of the major vaccines used to fight COVID-19, is the son of Turkish immigrants who moved to Cologne, Germany, where his father worked in a Ford factory. His father was one of 2.5 million Turkish "guest workers" recruited to Germany as cheap, temporary migrant labor.

As a boy, Şahin was a dedicated and diligent student. He was the only Turkish student at his primary school. At first, his teachers recommended him for the *Hauptschule,* the vocational track for those who aren't "college material." Due to the intervention of a neighbor who recognized the boy's promise, Şahin went on to *Gymnasium,* the most advanced of Germany's three tiers of secondary school. From there he attended the University of Cologne, where he earned a medical degree. He met his future wife, Özlem Türeci, another Turkish immigrant, at Saarland University in Homburg. The couple continued to teach and conduct research on molecular medicine and immunology until 2001, when they created a company, BioNTech, with their former university professor, Christoph Huber, an Austrian cancer specialist who taught at the Johannes-Gutenberg University Mainz.

Şahin and Türeci not only were key to developing the COVID-19 Pfizer vaccine but have also been significant in developing individualized cancer treatments. Their research may also lead to a vaccine for HIV-AIDS. One principle that they have reiterated is the need for international cooperation, information sharing, and research for the public good. Not coincidentally, although they do significant amounts of pro bono work and are dedicated philanthropists, they have also become the first Turkish guest workers to be among Germany's hundred wealthiest people.[4]

Their story reminds us of the incredible good that is possible in higher education. Yet it is always the case that exceptions do not prove the rule. In order for more forms of collaboration to happen, much needs to change. The good news is that we already know what works, what doesn't, what we should be fighting for in higher education, and what is simply legacy infrastructure, designed over a hundred years ago, for a different time and place, and no longer useful for the world we live in now.

What if we—you, your college, your colleagues, all of us—are the people we have been waiting for?

Virtually every college and university mission statement presents our values in the loftiest terms. What if we treated our mission statements like higher education's learning outcomes? What if we engaged in a little backwards planning and redesigned our universities to align everything we do with those statements? We would be looking at a truly transformed higher education if we simply did what we say we do.

Many universities around the world see their mission as offering a benefit to their local communities and beyond. For instance, Sorbonne Université's strategic plan includes: "Acting in a Global World," "Participating Fully in Open Science, Digital, and Data Revolutions," and "Understanding, Learning, and Entrepreneurship in a Changing World."[5] That kind of global engagement is sharply focused on publishing for a public audience and using and creating open-source resources—the opposite of hoarding information to publish only for individual credit and gain. The University of Delhi frames its own mission statement as a commitment to "acting as a catalyst in shaping a bright and sustainable future of our nation and that of the whole world by acting as a bridge between the University community and the community at large." A fulfillment of that promise at every level would include making environmental sustainability a university-wide priority and hiring and rewarding service to the community as much as, if not more than, research.

Or consider the mission statement of Texas A&M University, one of the largest public universities in the United States. Texas A&M dedicates itself to the preparation of students "to assume roles in leadership, responsibility and service to society. Texas A&M assumes as its historic trust the maintenance of freedom of inquiry and an intellectual environment nurturing the human mind and spirit. It welcomes and seeks to serve persons of all racial, ethnic and geographic groups as it addresses the needs of an increasingly diverse population and a global economy."

This is a worthy mission for all of higher education. Diversity is too often mistaken as sufficient change, without revolutionizing the core curriculum or business structure. It feels like hypocrisy—and it is. To truly enact it would mean hiring a more diverse body of faculty whose lived experiences mirror those of our students. Most importantly, the university would need to devote more resources and funds to those faculty to give them the authority, time, and bandwidth to help reshape and transform the academy. Anything less, quite simply, falls short of our goals.

If every university followed these missions—of purpose, invention, innovation, discovery, diversity, inclusion, inquiry, intellectual freedom, nurturing the human mind and spirit, internationalism, creativity, leadership, the future—higher education would have its priorities straight.

Unfortunately, most universities worldwide are structured less to reflect the goals we announce in our mission statements and strategic plans than to trumpet such things as "citation counts" on research papers. The disconnect between our mission statements and our rewards for faculty (as teachers or as community and institutional citizens) are yet another product of being stuck with an inheritance that is, in today's world, irrelevant to our students' needs. Perhaps no college president addressing a board of trustees, potential donors, or a state educational committee has ever—*ever!*—used faculty citation count to argue for increased funding or a large contribution to the institution's endowment. Citation count is not what inspires the students we recruit, nor the public we wish to inspire.

All this sounds like a lesson plan for the New College Classroom. What comes after transformation in our classrooms? Once we have changed ourselves, once we have changed our classrooms, we need to change our institutions and workplaces to have an impact on society as a whole. It's that simple and that complicated if our ultimate ambition (as our mission statements proclaim) is to change the world.

We can do this.

We are the people we've been waiting for.

NOTES

ACKNOWLEDGMENTS

INDEX

Notes

Introduction

1. Sarah D. Sparks, "Getting Feedback Right: A Q&A with John Hattie," *Education Week*, June 19, 2018, www.edweek.org/ew/articles/2018/06/20/getting-feedback-right-a-qa-with-john.html.

2. Jay Howard and Roberta Baird, "The Consolidation of Responsibility and Students' Definitions of Situation in the Mixed-Age College Classroom," *Journal of Higher Education* 71 (2000): 700–721.

3. Scott Freeman et al., "Active Learning Increases Student Performance in Science, Engineering, and Mathematics," *Proceedings of the National Academy of Sciences* 111, no. 23 (2014): 8410–8415.

4. Freeman et al., "Active Learning."

5. E. J. Theobald et al., "Active Learning Narrows Achievement Gaps for Underrepresented Students in Undergraduate Science, Technology, Engineering, and Math," *Proceedings of the National Academy of Sciences* 117, no. 12 (2014): 6476–6483.

6. Mauricio Marrone, Murray Taylor, and Mara Hammerle, "Do International Students Appreciate Active Learning in Lectures?" *Australasian Journal of Information Systems* 22 (2018).

7. Freeman et al., "Active Learning."

8. Sarah L. Eddy and Kelly A. Hogan, "Getting under the Hood: How and for Whom Does Increasing Course Structure Work?" *CBE—Life Sciences Education* 13, no. 3 (2014): 453–468.

9. We have been collecting these examples for years, along with our esteemed colleague, Tatiana Ades, in a "Progressive Pedagogy" group that we created on HASTAC.org (www.hastac.org/groups/progressive-pedagogy-group). While we sample many in our book, we found more examples of innovative teaching than could possibly fit here, but the interviews that we and Ades conducted are available in full detail on the site.

10. Jal Mehta and Sarah Fine, *In Search of Deeper Learning: The Quest to Remake the American High School* (Cambridge, MA: Harvard University Press, 2019), 3–4, 24.

11. Steven L. Berg, Facebook post and personal correspondence, May 4 and 6, 2021. See also Berg, *Promoting Student Transformation at a Community College: If Everything Happens That Can't Be Done* (Manifold, 2020), https://cuny.manifoldapp.org/projects/promoting-student-transformation-at-a-community-college.

12. Robert B. Barr and John Tagg, "From Teaching to Learning—A New Paradigm for Undergraduate Education," *Change: The Magazine of Higher Learning* 27, no. 6 (1995): 12–26.

13. For an exhaustive survey of a wide range of these methods, see Coalition for Psychology in Schools and Education, "Top 20 Principles from Psychology for PreK–12 Teaching and Learning," American Psychological Association, 2015, www.apa.org/ed/schools/cpse/top-twenty-principles.pdf.

14. Alfie Kohn, "Progressive Education," *Alfie Kohn,* www.alfiekohn.org/article/progressive-education/.

15. Felicia Rose Chavez, *The Anti-Racist Writing Workshop: How to Decolonize the Creative Classroom* (Chicago: Haymarket, 2021); Henry Giroux, *On Critical Pedagogy,* 2nd ed. (London: Bloomsbury Academic, 2020); Max Liboiron, *Pollution Is Colonialism* (Durham, NC: Duke University Press, 2021); Bettina Love, *We Want to Do More Than Survive: Abolitionist Teaching and the Pursuit of Educational Freedom* (Boston: Beacon Press, 2019); Maria Popova, "Fixed vs. Growth: The Two Basic Mindsets That Shape Our Learning," January 29, 2014, www.brainpickings.org/2014/01/29/carol-dweck-mindset/; Sandy Grande, ed., *Red Pedagogy: Native American Social and Political Thought,* 10th anniv. ed. (New York: Rowman and Littlefield, 2015); Carla Shedd, *Unequal City: Race, Schools, and Perceptions of Injustice* (Russell Sage Foundation, 2015); Helen Verran, *Science and an African Logic* (Chicago: University of Chicago Press, 2001).

16. Christina Katopodis, "A Lesson Plan for Democratic Co-Creation," December 13, 2018, HASTAC, www.hastac.org/blogs/ckatopodis/2018/12/13/lesson-plan-democratic-co-creation-forging-syllabus-students-students; Christina Katopodis, "Writing Learning Outcomes with Your Students," February 19, 2019, HASTAC, www.hastac.org/blogs/ckatopodis/2019/02/19/writing-learning-outcomes-your-students.

17. Beverly Daniel Tatum, *Why Are All the Black Kids Sitting Together in the Cafeteria? And Other Conversations about Race,* 20th anniv. ed. (New York: Basic Books, 2017). See also Estela M. Bensimon, *Confronting Equity Issues on Campus* (Sterling, VA: Stylus, 2012).

18. Carl E. Wieman, "Active Learning with Carl E. Wieman: Don't Lecture Me," *Lindau Nobel Laureate Meetings,* November 24, 2019, www.lindau-nobel.org/blog-active-learning-with-carl-e-wieman-dont-lecture-me/.

19. Carl E. Wieman, *Improving How Universities Teach Science: Lessons from the Science Education Initiative* (Cambridge, MA: Harvard University Press, 2017), 6–7.

20. Wieman, "Active Learning."

21. Cathy N. Davidson, *Now You See It: How the Brain Science of Attention Will Change the Way We Live, Work, and Learn* (New York: Viking-Penguin, 2011).

22. Michel de Certeau, *The Practice of Everyday Life* (Berkeley: University of California Press, 1984).

23. Colleen Flaherty, "Required Pedagogy," *Inside Higher Ed,* December 13, 2019; "Graduate Programs Requiring Instruction in Teaching (Inc. For-Credit Courses)," crowd-sourced list, 2019, https://docs.google.com/document/d/1qAUVazIBzHgXp8VZwoEIUvQy7q05x3eEUX2zM2qQb_Y/edit.

24. Beth McMurtrie, "Why the Science of Teaching Is Often Ignored," *Chronicle of Higher Education,* January 3, 2022, https://www.chronicle.com/article/why-the-science-of-teaching-is-often-ignored.

25. Louis Deslauriers, Logan S. McCarty, Kelly Miller, Kristina Callaghan, and Greg Kestin, "Measuring Actual Learning versus Feeling of Learning in Response to Being Actively Engaged in the Classroom," *Proceedings of the National Academy of Sciences* 116, no. 39 (2019): 19251–19257.

1. Why Change Now?

1. On Charles Eliot, see Cathy N. Davidson, *The New Education: How to Revolutionize the University to Prepare Students for a World in Flux* (New York: Basic Books, 2017).

2. Morris Cooke, "Academic and Industrial Efficiency: A Report to the Carnegie Commission for the Advancement of Teaching," Carnegie Foundation for the Advancement of Teaching (1910; rpt. London: Forgotten Books, 2015).

3. For a more detailed discussion of late nineteenth-century educational reform, see Davidson, *New Education.*

4. Adam S. Cohen, "Harvard's Eugenics Era," *Harvard Magazine,* March–April 2016, www.harvardmagazine.com/2016/03/harvards-eugenics-era.

5. Among the many books and articles on these exclusionary practices, see Jerome Karabel, *The Chosen: The Hidden History of Admission and Exclusion at Harvard, Yale, and Princeton* (Boston: Houghton Mifflin, 2005).

6. "Paul Henry Hanus, 1855–1941," About Harvard Graduate School of Education, https://www.gse.harvard.edu/about/history/deans/hanus.

7. Davidson, *New Education,* 17–46; Jonathan Zimmerman, *The Amateur Hour: A History of College Teaching in America* (Baltimore: Johns Hopkins University Press, 2020).

8. Bruce Mau, *MC24: Bruce Mau's 24 Principles for Designing Massive Change in Your Life and Work* (New York: Phaidon Press, 2020), 90.

9. See Emma Dorn, Frédéric Panier, Nina Probst, and Jimmy Sarakatsannis, "Back to School: A Framework for Remote and Hybrid Learning amid COVID-19," McKinsey & Company, August 31, 2020, www.mckinsey.com/industries/public-and-social-sector/our-insights/back-to-school-a-framework-for-remote-and-hybrid-learning-amid-covid-19#; "How Countries Are Using Edtech (Including Online Learning, Radio, Television, Texting) to Support Access to Remote Learning during the COVID-19 Pandemic," World Bank, April 2, 2020, https://reliefweb.int/report/austria/how-countries-are-using-edtech-including-online-learning-radio-television-texting.

10. Leslie Davis and Richard Fry, "College Faculty Have Become More Racially and Ethnically Diverse but Remain Far Less So Than Students," Pew Research Center, July 31, 2019, www.pewresearch.org/fact-tank/2019/07/31/us-college-faculty-student-diversity/. Interestingly, the one ethnic group that was the exception were a category collectively grouped as "Asians" in this study, with "11 percent of professors and 7 percent of students." See also Colleen Flaherty, "Professors Still More Likely Than Their Students to Be White," *Inside Higher Ed,* August 1, 2019, www.insidehighered.com/quicktakes/2019/08/01/professors-still-more-likely-students-be-white.

11. Aaron Clauset, Samuel Arbesman, Daniel B. Larremore, "Systematic Inequality and Hierarchy in Faculty Hiring Networks," *Science Advances* 1, no. 1 (February 12, 2015): 1400005.

12. Robert Oprisko, "Superpowers: The American Academic Elite," *Georgetown Public Policy Review,* December 3, 2012, http://gppreview.com/2012/12/03/superpowers-the-american-academic-elite/.

13. Scholars of color face a range of other differences, biases, and attitudes (from both peers and students). For a superb analysis of the complexities of race and income inequality in higher education, see Anthony Abraham Jack, *The Privileged Poor: How Elite Colleges Are Failing Disadvantaged Students* (Cambridge, MA: Harvard University Press, 2019), 1.

14. For an excellent discussion of the social and racial inequality enacted through school defunding, see Noliwe M. Rooks, *Cutting School: Privatization, Segregation, and the End of Public Education* (New York: New Press, 2020).

15. Raj Chetty includes many studies he and his team are conducting on his website: www.rajchetty.com/.

16. "2021 Top Performers on Social Mobility: National Universities," *U.S. News and World Report,* www.usnews.com/best-colleges/rankings/national-universities/social-mobility, accessed June 10, 2021; "2021 Top Performers on Social Mobility: Regional Universities North," *U.S. News and World Report,* www.usnews.com/best-colleges/rankings/regional-universities-north/social-mobility, accessed June 10, 2021.

17. Kandice Chuh, "Pedagogies of Dissent for Asian American Studies," Thursday Dialogues, September 7, 2017, Futures Initiative, The Graduate Center, CUNY, Panel Presentation, www.hastac.org/opportunities/pedagogies-dissent-asian-american-studies.

18. Tia Brown McNair et al., *Becoming a Student-Ready College: A New Culture of Leadership for Student Success* (San Francisco: Jossey-Bass, 2016).

2. *Structuring Active Learning*

1. John Dewey made this statement often and in slightly varied forms, including in *My Pedagogic Creed* (1897) and *Democracy and Education* (1916).

2. Jerome S. Bruner, Jacqueline J. Goodnow, and George A. Austin, *A Study of Thinking* (New York: John Wiley and Sons, 1956).

3. David Wood, Jerome S. Bruner, and Gail Ross, "The Role of Tutoring in Problem Solving," *Journal of Child Psychiatry and Psychology* 17, no. 2 (1976): 89–100; Anat Ninio and Jerome Bruner, "The Achievement and Antecedents of Labelling," *Journal of Child Language* 5 (1978): 1–15.

4. Lev Vygotsky, *Thought and Language,* translated by Eugenia Hanfmann and Gertrude Vakar (Cambridge, MA: MIT Press, 1932).

5. Flower Darby and James M. Lang, *Small Teaching Online: Applying Learning Science in Online Classes* (San Francisco: Jossey-Bass, 2019), 12–13; James M. Lang, *Small Teaching: Everyday Lessons from the Science of Learning* (San Francisco: Jossey-Bass, 2016), 41–62.

6. Susana Claro, David Paunesku, and Carol S. Dweck, "Growth Mindset Tempers the Effects of Poverty on Academic Achievement," *Proceedings of the National Academy of Sciences* 113, no. 31 (2016): 8664–8668.

7. Steven M. Singer, "Six Problems with a Growth Mindset in Education," *Gadfly on the Wall,* August 12, 2019, https://gadflyonthewallblog.com/2019/08/12/six-problems-with-a-growth-mindset-in-education/.

8. Toby Young, "A Myth That Keeps Growing and Growing: 'Growth Mindset' Requires Children to Believe Something Demonstrably False," *The Spectator,* January 21, 2017, www.spectator.co.uk/article/a-myth-that-keeps-growing-and-growing.

9. For more on environmental factors, see David Moreau, Brooke N. Macnamara, and David Z. Hambrick, "Overstating the Role of Environmental Factors in Success: A Cautionary Note," *Current Directions in Psychological Science* 28, no. 1 (2019): 28–33.

10. For an excellent article summarizing the different theoretical positions (and even feuds) around mindset theory, see Lydia Denworth, "Debate Arises over Teaching 'Growth Mindsets' to Motivate Students," *Scientific American,* August 12, 2019; see also David S. Yeager et al., "A National Experiment Reveals Where a Growth Mindset Improves Achievement," *Nature* 573 (2019): 364–369.

11. Beronda L. Montgomery, *Lessons from Plants* (Cambridge, MA: Harvard University Press, 2021), 124–125.

12. Jennifer Goodman, "Trial and Error: Flipped Course Boosts Passing Rates to 80+ Percent," *Inside Higher Ed,* May 10, 2017, www.insidehighered.com/digital-learning/article/2017/05/10/trial-and-error-lehman-and-hunter-colleges-boost-chemistry.

13. Eric Mazur, *Peer Instruction: A User's Manual* (Upper Saddle River, NJ: Prentice Hall, 1997).

14. Craig Cameron and Jennifer Dickfos, "Peer Review of Teaching Law to Business Students in Traditional and Flipped Lecture Environments," in *Teaching for Learning and Learning for Teaching,* edited by Christopher Klopper and Steve Drew (Rotterdam: Sense, 2015), 99–116.

15. Goodman, "Trial and Error."

16. "Flipping the Classroom," *Economist,* September 17, 2011; Susan D. Blum, "Learning In and Out of School," *Susan D. Blum,* July 29, 2013, www.susanblum.com/blog/learning-in-and-out-of-school; Lauren Garcia and Tressie McMillan Cottom, "Why You Should Consider an 'Unconference' for Your Next Academic Meeting," *Chronicle of Higher Education,* February 24, 2020, www.chronicle.com/article/why-you-should-consider-an-unconference-for-your-next-academic-meeting/.

3. Teaching Is Mentoring

1. On modern applications of Greek mentorship, see B. R. J. O'Donnell, "*The Odyssey*'s Millennia-Old Model of Mentorship," *Atlantic,* October 13, 2017.

2. Christina Katopodis, “A Pedagogy of Self-Care for a Post-Pandemic Fall,” *Hybrid Pedagogy,* July 29, 2021, https://hybridpedagogy.org/pedagogy-of-self-care/.

3. bell hooks, *Teaching to Transgress: Education as the Practice of Freedom* (New York: Routledge, 1994), 13.

4. Maha Bali, “Pedagogy of Care—Gone Massive,” *Hybrid Pedagogy,* April 20, 2015, https://hybridpedagogy.org/pedagogy-of-care-gone-massive/; Maha Bali, “Pedagogy of Care: Covid-19 Edition,” *Reflecting Allowed,* May 28, 2020, https://blog.mahabali.me/educational-technology-2/pedagogy-of-care-covid-19-edition/.

5. See Yusef Waghid, *Towards a Philosophy of Caring in Higher Education: Pedagogy and Nuances of Care* (London: Palgrave MacMillan, 2019), 89–90.

6. Adashima Oyo, “The Last Page,” HASTAC, January 29, 2020, www.hastac.org/blogs/adashima-oyo/2020/01/29/last-page.

7. “Cornerstone Integrated Liberal Arts,” Purdue University, www.cla.purdue.edu/academic/cornerstone/index.html.

8. Tom Mullaney (@firstgenprofessor), “Your Prof WANTS to Meet You. Go to Office Hours,” TikTok, March 24, 2021, www.tiktok.com/@firstgenprofessor/video/6943287034123390214; see also Tom Mullaney, “How Academia Works,” YouTube, www.youtube.com/channel/UClgd2-Rsz-CAv0UqMKHZe8g.

9. Maryellen Weimer, “Office Hours Alternative Resonates with Students,” *Faculty Focus,* February 15, 2019, www.facultyfocus.com/articles/teaching-and-learning/office-hours-alternative-resonates-students/.

10. Sara Ahmed, *Complaint!* (Durham, NC: Duke University Press, 2021).

11. Sandy Grande, *Red Pedagogy: Native American Social and Political Thought* (Lanham, MD: Rowman and Littlefield, 2004), 19. See also Eve Tuck and K. Wayne Yang, “Decolonization Is Not a Metaphor,” *Decolonization: Indigeneity, Education & Society* 1, no. 1 (2012): 1.

12. Gabriella Gutiérrez y Muhs et al., eds., *Presumed Incompetent: The Intersections of Race and Class for Woman in Academia* (Logan: Utah State University Press, 2021).

13. Nicole Truesdell, “Black Lives, Black Women, and the Academy: ‘Doing’ Equity and Inclusion at PWIs,” in *Difficult Subjects: Insights and Strategies for Teaching about Race, Sexuality, and Gender,* edited by Badia Ahad-Legardy and OiYan A. Poon (Sterling, VA: Stylus Press, 2018), 139.

14. The Hope Center for College, Community and Justice, http://saragoldrickrab.com/research/; “The SEEK Program,” City College of New York, www.ccny.cuny.edu/financialaid/seek, accessed June 10, 2021; “The Percy Ellis Sutton SEEK Program,” City College of New York, https://www.ccny.cuny.edu/seek, accessed June 10, 2021; “SEEKing Opportunity for All CUNY Students,” CUNY Matters, November 22, 2019,

www1.cuny.edu/sites/matters/2019/11/22/seek/, accessed June 10, 2021; Alexis Gravely, "Help for Community College Students," *Inside Higher Ed,* July 8, 2021, www.insidehighered.com/news/2021/07/08/bill-provide-community-college-students-support-services-may-have-new-path-forward.

15. Kristen Gillespie-Lynch, "Is Universal Design Enough? Learning from the Neurodiversity Movement How to Engage Diverse Learners," Transformative Learning in the Humanities, City University of New York, March 26, 2021.

16. See also Stephen Shore, ed., *Ask and Tell: Self Advocacy and Disclosure for People on the Autism Spectrum* (Shawnee Mission, KS: Autism Asperger Publishing, 2004).

17. Todd McCullough, "Five Essential Mechanisms for Supporting Non-Traditional Student Success," *The EvoLLLution,* April 16, 2013, https://evolllution.com/opinions/essential-mechanisms-supporting-non-traditional-student-success/.

18. "Pioneer Connections," *Volunteer Community College,* www.volstate.edu/sites/default/files/documents/veterans/Pioneer_Connections_Faculty_Staff_Reference.pdf.

4. Before the First Class

1. For an extensive account of the history of "syllabus," see William Germano and Kit Nicholls, *Syllabus: The Remarkable, Unremarkable Document That Changes Everything* (Princeton, NJ: Princeton University Press, 2020).

2. Kevin Gannon offers a useful guide for navigating this balance in his advice guide: Gannon, "How to Create a Syllabus," n.d., *Chronicle of Higher Education* website, www.chronicle.com/interactives/advice-syllabus, accessed February 16, 2022.

3. For sample syllabi, see the Open Syllabus Project (https://opensyllabus.org/) founded at the American Assembly, which encompasses countless projects in all fields and worldwide.

4. Kathy Klein, associate professor of occupational therapy at Stockton University in Galloway, New Jersey, writes about her journey and how it transformed her classroom and made her whole course more engaging. See Kathy Klein, "Give Your Syllabus a Makeover and Watch Your Classroom Transform," *NOBA Blog,* March 6, 2019, https://nobaproject.com/blog/2019-03-06-give-your-syllabus-a-makeover-and-watch-your-classroom-transform.

5. Tona Hangen, "Extreme Makeover, Syllabus Edition," *Tona Hangen,* January 3, 2011, www.tonahangen.com/2011/01/syllabus-makeover/.

6. Hangen, "Extreme Makeover, Syllabus Edition."

7. Angela Jenks (@angelacjenks), "I've switched to using the interactive syllabus to walk students through the syllabus and ask them to respond. I set it up as a Canvas

survey so they get credit for completing it and I can respond directly to any questions they have." See *Twitter,* June 19, 2020, 2:33 p.m., https://twitter.com/angelacjenks/status/1274047553068130304?s=20.

8. Catherine Bovill, "Co-creation in Learning and Teaching: The Case for a Whole-Class Approach in Higher Education," *Higher Education* 79 (2020): 1023–1037, https://link.springer.com/article/10.1007/s10734-019-00453-w.

9. Peter Armbruster, Maya Patel, Erika Johnson, and Martha Weiss, "Active Learning and Student-Centered Pedagogy Improve Student Attitudes and Performance in Introductory Biology," *CBE Life Sciences Education* 8 (2009): 203–213; Jeannie D. DiClementi and Mitchell M. Handelsman, "Empowering Students: Class-Generated Course Rules," *Teaching of Psychology* 32 (2005): 18–21; Lisl Walsh, "Sample Day 1 Student-Led Syllabus Design," *EIDOLON,* July 11, 2016, https://eidolon.pub/sample-day-1-student-led-syllabus-design-8a7ae40e7325.

10. Biswas-Diener uses Harrison Owen's Open Space Technology as a model. Owen has applied self-organization methods to meetings of 5 to 2,000 people in 134 different countries. See Harrison Owen, *Open Space Technology: A User's Guide,* 3rd ed. (Oakland: Berrett-Koehler, 2008).

11. On constructing a learner-centered syllabus, see Aaron S. Richmond, "Constructing a Learner-Centered Syllabus: One Professor's Journey," *IDEA,* September 2016, www.ideaedu.org/Portals/0/Uploads/Documents/IDEA%20Papers/IDEA%20Papers/PaperIDEA_60.pdf.

12. Howard Rheingold, "Digital Journalism Workspace: Winter Quarter, 2010," *Social Media Classroom,* http://socialmediaclassroom.com/digitaljournalism09/.

13. Howard Rheingold, *Net Smart: How to Thrive Online* (Cambridge, MA: MIT Press, 2012).

14. "Credit," *NYS Higher Education Services Corporation,* June 27, 2020, www.hesc.ny.gov/partner-access/financial-aid-professionals/tap-and-scholarship-resources/tap-coach/31-credit.html.

15. Peter Jacobs, "Here's the Insane Amount of Time Student-Athletes Spend on Practice," *Business Insider,* January 27, 2015, www.businessinsider.com/college-student-athletes-spend-40-hours-a-week-practicing-2015-1.

16. "About the Open Syllabus Project," *Open Syllabus Explorer,* June 27, 2020, https://blog.opensyllabus.org/about-the-open-syllabus-project/.

17. bell hooks, *Teaching to Transgress: Education as the Practice of Freedom* (New York: Routledge, 1994), 13.

18. See Elizabeth Barre, "How Much Should We Assign? Estimating Out of Class Workload," Rice University Teaching and Learning Center, July 11, 2016, https://cte.rice.edu/blogarchive/2016/07/11/workload, accessed May 3, 2020; Alexander C. McCormick, "It's about Time: What to Make of Reported Declines in How Much Students

Study," *Liberal Education* 97, no. 1 (Winter 2011), www.aacu.org/publications-research/periodicals/its-about-time-what-make-reported-declines-how-much-college.

19. Some of the most engaging, innovative, and student-centered textbooks can be found in *Reacting to the Past,* a series of games developed by colleagues at Barnard College and beyond, published by W. W. Norton. Even better, participating in *Reacting to the Past* comes with access to a Facebook group for live support. The group is made up of experienced faculty who have run these games in their classrooms, and they offer generous support to those trying these games out for the first time. See "Published Games," *Barnard College: Reacting to the Past,* https://reacting.barnard.edu/games.

20. Joan Petersen and Susan McLaughlin, "Laboratory Exercises in Microbiology: Discovering the Unseen World through Hands-On Investigation," *CUNY Academic Works,* 2016, https://academicworks.cuny.edu/qb_oers/16.

21. Ke Xin, "Welcome to Help Your Math," *Help Your Math,* http://helpyourmath.com/.

22. Salomé Martínez, "A School Year from Home: How Chile Has Taught Math during the Pandemic," The National Academies of Sciences, Engineering, Medicine, July 23, 2020, www.nationalacademies.org/event/07-23-2020/a-school-year-from-home-how-chile-has-taught-math-during-the-pandemic#sectionEventMaterials; Alicia en el país de las probabilidades, Centro de Modelamiento Matemático (CMM), https://cmmedu.uchile.cl/innovaciones-para-el-aula/alicia-en-el-pais-de-las-probabilidades/.

23. Ilarion (Larry) Merculieff and Libby Roderick, *Stop Talking: Indigenous Ways of Teaching and Learning and Difficult Dialogues in Higher Education* (Fairbanks: University of Alaska Press, 2013), 12.

24. Audre Lorde, *"I Teach Myself in Outline," Notes, Journals, Syllabi & an Excerpt from* Deotha, edited by Miriam Atkin and Iemanjá Brown, *Lost and Found* 7, no. 1 (Fall 2017): 28.

25. Anne Gulick, personal correspondence, April 3, 2020.

26. Danica Savonick, "Timekeeping as Feminist Pedagogy," *Inside Higher Ed,* June 27, 2017, www.insidehighered.com/advice/2017/06/27/how-social-hierarchies-influence-who-gets-most-time-speak-classrooms-essay.

27. Christopher Karpowitz, Tali Mendelberg, and Lee Shaker, "Gender Inequality in Deliberative Participation," *American Political Science Review* 106, no. 3 (2012): 533–547. For a study of racial disparities in meetings and in collaborative work settings, see Drew S. Jacoby-Senghor, Stacey Sinclair, and J. Nicole Shelton, "A Lesson in Bias: The Relationship between Implicit Racial Bias and Performance in Pedagogical Contexts," *Journal of Experimental Social Psychology* 63 (2016): 50–55; Gabriella Gutiérrez y Muhs et al., eds., *Presumed Incompetent: The Intersections of Race and Class for Woman in Academia* (Logan: Utah State University Press, 2021); Mahajoy A.

Laufer, "Black Students' Classroom Silence in Predominantly White Institutions of Higher Education" (MA thesis, Smith College, Northampton, MA, 2012), https://scholarworks.smith.edu/cgi/viewcontent.cgi?article=1716&context=theses.

28. Dina Limandri, "Active Listening: Developing Skills for Patient Advocacy in Health Care," Open Educational Resources, CUNY Academic Works, May 25, 2014, https://academicworks.cuny.edu/kb_oers/1/.

29. Abdelrahman Mohamed Ahmed and Mohamed Eltahir Osman, "The Effectiveness of Using WiziQ Interaction Platform on Students' Achievement, Motivation, and Attitudes," *Turkish Online Journal of Distance Education* 21, no. 1 (2020): 19–30.

30. See Emma Dorn et al., "Back to School: A Framework for Remote and Hybrid Learning amid COVID-19," McKinsey, August 31, 2020, www.mckinsey.com/industries/public-and-social-sector/our-insights/back-to-school-a-framework-for-remote-and-hybrid-learning-amid-covid-19#.

31. "About," Academics for Black Lives, www.academics4blacklives.com/about.

32. Geoffrey A. Fowler, "An Early Report Card on Massive Open Online Courses," *Wall Street Journal,* October 8, 2013.

33. Dorn et al., "Back to School."

34. Farah Jasmine Griffin, "Teaching African American Literature during COVID-19," *Boston Review,* May 21, 2020, http://bostonreview.net/arts-society/farah-jasmine-griffin-teaching-african-american-literature-during-covid-19.

5. The First Class

1. Guy McHendry, "About," *Interactive Syllabus,* June 27, 2020, http://www.interactivesyllabus.com/about.html.

2. Louis Deslauriers et al., "Measuring Actual Learning versus Feeling of Learning in Response to Being Actively Engaged in the Classroom," *PNAS* 116, no. 39 (2019): 19251–19257; Peter Reuell, "Lessons in Learning: Study Shows Students in 'Active Learning' Classrooms Learn More Than They Think," *Harvard Gazette,* September 4, 2019, https://news.harvard.edu/gazette/story/2019/09/study-shows-that-students-learn-more-when-taking-part-in-classrooms-that-employ-active-learning-strategies/.

3. Leonora G. Weil et al., "The Development of Metacognitive Ability in Adolescence," *Consciousness and Cognition* 22, no. 1 (March 2013): 264–271.

4. Marilyn Price-Mitchell, "Metacognition: Nurturing Self-Awareness in the Classroom," *Edutopia,* April 7, 2015, www.edutopia.org/blog/8-pathways-metacognition-in-classroom-marilyn-price-mitchell.

5. "Educational Inequity Is Solvable," *Solvable,* interview with Anne Applebaum, October 2, 2019, https://podcasts.apple.com/us/podcast/educational-inequity-is-solvable/id1463448386?i=1000451988495; Tatiana Ades, "How to Change Our Classrooms (and Digital Spaces) to Empower Girls: Insights from Dr. Urvashi Sahni," HASTAC, January 19, 2020, www.hastac.org/blogs/tianaades/2020/01/19/how-change-our-classrooms-and-digital-spaces-empower-girls-insights-dr.

6. See Barbara Daley, "Constitution Study Guide," *Adult Education at Southwestern Illinois College,* https://sites.google.com/site/constitutionstudyguide/home/parts-of-the-constitution.

7. Christina Katopodis, "Every Fall Syllabus Needs an 'Or' Option," HASTAC, June 4, 2020, www.hastac.org/blogs/ckatopodis/2020/06/05/every-fall-syllabus-needs-or-option.

6. *Activities for Any Day of the Term*

1. See Darlene Christopher, *The Successful Virtual Classroom: How to Design and Facilitate Interactive and Engaging Live Online Learning* (New York: American Management Association, 2014), 103.

2. Judith Davidson, "Activities for Helping Students Learn One Another's Name," Faculty Focus, January 24, 2014, www.facultyfocus.com/articles/teaching-and-learning/activities-helping-students-learn-one-anothers-name/.

3. For more detailed examples of fishbowl techniques, see Diana Fuss and William A. Gleason, eds., *The Pocket Instructor: Literature: 101 Exercises for the College Classroom* (Princeton, NJ: Princeton University Press, 2015).

4. "The College Prep Mathematics Program Is Problem-Based and Student-Centered," College Prep, www.college-prep.org/academics/course-offerings/math--computer-science.

5. Frances Tran, "Making Time for Listening Dyads in the Classroom," HASTAC, October 16, 2017, www.hastac.org/blogs/francest/2017/10/16/making-time-listening-dyads-classroom.

6. On video conferencing fatigue, see Susan D. Blum, "Why We're Exhausted by Zoom," *Inside Higher Ed,* April 22, 2020, www.insidehighered.com/advice/2020/04/22/professor-explores-why-zoom-classes-deplete-her-energy-opinion.

7. Deborah M. Kolb and Jessica L. Porter, *Negotiating at Work: Turn Small Wins into Big Gains* (San Francisco: Jossey-Bass, 2015).

8. Steven L. Berg, *Promoting Student Transformation at a Community College: If Everything Happens That Can't Be Done* (Manifold, 2020), https://cuny.manifoldapp.org/projects/promoting-student-transformation-at-a-community-college.

7. Democratic and Antiracist Pedagogy

1. Eve Tuck and K. Wayne Yang, "Decolonization Is Not a Metaphor," *Decolonization: Indigeneity, Education & Society* 1, no. 1 (2012): 28, 35–36.

2. Shashi Jayakumar, "Commentary: Why Did George Floyd Protests Gain Traction Worldwide—Including Asia?" *Channel News Asia: Singapore Edition,* www.channelnewsasia.com/news/commentary/george-floyd-protests-black-lives-matter-asia-racism-race-12935364.

3. "Philippines' 'War on Drugs,'" Human Rights Watch, www.hrw.org/tag/philippines-war-drugs#.

4. "Anti-Racism Training," Academics for Black Lives, www.academics4blacklives.com/anti-racism-training.

5. Anthony Rebora, "Widening the Lens: A Conversation with Beverly Daniel Tatum," *Educational Leadership* 76, no. 7 (April 2019): 30–33.

6. Mahajoy A. Laufer, "Black Students' Classroom Silence in Predominantly White Institutions of Higher Education" (MA thesis, Smith College, Northampton, MA, 2012), https://scholarworks.smith.edu/theses/639; Jennifer J. Lee and Janice McCabe, "Who Speaks and Who Listens: Revisiting the Chilly Climate in College Classrooms," *Gender and Society* 35, no. 1 (2021): 32–60.

7. Danica Savonick and Cathy N. Davidson, "Gender Bias in Academe: An Annotated Bibliography," HASTAC, May 1, 2018, www.hastac.org/blogs/superadmin/2015/01/26/gender-bias-academe-annotated-bibliography-important-recent-studies.

8. On the question stacking controversy, see Scott Jaschik, "Should White Boys Still Be Allowed to Talk?" *Inside Higher Ed,* February 18, 2019, www.insidehighered.com/news/2019/02/18/essay-about-how-white-male-students-dominate-discussions-sets-debate-dickinson-and.

9. Subramaniam Ananthram, Dawn Bennett, and Sherry Bawa, "It's Not Lack of Confidence That's Holding Back Women in STEM," *The Conversation,* March 14, 2021, https://theconversation.com/its-not-lack-of-confidence-thats-holding-back-women-in-stem-155216.

10. Klara Sedova et al., "Do Those Who Talk More Learn More? The Relationship between Student Classroom Talk and Student Achievement," *Learning and Instruction* 63 (October 2019), 101217, www.sciencedirect.com/science/article/pii/S0959475218303839.

11. On the progressive stack and related research, see Gina Quattrochi, "When the System Itself Is the Problem," Bailey House blog post, November 19, 2011, now unavailable; Danica Savonick, "Creating Spaces for Conversation: Three Strategies," HASTAC, February 16, 2016, www.hastac.org/blogs/danicasavonick/2016/02/16/creating-spaces-conversation-three-strategies; Kevin Gannon, "The Progressive

Stack and Standing for Inclusive Teaching," *The Tattooed Professor,* October 20, 2017, www.thetattooedprof.com/2017/10/20/the-progressive-stack-and-standing-for-inclusive-teaching/.

12. Jesús Treviño, "Diversity and Inclusiveness in the Classroom," Arizona State University, https://humanities.arizona.edu/files/Classroom%20Dialogue%20Guide%20.pdf.

13. Treviño, "Diversity and Inclusiveness in the Classroom."

14. Melissa Schieble, Amy Vetter, and Kahdeidra Monét Martin, *Classroom Talk for Social Change: Critical Conversations in English Language Arts* (New York: Teachers College Press, 2020), 66–68.

15. Dian Million, "Felt Theory: An Indigenous Feminist Approach to Affect and History," *Wicaszo Sa Review* 24, no. 2 (2009): 54, 61.

16. Barbara Applebaum, *Being White, Being Good: White Complicity, White Moral Responsibility, and Social Justice Pedagogy* (Lanham, MD: Lexington Books, 2010), 107.

17. Adriana Estill, "Feeling Our Way to Knowing: Decolonizing the American Studies Classroom," in *Difficult Subjects: Insights and Strategies for Teaching about Race, Sexuality, and Gender,* edited by Badia Ahad-Legardy and OiYan A. Poon, 113–128 (Sterling, VA: Stylus, 2018).

18. Felicia Rose Chavez, *The Anti-Racist Writing Workshop: How to Decolonize the Creative Classroom* (Chicago: Haymarket Books, 2021), 10.

19. On terms such as *race, ethnic, white,* and so on, see Nell Irvin Painter, *The History of White People* (New York: W. W. Norton, 2011); Noel Ignatiev, *How the Irish Became White* (New York: Routledge, 1995); Isabel Wilkerson, *Caste: The Origins of Our Discontents* (New York: Random House, 2020).

20. For an excellent theoretical discussion of how aesthetics and ideology intermingle, see Kandice Chuh, *The Difference Aesthetics Makes: On the Humanities "After Man"* (Durham, NC: Duke University Press, 2019).

21. Chavez, *Anti-Racist Writing Workshop,* 170.

22. Chavez, *Anti-Racist Writing Workshop,* 169.

23. For a succinct overview of the political controversy and a general discussion of Critical Race Theory, see Janel George, "A Lesson on Critical Race Theory," American Bar Association, January 11, 2021, www.americanbar.org/groups/crsj/publications/human_rights_magazine_home/civil-rights-reimagining-policing/a-lesson-on-critical-race-theory/, accessed November 8, 2021.

24. Derrick A. Bell Jr., "*Brown v. Board of Education* and the Interest-Convergence Dilemma," *Harvard Law Review* 93, no. 3 (1980): 518–533; Derrick A. Bell, "Who's Afraid of Critical Race Theory?" *University of Illinois Law Review,* no. 4 (1995):

893–910; Kimberlé Crenshaw et al., eds., *Critical Race Theory: The Key Writings That Formed the Movement* (New York: New Press, 1995); Kimberlé Crenshaw, "Race, Reform, and Retrenchment: Transformation and Legitimation in Antidiscrimination Law," *Harvard Law Review* 101, no. 7 (1988): 1331–1387; Richard Delgado and Jean Stefancic, eds., *Critical Race Theory: The Cutting Edge,* 3rd ed. (Philadelphia: Temple University Press, 2013), 6.

25. Stephen Sawchuk, "What Is Critical Race Theory and Why Is It under Attack?" *Education Week,* May 18, 2021, www.edweek.org/leadership/what-is-critical-race-theory-and-why-is-it-under-attack/2021/05, accessed October 28, 2021.

26. "Being Antiracist," National Museum of African American History and Culture, https://nmaahc.si.edu/learn/talking-about-race/topics/being-antiracist, accessed May 24, 2021.

27. Ibram X. Kendi, *How to Be an Antiracist* (New York: One World, 2019); Ibram X. Kendi, *Stamped from the Beginning: The Definitive History of Racist Ideas in America* (New York: Bold Type Books, 2016).

28. "Antiracism Starts with You," Boston University Center for Antiracist Research, www.bu.edu/antiracism-center/, accessed June 10, 2021.

29. Ibram X. Kendi, "The Antiracist Reading List: 38 Books for Those Open to Changing Themselves, and Their World," *Atlantic,* February 12, 2019.

30. Colleen Walsh, "Making Higher Education Anti-Racist," *Harvard Gazette,* November 20, 2020, https://news.harvard.edu/gazette/story/2020/11/ibram-x-kendi-discusses-antiracism-in-education/, accessed June 10, 2021.

8. Group Work Without the Groans

1. Eric Ravenscraft, "An Adult's Guide to Social Skills, for Those Who Were Never Taught," *New York Times,* January 23, 2020.

2. Joshua Lederberg, Keith Uncapher, and William Allan Wulf, "Towards a National Collaboratory: Report of an Invitational Workshop at the Rockefeller University, March 17–18, 1989," Conference Paper and Proceedings, n.p.,1989.

3. Lydia Belatèche, "Far from Remote: Zooming with Advanced Students of French at the U," University of Minnesota Language Center, November 12, 2020, https://cla.umn.edu/language-center/news-events/news/far-remote-zooming-advanced-students-french-u.

4. Christina Katopodis, "How Prof Bruns Helps 1st Year College Students Speak in Class," HASTAC, November 19, 2019, www.hastac.org/blogs/ckatopodis/2019/11/20/how-prof-bruns-helps-1st-year-college-students-speak-class.

5. Cathy N. Davidson, "Recognizing Leadership and Group Classroom Methods of Virginia Yonkers, Univ of Albany," HASTAC, November 15, 2019, www.hastac.org

/blogs/cathy-davidson/2019/11/15/recognizing-leadership-and-group-classroom-methods-prof-virginia.

6. Mesrure Tekay, interview with Christina Katopodis, August 10, 2020.

7. Andrew Hopkins, *Disastrous Decisions: The Human and Organisational Causes of the Gulf of Mexico Blowout* (Macquarie Park, Australia: CCH Australia, 2012).

8. Tatiana Ades, "Learning How to Strengthen Communities with Prof Osteen," HASTAC, December 10, 2019, www.hastac.org/blogs/tianaades/2019/12/10/learning-how-strengthen-communities-prof-osteen.

9. Beth McMurtrie cites the survey conducted by Vikki Katz in "Teaching: What Students Want Their Professors to Know," *Teaching Newsletter,* September 24, 2020, *Chronicle of Higher Education,* www.chronicle.com/newsletter/teaching/2020-09-24.

10. See also Cathy N. Davidson and Christina Katopodis, "Eight Ways to Improve Online Learning," *Inside Higher Ed,* October 28, 2020, www.insidehighered.com/advice/2020/10/28/advice-how-successfully-guide-students-group-work-online-opinion.

11. Dr. Fridman's approach grows out of research demonstrating that social sensitivity, equality of turn taking, and psychological safety were the strongest predictors of innovation and high performance. See Charles Duhigg, *Smarter Faster Better: The Secrets of Being Productive in Life and Business* (New York: Random House, 2016).

12. "What Is Service-Learning?" Suffolk University, www.suffolk.edu/student-life/student-involvement/community-public-service/service-learning/what-is-service-learning.

13. "Five Keys to a Successful Google Team," *re:Work,* https://rework.withgoogle.com/blog/five-keys-to-a-successful-google-team/.

14. Michael Yarbrough, "COVID-19 at CUNY: A Class Project," CUNY John Jay College, https://johnjay.digication.com/covid19-at-cuny/home-1.

15. Richard J. Light, *Making the Most of College: Students Speak Their Minds* (Cambridge, MA: Harvard University Press, 2004).

16. Benjamin S. Bloom, *Taxonomy of Educational Objectives* (Boston: Allyn and Bacon, 1956). See also John Biggs and Kevin Collis, *Evaluating the Quality of Learning: The SOLO Taxonomy (Structure of the Observed Learning Outcome)* (New York: Academic Press, 1982); Örjan Dahlström, "Learning during a Collaborative Final Exam," *Educational Research and Evaluation* 18, no. 4 (2012): 321–332; John F. Zipp, "Learning by Exams: The Impact of Two-Stage Cooperative Tests," *Teaching Sociology* 35 (2007): 62–76; "Higher Order Thinking: Bloom's Taxonomy," The Learning Center, University of North Carolina Chapel Hill, https://learningcenter.unc.edu/tips-and-tools/higher-order-thinking/.

9. Research That Inspires Creativity

1. Ann Powers, "Keynote Conversation with Alanis Morissette," *Pop Talks,* September 10, 2020, www.soundinthesignals.com/2020/09/alanis-morissette-keynote-conversation.html.

2. On teaching critical thinking through thoughtful, polished writing, see John C. Bean, *Engaging Ideas: The Professor's Guide to Integrating Writing, Critical Thinking, and Active Learning in the Classroom,* 2nd ed. (San Francisco: Jossey-Bass, 2011); John Warner, *Why They Can't Write: Killing the Five-Paragraph Essay and Other Necessities* (Baltimore: Johns Hopkins University Press, 2018).

3. Linda Tuhiwai Te Rina Smith, *Decolonizing Methodologies: Research and Indigenous Peoples,* 2nd ed. (London: Zed Books, 2012), 25.

4. Bathsheba Demuth, *Floating Coast: An Environmental History of the Bering Strait* (New York: W. W. Norton, 2019), 4.

5. "MSU Uses $1.5M Mellon Foundation Grant to Build Massive Slave Trade Database," *MSU Today,* January 9, 2018, https://msutoday.msu.edu/news/2018/msu-uses-15m-mellon-foundation-grant-to-build-massive-slave-trade-database/.

6. "The 1870 Brick Wall," *Lowcountry Africana: African American Genealogy in SC, GA, and FL,* https://lowcountryafricana.com/the-1870-brick-wall/.

7. Flore Mietton et al., "Selective BET Bromodomain Inhibition as an Antifungal Therapeutic Strategy," *Nature Communications* 8 (2017), 15482; Emily Gersema, "International Team Uncovers New Approach to Combat Deadly Fungal Infection," *USC Dornsife,* June 20, 2017, https://dornsife.usc.edu/news/stories/2622/international-team-uncovers-new-approach-to-combat-deadly-fungal/.

8. Danielle Batist, "'Design Thinking' Approach Aims to Train Dutch Students' Ability to Solve Problems," *U.S. News & World Report,* December 4, 2019.

9. Meghan Bogardus Cortez, "Solving Real-World Problems Is Key to Ed Tech Success," *EdTech,* September 19, 2017, https://edtechmagazine.com/k12/article/2017/09/solving-real-world-problems-key-ed-tech-success.

10. Ann M. Pendleton-Jullian and John Seely Brown, *Design Unbound: Designing for Emergency in a White Water World* (Cambridge, MA: MIT Press, 2018), 28.

11. Pendleton-Jullian and Brown, *Design Unbound,* 210–216.

12. Maureen Haaker and Bethany Morgan Brett, "Developing Research-Led Teaching: Two Cases of Practical Data Reuse in the Classroom," *SAGE* 7, no. 2 (April–June 2017), 1–9. See also a 2002 workshop by Angela Brew from Macquarie University in Australia titled "Enhancing the Quality of Learning through Research-Led Teaching," www.researchgate.net/publication/228978625_Enhancing_the_quality

_of_learning_through_research-led_teaching; Philip Cook and Denise Sweeney, "Research-Led Teaching: Theory, Practice, and Policy," Learning and Teaching Conference 2013, University of Leicester, www2.le.ac.uk/offices/academic-practice/resources/learning-teaching-conference/workshop-resources/ResearchLedTeaching%20PC%20Changes%202.pdf; Angela Brew, "Research and Teaching from the Students' Perspective," International Policies and Practices for Academic Enquiry: An International Colloquium, Marwell Conference Centre, Winchester, UK, April 19–21, 2007; David Hodge, Kira Pasquesi, and Marissa Hirsh, "From Convocation to Capstone: Developing the Student as Scholar," keynote address, Association of American Colleges and Universities Network for Academic Renewal Conference, Long Beach, CA, April 19–21, 2007, www.miami.muohio.edu/president/reports_and_speeches/pdfs/From_Convocation_to_Capstone.pdf.

13. This is one core element of Universal Design for Learning (UDL), developed by the Center for Applied Special Technology (CAST). See Kirsten T. Behling and Thomas J. Tobin, *Reach Everyone, Teach Everyone: Universal Design for Learning in Higher Education* (Morganstown: West Virginia University Press, 2018), 129.

14. See Pooja K. Agarwal and Patrice M. Bain, *Powerful Teaching: Unleash the Science of Learning* (San Francisco: Jossey-Bass, 2019), 187–190.

15. Judith V. Boettcher and Rita-Marie Conrad, *The Online Teaching Survival Guide: Simple and Practical Pedagogical Tips,* 2nd ed. (San Francisco: Jossey-Bass, 2016), 267.

16. Raewyn Connell, *The Good University: What Universities Actually Do and Why It's Time for Radical Change* (London: Zed Books, 2019), 48–49.

17. Andrea A. Lunsford, Jenn Fishman, and Warren M. Liew, "College Writing, Identification, and the Production of Intellectual Property: Voices from the Stanford Study of Writing," *College English* 75, no. 5 (May 2013): 470–492.

18. Katherine Schulten, "Writing for an Audience beyond the Teacher: 10 Reasons to Send Student Work Out into the World," *New York Times,* November 15, 2018.

19. "Past Problems," ICPC International Collegiate Programming Contest, https://icpc.global/worldfinals/problems.

20. Katherine Schulten, "Show Us Your Generation: A Photo Contest for Teenagers," *New York Times,* September 5, 2018.

21. Ulla-Maaria Koivula, "From Italy: 10 Creative Ideas for Teaching Remotely," *Thinglink Blog,* March 30, 2020, https://blog.thinglink.com/marketing/10-creative-ideas-for-teaching-remotely.

22. On how to avoid surveillance online, see Erin Rose Glass, "Ten Weird Tricks for Resisting Surveillance Capitalism in and through the Classroom . . . Next Term!" HASTAC, December 28, 2018, www.hastac.org/blogs/erin-glass/2018/12/27/ten-weird-tricks-resisting-surveillance-capitalism-and-through-classroom.

23. "Examples of Undergraduate Research," Office of the Provost, Virginia Commonwealth University, https://provost.vcu.edu/initiatives/urop/examples/.

24. Enoch Chan, Michael George Botelho, and Gordon Tin-Chun Wong, "A Flipped Classroom, Same-Level Peer-Assisted Learning Approach to Clinical Skill Teaching for Medical Students," *PLOS One* 16, no. 10 (2021), e0258926.

10. Feedback That Really Works

1. Victoria Pitts-Taylor, class lecture, The Graduate Center, CUNY, Fall 2013.

2. Eve Kosofsky Sedgwick, "Paranoid Reading and Reparative Reading; or, You're So Paranoid, You Probably Think This Introduction Is about You," in *Novel Gazing: Queer Readings in Fiction,* edited by Eve Kosofsky Sedgwick (Durham, NC: Duke University Press, 1997).

3. Filip Dochy, Mien R. Segers, and Dominique Sluijsmans, "The Use of Self-, Peer and Co-assessment in Higher Education: A Review," *Studies in Higher Education* 24, no. 3 (October 1999): 331–350.

4. Felicia Rose Chavez, *The Anti-Racist Writing Workshop: How to Decolonize the Creative Classroom* (Chicago: Haymarket Books, 2021).

5. John Hattie and Helen Timperley, "The Power of Feedback," *Review of Educational Research* 77, no. 1 (March 2007): 82.

6. See also John Hattie, "Influences on Student Learning," inaugural professorial address, University of Auckland, NZ, 1999, www.arts.auckland.ac.nz/staffindex.cfm?P=8650; John Hattie, John Biggs, and Nola Purdie, "Effects of Learning Skills Intervention on Student Learning: A Meta-Analysis," *Review of Research in Education* 66 (1996): 99–136.

7. Hattie and Timperley, "Power of Feedback," 86.

8. J. S. Bruner, "The Act of Discovery," *Harvard Educational Review* 31, no. 1 (1961); Seymour Papert and Idit Harel, eds., *Constructionism: Research Reports and Essays 1985–1990* (Norwood, NJ: Ablex, 1991).

9. Douglas Stone and Sheila Heen, *Thanks for the Feedback: The Science and Art of Receiving Feedback Well Even When It Is Off-Base, Unfair, Poorly Delivered, and, Frankly, You're Not in the Mood* (New York: Penguin, 2015), 273–274.

10. David Gooblar, *The Missing Course: Everything They Never Taught You about College Teaching* (Cambridge, MA: Harvard University Press, 2019), 130.

11. Jack Zenger and Joseph Folkman, "The Assumptions That Make Giving Tough Feedback Even Tougher," *Harvard Business Review,* April 30, 2015, https://hbr.org/2015/04/the-assumptions-that-make-giving-tough-feedback-even-tougher.

12. Quoted in Maria Popova, "Fixed v. Growth: The Two Basic Mindsets That Shape Our Lives," *Brain Pickings,* January 29, 2014, www.brainpickings.org/2014/01/29/carol-dweck-mindset/.

13. Carol Dweck, *Mindset: The New Psychology of Success* (New York: Random House, 2006).

14. Emma Briggs, "How to Give Feedback with a Growth-Mindset Approach," NeuroLeadership Institute, July 16, 2019, https://neuroleadership.com/your-brain-at-work/feedback-strategies-growth-mindset/.

15. Cate Denial, "Making the Grade," *Cate Denial,* October 16, 2017, https://catherinedenial.org/blog/uncategorized/making-the-grade/.

16. S. W. VanderStoep, P. R. Pintrich, and A. Fagerlin, "Disciplinary Differences in Self-Regulated Learning in College Students," *Contemporary Educational Psychology* 21, no. 4 (1996): 345–362.

17. Sarah J. Schendel, "What You Don't Know (Can Hurt You): Using Exam Wrappers to Foster Self-Assessment Skills in Law Students," *Pace Law Review* 40 (2020): 154. See also M. C. Lovett, "Make Exams Worth More Than the Grade: Using Exam Wrappers to Promote Metacognition," in *Using Reflection and Metacognition to Improve Student Learning: Across the Disciplines, Across the Academy,* edited by M. Kaplan et al., 18–52 (Sterling, VA: Stylus, 2013).

18. Starr Sackstein, "Shifting the Grading Mindset," in *Ungrading: Why Rating Students Undermines Learning (and What to Do Instead),* edited by Susan D. Blum (Morgantown: West Virginia University Press, 2020), 76–77.

19. Stone and Heen, *Thanks for the Feedback,* 299.

20. See José Antonio Bowen and C. Edward Watson, *Teaching Naked Techniques: A Practical Guide to Designing Better Classes* (San Francisco: Jossey-Bass, 2017), 8.

21. Carl E. Wieman, *Improving How Universities Teach Science: Lessons from the Science Education Initiative* (Cambridge, MA: Harvard University Press, 2017), 171–173.

22. Ted Dintersmith, "Prepare Our Kids for Life, Not Standardized Tests," *TEDx Talk,* August 15, 2015, www.youtube.com/watch?v=Rvhb9aoyeZs.

23. For an example of self- and peer-evaluation form, see Christina Katopodis and Cathy N. Davidson, "Contract Grading and Peer Review," in Blum, *Ungrading,* 105–122.

24. bell hooks, *Teaching to Transgress: Education as the Practice of Freedom* (New York: Routledge, 1994), 206.

25. Lillian MacNell, Adam Driscoll, and Andrea N. Hunt, "What's in a Name: Exposing Gender Bias in Student Ratings of Teaching," *Innovative Higher Education* 40 (2015): 291–303, https://doi.org/10.1007/s10755-014-9313-4; Kristina M. W. Mitchell and

Jonathan Martin, "Gender Bias in Student Evaluations," *PS: Political Science and Politics* 51, no. 3 (2018): 648–652.

26. Kerry Chavez and Kristina M. W. Mitchell, "Exploring Bias in Student Evaluations: Gender, Race, and Ethnicity," *PS: Political Science and Politics* 53, no. 2 (2020): 270–274.

27. See Danica Savonick and Cathy N. Davidson, "Gender Bias in Higher Ed," *LSE Blog,* March 8, 2017, https://blogs.lse.ac.uk/impactofsocialsciences/2017/03/08/newly-updated-for-international-womens-day-gender-bias-in-academe-bibliography/; Chavella Pittman, "Addressing Incivility in the Classroom," in *Difficult Subjects: Insights and Strategies for Teaching about Race, Sexuality, and Gender,* edited by Badia Ahad-Legardy and OiYan A. Poon (Sterling, VA: Stylus Press, 2018), 66–67; Pittman references Dalton State College psychology professor Christy Price's work on student preferences for "classroom environments that are active, collaborative, and participatory." See Price, "Why Don't My Students Think I'm Groovy?" *The Teaching Professor* 23, no. 1 (2009): 7–10.

28. Pittman, "Addressing Incivility," 67.

11. *Grades*—Ugh!

1. An earlier version of this discussion appeared in Christina Katopodis and Cathy N. Davidson, "Contract Grading and Peer Review," in *Ungrading: Why Rating Students Undermines Learning (and What to Do Instead),* edited by Susan D. Blum (Morgantown: West Virginia University Press, 2020).

2. Dehui Hu, Joshua Von Korff, and N. Sanjay Rebello, "Assessing Transfer of Learning in Problem Solving from the Perspective of Preparation for Future Learning," Physics Education Research Conference, Portland, Oregon, 2013, 189–192, www.compadre.org/Repository/document/ServeFile.cfm?ID=13165&DocID=3712.

3. Jesse Stommel, "How to Ungrade," in Blum, *Ungrading,* 25–41; Alfie Kohn, "Foreword," in Blum, *Ungrading,* xiii–xx; Susan D. Blum, "Introduction: Why Ungrade? Why Grade?" in Blum, *Ungrading,* 2.

4. Paulo Freire, *Pedagogy of the Oppressed* (New York: Herder and Herder, 1972).

5. Cate Denial, "More Thoughts about Grades," *Cate Denial,* December 11, 2019, https://catherinedenial.org/blog/uncategorized/more-thoughts-about-grades/.

6. On the history of grading, see Blum, "Introduction," 6.

7. Neil Postman, *Technopoly: The Surrender of Culture to Technology* (New York: Alfred A. Knopf, 1992).

8. Cathy N. Davidson, *The New Education: How to Revolutionize the University to Prepare Students for a World in Flux* (New York: Basic Books, 2017), 193–226.

9. Arthur Chiaravalli, "Grades Stifle Student Learning. Can We Learn to Teach without Grades?" in Blum, *Ungrading,* 83.

10. @OnlineCrsLady, "the thing is that there ARE real measures out there. if you teach typing, you can measure typing speed, accuracy, etc. with typing test. but letting ABCDF letter grades be stand-ins for real assessments of learning in a course seems ridiculous to me. grades are not real measures." Twitter, November 5, 2021, 4:05 p.m., https://twitter.com/OnlineCrsLady/status/1456714365013463043?s=20.

11. Astrid Poorthuis et al., "Do Grades Shape Students' School Engagement? The Psychological Consequences of Report Card Grades at the Beginning of Secondary School," *Journal of Educational Psychology* 107, no. 3 (2014): 842–854.

12. Hall P. Beck, Sherry Rorrer-Woody, and Linda G. Pierce, "The Relations of Learning and Grade Orientations to Academic Performance," *Teaching of Psychology* 18, no. 1 (February 1991): 35–37.

13. Matt Townsley and Tom Buckmiller, "What Does the Research Say about Standards-Based Grading?" *McTownsley,* January 14, 2016, http://mctownsley.net/standards-based-grading-research/, accessed October 22, 2020. See also Matt Townsley and Nathan L. Wear, *Making Grades Matter: Standards-Based Grading in a Secondary PLC at Work* (Bloomington, IN: Solution Tree, 2020).

14. See also Kohn, "Foreword," xiii–xx; Blum, "Introduction," 2.

15. Alfie Kohn, "Can Everyone Be Excellent?" *New York Times,* June 16, 2019.

16. Kohn, "Can Everyone Be Excellent?"

17. Stuart Rojstaczer, "Grade Inflation," http://gradeinflation.com/; Stuart Rojstaczer and Christopher Healy, "Where A Is Ordinary: The Evolution of American College and University Grading, 1940–2009," *Teachers College Record* 114, no. 7 (2012): 1–23.

18. Jenny Anderson, "Rich Kids' Grades Are Rising Faster, and Intelligence Probably Isn't the Reason Why," *Quartz,* August 21, 2017, https://qz.com/1058J476/grade-inflation-is-the-worst-at-rich-private-schools-disadvantaging-poor-students/.

19. Blum, ed., *Ungrading.*

20. Blum, "Introduction," 4.

21. Quoted as the epigraph to Blum, ed., *Ungrading.*

22. Ruth Butler, "Enhancing and Undermining Intrinsic Motivation: The Effects of Task-Involving and Ego-Involving Evaluation on Interest and Performance," *British Journal of Educational Psychology* 58, no. 1 (1988): 1–14; Chiaravalli, "Grades Stifle Student Learning," 82; William Dylan, *Embedded Formative Assessment* (Bloomington, IN: Solution Tree, 2018).

23. Ruth Butler, "Task-Involving and Ego-Involving Properties of Evaluation: Effects of Different Feedback Conditions on Motivational Perceptions, Interest, and Performance," *Journal of Educational Psychology* 79, no. 4 (1987): 474–482.

24. Rosalie Metro, "Humane Assessment Shouldn't Happen Only during a Pandemic," *Inside Higher Education,* September 9, 2020, www.insidehighered.com/views/2020/09/09/new-approaches-assessment-can-promote-student-success-times-crisis-well-normalcy.

25. John Warner, "A Final Nail in the Coffin for Turnitin?" *Inside Higher Ed,* September 18, 2019, www.insidehighered.com/blogs/just-visiting/final-nail-coffin-turnitin. See also John Warner, *Why They Can't Write: Killing the Five-Paragraph Essay and Other Necessities* (Baltimore: Johns Hopkins University Press, 2018).

26. Asao B. Inoue, *Labor-Based Grading Contracts: Building Equity and Inclusion in the Compassionate Writing Classroom* (Fort Collins, CO: WAC Clearinghouse / Boulder: University Press of Colorado, 2019), 129–168, https://wac.colostate.edu/books/perspectives/labor/.

27. For an example of a contract that Cathy offered second- and third-year students in a course in the Information Science and Studies program at Duke University, see Katopodis and Davidson, "Contract Grading and Peer Review," 105–122.

28. Courtney Sobers Swindell, email correspondence, January 2, 2021.

29. See Cathy N. Davidson, "Essential Tool Kit for Peer Learning and Peer Teaching," HASTAC, August 29, 2019, www.hastac.org/blogs/cathy-davidson/2013/06/04/essential-tool-kit-peer-learning-and-peer-teaching.

30. For a thorough study of peer-evaluation and badging, see E. A. O'Connor and A. McQuigge, "Exploring Badging for Peer Review, Extended Learning and Evaluation, and Reflective / Critical Feedback within an Online Graduate Course," *Journal of Educational Technology Systems* 42, no. 2 (2013): 87–105.

31. See also R. Shields and R. Chugh, "Digital Badges—Rewards for Learning?" *Education and Information Technologies* 22, no. 4 (2017): 1817–1824.

32. Greg Linden, Brent Smith, and Jeremy York, "Amazon.com Recommendations Item-to-Item Collaborative Filtering," *IEEE Internet Computing* 7, no. 1 (January–February 2003): 76–80.

33. Eva L. Baker, "2007 Presidential Address—The End(s) of Testing," *Educational Researcher* 36, no. 6 (2007): 309–317.

34. For more about badging, see Cathy N. Davidson, "About the Digital Media and Learning Competitions," HASTAC, www.hastac.org/dml-competitions/competitions-home/about-digital-media-learning-competition, accessed October 21, 2020. See also Doug Belshaw, "10 Platforms for Issuing Open Badges," February 19, 2019, https://blog.weareopen.coop/10-platforms-for-issuing-open-badges-f249cf609d42.

35. Siqi Tu, "Event Recap: Classrooms and Social Justice: Why Start with Pedagogy?" *Futures Initiative,* October 4, 2018, https://futuresinitiative.org/blog/2018/10/04/event-recap-classroom-and-social-justice-why-start-with-pedagogy/.

36. Jonathan Sterne, "Multiple Choice Exam Theory: Remote Learning Edition," *Super Bon,* June 11, 2020, https://superbon.net/2020/06/11/multiple-choice-exam-theory-remote-teaching-edition/.

37. H. Ebbinghaus, *Memory: A Contribution to Experimental Psychology* (New York: Dover, 1885).

38. See, for example, Daniel L. Schacter et al., "The Future of Memory: Remembering, Imagining, and the Brain," *Neuron* 76, no. 4 (2012): 677–694.

39. Sterne, "Multiple Choice Exam Theory."

40. Virginia Yonkers (@Comprof1), "I had a great economics prof (though didn't know it at the time) who used Multiple choice to start the convo. You chose the answer then had to explain your choice. Correct with good explanation could get the same grade as incorrect with good explanation," Twitter, November 11, 2020, 8:35 A.M., https://twitter.com/Comprof1/status/1326518975753293824; Virginia Yonkers (@Comprof1), "I write poor multiple choice (and don't like using them). But our Teaching Center suggested that I use this as a discussion starter in class. It is a great way to get groups discussion concepts but also teaching the vocab of my subject," Twitter, November 11, 2020, 8:35 A.M., https://twitter.com/Comprof1/status/1326518975753293824.

12. What Could Possibly Go Wrong?

1. For more "teaching fails," see *The Journal of Interactive Technology and Pedagogy.*

2. Ginia Bellafante, "Raising Ambitions: The Challenge in Teaching at Community Colleges," *New York Times,* December 19, 2014.

3. We decided to publish all of the materials in this course in a free open-source book. See Cathy N. Davidson and Eduardo Vianna, eds., *I Wake Up Counting: A Guide to Transformative Teaching and Learning in the Humanities and Social Sciences,* Tatiana Ades, general editor (New York: Manifold Edition, 2021).

4. R. C. Wilson et al., "The Eighty Five Percent Rule for Optimal Learning," *Nature Communications* 10, no. 1 (2019), 4646.

5. bell hooks, *Teaching Community: A Pedagogy of Hope* (New York: Routledge, 2003), 92.

Conclusion: Changing the World

1. "Full Syllabus," *Radical Hope: Inspiring Sustainability Transformations through Our Past: A Group Sourced Syllabus,* https://radicalhopesyllabus.com/syllabi/, accessed June 10, 2021.

2. "Torn Apart / Separados Allies Directory," Columbia University, https://xpmethod.columbia.edu/torn-apart/allies.html.

3. "NIH to Launch Public-Private Partnership to Speed COVID-19 Vaccine and Treatment Options," National Institutes of Health, April 17, 2020, www.nih.gov/news-events/news-releases, accessed April 8, 2021; James C. Robinson, "Funding of Pharmaceutical Innovation During and After the COVID-19 Pandemic," *JAMA* 325, no. 9 (2021): 825–826; Jessica Kent, ed., "Healthcare Data Sharing Connects the Dots for COVID-19 and Beyond," July 31, 2020, http://healthitanalytics.com/features. Even big pharmaceutical companies, normally rivals, put competition aside and worked together to produce and distribute vaccines quickly. See Jared S. Hopkins, "To Make More Covid-19 Vaccines, Rival Drugmakers Team Up: Sanofi and Novartis Are among the Big Pharmaceutical Companies That Have Agreed to Help Make a Competitor's Shots," *Wall Street Journal,* February 23, 2021; Matt Levine, "Money Stuff: The Vaccine Is Not a Competition," *Bloomberg,* February 24, 2021, www.bloomberg.com/news/newsletters.

4. "Coronavirus: Turkish Germans Raise New Covid Vaccine Hopes," *BBC News,* November 10, 2020, www.bbc.com/news/world-europe-54886883, accessed May 1, 2021; Philip Oltermann, "Uğur Şahin and Özlem Türeci: German 'Dream Team' behind Vaccine," *Guardian,* November 10, 2020; "Uğur Şahin," Wikipedia, https://en.wikipedia.org/wiki/U%C4%9Fur_%C5%9Eahin, accessed June 6, 2021; "Özlem Türeci," Wikipedia, https://en.wikipedia.org/wiki/%C3%96zlem_T%C3%BCreci, accessed June 6, 2021.

5. "The Strategic Plan," Sorbonne Université, November 25, 2019, www.sorbonne-universite.fr/en/university/about-us/strategic-plan.

Acknowledgments

In writing this book, we have incurred many debts. We would like to thank all of our colleagues throughout the City University of New York's many campuses, at the Graduate Center's Futures Initiative, the CUNY Innovative Teaching Academy, Transformative Learning in the Humanities, and at HASTAC ("haystack": Humanities, Arts, Science, and Technology Alliance and Collaboratory). We are grateful for the conscientiousness and care of our agent, Deirdre Mullane, our editor, Andrew J. Kinney, and all of the editors and others at Harvard University Press.

Personally, I (Cathy) would like to thank my partner, Ken Wissoker, for his loving support, capacious intellect, and generous spirit. I'm grateful to my colleagues Lauren Melendez, Katina Rogers, and Adashima Oyo for their tireless energy and dedication to making higher education a more humane space. I thank my friends (and co-teachers) Racquel Gates and Michael Gillespie for their constant insights and energy; my Second Sundays science fiction writing group; my colleagues Herman Bennett, Frances Bronet, Ana Mari Cauce, Kandice Chuh, Michelle Fine, Ofelia Garcia, Matt Gold, Dianne Harris, Sharon Holland, Carla Shedd, Priscilla Wald, and Bianca Williams for their engagement with these ideas. I wish to thank everyone who joins in leading HASTAC, especially co-director Jacqueline Wernimont of Dartmouth College. I cofounded HASTAC in 2002 and, with over eighteen thousand members, it is now known as one of the world's first and oldest academic social networks. There are so many other colleagues I learn from every day. You know who you are; I wish I could name you all. Tatiana Ades, Jacqueline Cahill, Dasharah Green, and Danica Savonick were research assistants during parts of this project and continue to be deeply valued colleagues. I also thank Charles Davidson and Susan Brown; Karina Davidson; my sisters (Mary Lou Shioji Notari, Sharon Notari, and Debbie McGrath); my cousin Mari Krasney; my father, Paul Notari; and my mother-in-law, Barbara Wissoker (and all of my Wissoker family) who remained strong during a very difficult time for our family.

I (Christina) thank my partner, Erik Wohlmuth, for his unwavering support and depth of insight, and our tiny human, William, who has filled our lives with joy when the world was in crisis. I've been fortunate to have vibrant scholar-teacher communities like the Academic Center for Excellence in Research and Teaching (ACERT) at Hunter College; the Center for the Humanities, English PhD program, Futures Initiative, New Media Lab, and Teaching and Learning Center at the Graduate Center; and the Innovative Teaching Academy and Office of Academic Affairs at CUNY. I am grateful to have had the privilege to cocreate syllabi with such brave, curious, and hard-working students—they have shaped my pedagogy most of all, and their ideas and feedback have been with me throughout the writing of this book. I am honored to be among teachers who inspire me every day: Alicia Andrzejewski, Austin Bailey, Sindija Franzetti, Alicia Green Gennaro, Bethany Holmstrom, Kashema Hutchinson, Jack Kenigsberg, Kahdeidra Monét Martin, Kaitlin Mondello, and Jacinta Yanders. To my peers in our writing groups, my Manifold mentors, fellow academic mamas, my collaborators, and delightful officemates—thank you for cheering on this work. I thank the educators who inspired me to become a teacher:

Mrs. (Laura) Dreyer, Señora (Linda) Thompson, and Mr. (Ronald) Miller. I thank my family, especially my parents, Mary Brooks and John Katopodis, who imparted a thirst for lifelong learning; and my grandparents, Nonda and Yola Katopodis, and Bernard and Helen Kawecki, who sacrificed everything so that their children and grandchildren would have an education.

Together, we thank all of the scholars and instructors whose research we studied, classes we visited, and ideas we have shared. To all our colleagues in the public humanities who share their experiences on #AcademicTwitter and on TikTok: we learn from you each and every day. We thank our colleagues in the Transformative Learning in the Humanities Program: Shelly Eversley, Grace Handy, Khanh Le, Jessica Murray, Annemarie Nicols-Grinenko, and Boya Wang. We thank the Andrew W. Mellon Foundation for their continuing support of our work and, more generally, of work designed to make higher education more equitable and relevant.

We are grateful to every student who fought for an education against all odds, inspiring us to raise the bar higher and higher. Finally, we thank one another. It's been a pleasure and sometimes a lifeline writing this book together in an isolating and dispiriting time. Amid tragedy and hardships, it has been a joy to work together on compelling ideas that offer the promise of meaning, hope, and the foundation for a better future.

Index